Indie Video Game Development Work

"With his characteristically open-minded approach, drawing on perspectives from economic policy through anthropology all the way to the space where the green ants dream, Styhre is in search of the elusive and ephemeral indie video game industry. Such an approach proves to be indispensable in order to do justice to a world where the passionate love of video games and the social norms of the indie scene on the one hand are paired with industrial logics, financial forces, and calculative, commercial action, on the other."

—Thomas Lennerfors, *Professor in Industrial Engineering and Management, Uppsala University*

Alexander Styhre

Indie Video Game Development Work

Innovation in the Creative Economy

palgrave
macmillan

Alexander Styhre
Gothenburg, Sweden

ISBN 978-3-030-45544-6 ISBN 978-3-030-45545-3 (eBook)
https://doi.org/10.1007/978-3-030-45545-3

This Palgrave Macmillan imprint is published by the registered company Springer Nature Switzerland AG.
The registered company address is: Gewerbestrasse 11, 6330 Cham, Switzerland

Preface

"The problem with fiction, it has to be plausible. That's not true with non-fiction," Tom Wolfe, American novelist and one of the pioneers of the New Journalism school, once remarked. This is an inspirational dictum for social science scholars inasmuch as we should not shy away from what appears to be implausible or even absurd. I believe that theoretical frameworks need to be "plausible" in the sense of being understandable and appear to be reasonable, but, when it comes to empirics, some results are "too good to be true" inasmuch as empirical conditions may vastly exceed what even the most imaginative mind would have been able to anticipate. Think, for instance, of the various evidence of opportunistic behaviour when it comes to executive decision making during the first decade of the new millennium, including the fabled Enron bankruptcy in 2001 and the AIG rescue activities in 2008–2009, offering inroads to a world wherein, for example, economic compensation in the form of bonuses is not so much a matter of performance as it is an entitlement, an attitude that represents a return to medieval or pre-modern aristocratic norms regarding God-given authority and privileges justified thereupon. Also when it comes to the effect of new digital media, some empirical outcomes are simply mind-boggling. Consider, for instance, the once relatively small Finnish video game company Rovio, which developed the massive hit *Angry Birds*, a casual video game that had been downloaded in excess of 1 billion times when my colleague interviewed a company representative in early February 2014. Tom Wolfe did not provide a yardstick for actually measuring degrees of plausibility but, for me personally, such unexpected (but not unanticipated) outcomes do not qualify as "plausible" in the conventional sense of the term. Yet, implausible things happen every now and then.

This is what is so deeply intriguing but also vexing about video game development, that the sheer creativity and ability to organize product development activities so that they result in a digital object that eventually are distributed all over the globe, and at the speed of light (financial capital also amass at an almost equally high speed) is the primary driver of the industry: video game developers can *de facto* emerge from obscurity, being socially, culturally, and not the least financially marginalized figures to become international superstars and overnight sensations. That was the case of Markus Persson, better known under his developer *non de plume* Notch (programming is a species of writing, even authorship, after all), whose company Mojang developed *Minecraft* that became a major hit as soon as it was released in 2011. Persson was suddenly a multi-millionaire who did not have to worry too much about the next game to develop (for two accounts of the *Minecraft* phenomenon, see Arnroth 2013; Goldberg and Larsson 2012). In September 2019, *The Guardian* listed *Minecraft* as "the best video game of the 21st century" (Stuart and MacDonald 2019), an accolade that is indicative of the significance of the video game. "With more than 175 m copies now sold on an array of devices from smart-phones to virtual-reality headsets, Minecraft has transcended the idea of what games are and what they can achieve," *The Guardian* stated. In 2018, Mojang reported a turnover in excess of 200 million euros and was named the most profitable developer studio in the entire industry (Swedish Games Industry 2019: 7). Such highly "implausible" and infrequent, yet not impossible, scenarios are what fuels the indie video game industry. Needless to say, most indie video game developers do not reasonably anticipate a career trajectory comparable to Notch's. Instead, video game development is initiated and justified by the love of video games and the video gaming experience, the ambition to turn novel gaming ideas and game concepts into functional digital objects through collaborative efforts with other individuals sharing this commitment to the "digital arts." Yet, there is a lingering thought that when the conditions are right and luck is surfacing, huge commercial successes can result in what is unexpected (but, again, not unanticipated), that is, "implausible." This ambition to make money is arguably not the principal motivator, but it is a form of icing on the cake or the sugar-coating on the pill that is hard to fully forget once the thought has struck one's mind. Especially in a world totally determined by digital distribution channels and online real-time reporting on sales, the chance of commercial and financial success is a constitutive feature of the industry.

So who are these "indie developers"? Keogh (2015) introduces the indie developer community in the following terms:

> [A] far more diverse range of creators, audiences, and modes of video games production and consumption has emerged with the rise of digital distribution and a proliferation of platforms. International corporate publishers now compete with—and draw influence from—smaller teams of individuals that are finding their own critical and commercial success in vibrant independent scenes. (Keogh 2015: 152)

This volume will report empirical materials from a study of indie developers in Sweden to better explain how what is called innovation-led growth is in fact predicated on the individual's ability to commit him or herself to innovative activities that are uncertain (not the least in terms of estimating market demand) and beset by the difficulty to raise money to finance the development work. Economists have consistently argued in favour of developed economies changing their production activities so that more sophisticated and knowledge-intensive work is conducted, while allegedly less demanding production activities are offshored to "developing economies" with lower production costs. One of the consequence is that professional work includes activities that are determined by a high degree of uncertainty, for example, basic research, new drug development, and the creation of new technologies such as "green energy," all of which are unified by the difficulty to anticipate market conditions and the wider socio-economic consequences of the new technologies (say, the development of automatic transportation systems, no longer demanding skilled and experienced drivers). Such development work may be part of the R&D activities of large corporations, generating the finance capital through their regular business activities, or on the basis of state-controlled investment agencies in, for example, basic research in the life sciences. At the same time, industries such as video game development fall outside of these regular financing systems inasmuch as the industry is relatively new, having a short history that stretches back to the 1980s or 1990s, and therefore has not yet accumulated the funds needed to support innovation work in the fringes of the industry, in, for example, indie development communities and businesses. Furthermore, video games are not yet consecrated to the level where it is eligible for state funding and subsidies, as in the case of the liberal arts (dramatic theatre, visual arts, literature, film, etc.), which makes video game development an exclusively market-based activity, operating outside of stated political interests and responsibilities. A current economic doctrine stipulates that small and enterprising industry sectors propel the capitalist economy and push it into new equilibrium, but policy makers and politicians, otherwise concerned with job creation and stable economic growth, are surprisingly reluctant to support industries that have the potential to carry such responsibilities. Until policy makers are presented with a *fait accompli*, they are largely unable to detect the weak market signals and respond to them in ways that support innovation-led growth. This is the predicament of the innovation-led economy: businesses at the fringe of the economy do not yet have the contacts with policy makers who would help them ensure a place on the political agenda. In practice, this means that especially financial concerns are left in the dark by policy makers, transferring the responsibility to raise the money needed to finance the development work to individual market actors.

This might sound like an overtly negative scenario, but, as a matter of fact, the Swedish video game is a success story in terms of job growth, turnover, and status and prestige on the global arena. "I think this is a very inspiring industry," an indie developer (Company M) remarked: "There are jobs and there is know-how that can be used elsewhere. If you are not directly involved in developing games, you can still participate in gamification, and such things [in other industries]." Most of these accomplishments have been made without any defined finance capital infusions, subsidies, or exemptions granted by the state. Instead, the Swedish video game has emerged and consolidated outside of a supportive economic policy framework. A study of indie video game developers therefore not only must include the behavioural and motivational factors that industry actors refer to when justifying their choice of career, but also should address the broader issues of economic policy and dominant economic ideas regarding the differences between, for example, imitation-led growth (as in the case of the expanding Chinese economy) and the innovation-led growth in many developed economies. The former category of theories is introduced and examined in the third chapter of this volume, whereas the latter issue is addressed in the second chapter. Under all conditions, innovation-led growth of the kind that, for example, the video game industry is representative of is fuelled by a passionate commitment to video games and digital media and gaming more widely, but it would be inadequate to ignore the economic conditions wherein such human skills and resources materialized into video games. Everyday work demands finance capital to pay salaries and acquire the resources needed, and therefore the formula for innovation-led growth necessarily includes both human resources and finance capital. A management studies view of video game development therefore needs to incorporate both production factors to fully understand how the innovation-led growth doctrine easily understates either of the two production factors. By the end of the day, innovation-led growth is not some kind of naturally occurring market phenomenon, emerging as some auxiliary benefit of liberal pro-market legislation, lenient regulatory control, and the presence of wise finance capital investors willing to commit their capital to enterprising activities. This free-market scenario is not the operational model for industrial policy. Instead, this volume simultaneously stipulates and substantiates the idea that innovation-led growth is based on a combination of economic, financial, legal, social, and cultural conditions that are complicated to disentangle when explaining specific successes in sectors of the economy, *after the fact*. This means that innovation-led growth cannot be a heavy-handed subsidizing of certain sectors and industries as such lack of discrimination between promising ventures and less viable business activities easily overprices entrepreneurial ventures and oversponsors low-quality entrepreneurs. For instance, in video game development, it is virtually impossible for industry actors to anticipate market success, and the chances of state-controlled innovation agency business developers and counsellors making predictions with higher precision than industry insiders are small and unreasonable to assume. Instead, innovation-led growth needs to operate through a variety of mechanisms to better assist local initiatives and to exploit emerging conditions. Expressed in more prosaic terms, industry policy conducive to innovation-led growth is a complicated pursuit, which demands an open-ended attitude towards emerging market properties. In showing these features of one of the current high-growth industries, this volume hopefully makes a more substantial contribution to the management studies literature than to merely report an empirical material that apprehends the nature of indie video development work. At least the volume is written with that intention.

Gothenburg, Sweden — Alexander Styhre

References

Arnroth, T. (2013). *Ett år med Mojang: Minecraft bakom kulisserna*. Stockholm: Publit.

Goldberg, D., & Larsson, L. (2012). *Minecraft: Block, pixlar och att göra sig en hacka: Historien om Markus "Notch" Persson och spelet som vände allt upp och ned*. Norstedt: Stockholm.

Keogh, B. (2015). Between Triple-A, indie, casual, and DIY. In K. Oakley & J. O'Connor (Eds.), *The Routledge companion to the cultural industries* (pp. 152–162). Abingdon: Routledge.

Stuart, K., & MacDonald, K. (2019, September 19). The 50 best video games of the 21st century. Retrieved September 20, 2019, from https://www.theguardian.com/games/2019/sep/19/50-best-video-games-of-the-21st-century

Swedish Games Industry. (2019). *Game development index 2019*, Stockholm. Retrieved September 30, 2019, from https://static1.squarespace.com/static/5a61edb7a803bb7a65252b2d/t/5d8a30a5c6a41508c50d8e6c/1569337529201/Spelutvecklarindex_digital_20190924.pdf

Acknowledgements

This research work is enabled on the basis of a research grant from the Swedish research agency FORTE (Grant Number 2017-00834). I am grateful for receiving funding to conduct the study. First of all, I would like to thank all the video game developers and video game industry representatives who have committed some of their time to the interviews conducted within the research project. Without the active and in many cases quite enthusiastic participation of these busy individuals, there would be previously little to say, at least on the basis of empirical grounds. Second, my colleague Björn Remneland-Wikhamn has made a first-rate contribution to this volume inasmuch as he conducted roughly half of the interviews that were included in the research project. Björn is a highly skilled and experienced interviewer and social science scholar, and his capacity to create interview situations wherein the informants speak freely about their view of the development work is exemplary. In addition, Björn is an excellent speaking partner with whom joint "brainstorming" is regularly rewarding and inspiring. Third, I would like to recognize the commissioning editor at Palgrave Macmillan, Jessica Harrison, for granting me a book contract. I have been fortunate to publish a number of books with Palgrave Macmillan over the years, and it has always been a pleasant experience to collaborate with the publisher's excellent staff.

Finally, I would like to thank my family, Sara, Simon, and Max, for helping me distract my mind outside of the work hours, which fortunately makes academic work something new to discover every morning when the new day begins.

Contents

CHAPTER 1

The Ethnographer's Dilemma: To Understand a World That Is Not Your Own While Avoiding to Misrepresenting It

Introduction: Claude Lévi-Strauss and the Anthropologist's Predicament

Scholars who are engaged in research and critical commentary on video games are referred to as "ludologists" (Keogh 2014), an academic specialism dedicated to the analysis of video games as digital artefact, as a source of experience, and as a cultural object. My concern is that I am not a gamer (even though I grew up in the 1980s as the first generation that could play video games on so-called "home computers" such as Commodore Vic-20 or Commodore ViC-64, and occasionally did so), nor am I particularly engaged in the intra-disciplinary debates that, for example, Keogh (2014) accounts for. Neither am I an activist that promotes, say, transgender interests (which I do not oppose either, if anyone care to know), nor pursue any other politically charged topic pertaining to video game production, promotion, or use. Instead, I am the schoolbook case of the uneventful and by any means "normal" cisgender-man, being, with Marguerite Duras' (2011: 27) memorable phrase (after recognizing her inability to attract any attention from people on the street, or otherwise having limited "celebrity capital"), "the triumph of banality." For me, as a business school scholar, trained and experienced from field studies in a variety of industries and sectors of the economy, video games are part of a highly innovative and expansive industry and is therefore a business that deserves attention regardless of the absence of personal or even private objectives. This means that I share with Keogh (2014) and other

A. Styhre, *Indie Video Game Development Work*,
https://doi.org/10.1007/978-3-030-45545-3_1

ludologists the ambition to shed light on video game production and consumption, but my angle on the business may be somewhat different than theirs. Yet the question remains, what could this outsider figure do with a set of first-hand empirical data in the absence of more detailed understandings and commitment to the video game as such? I will here consume some of my stipulated or imagined scholarly liberties to discuss this concern not so much as some epistemological afterthought, but as being an issue worthy of some detailed analysis and precise justification.

In many cases, methodological issues are the residual of scholarly work, the residual components of theoretical grandeur or explorative projects in a field of practice, an obligatory passage point that remains to be accounted for when all is said and done. Yet, the question of methodology is a core issue in scholarly work, being the anchoring point between theoretical ambitions and practical research work, the field and the scholar's desk. Methodology is present everywhere on the scholar's written pages, yet it remains curiously marginal to the overarching pursuit: to accumulate academic credibility and the various benefits that derive therefrom (e.g., salaried positions, received research grants, seats in prestigious editorial boards and decision-making communities). As this volume deals with a specific social and professional community with whom its author is not particularly familiar (at least not when the study was initiated), this book will open with a reflection regarding how to learn about a specific tribe or community with whom the researcher shares few beliefs, traditions, skills, and social norms, but without misrepresenting these people. The proposition is that this is no easy matter: the scholar's ambition is under the constant threat of being corrupted by misunderstanding, beliefs (inherited or learned), preferences, and a variety of other cognitive and behavioural conditions that the scholar cannot reasonably be assumed to command.

Philip Roth (2017: 381), the American author and one of the notable contemporary writers that in fact never received a Nobel Prize in literature, despite being rumoured to have been on the shortlist for decades, and being an accurate observer of the human condition, remarks that "Everybody has a hard work. All real work is hard." This statement serves at the same time as an observation regarding factual conditions and as a credo, a normative statement portraying "real work," that is, work that is conducted *de rigueur*, as what in fact demands the full commitment of the writer or anyone else doing what they do for a living. This is a proposition that applies also to the ethnographer's work. Claude Lévi-Strauss' *Tristes Tropiques*, first published in 1955, is an exemplary case of an anthropologist's sincere and confessional account of the ordeal of field work. The volume opens with Lévi-Strauss pithily remarking that "I hate travelling and explorers," before he account for his explorative travels into the Amazonas and elsewhere. In *Tristes Tropiques*, the anthropologist's work is far from glamorous but is beset by practical issues and concerns to be handled to be able to proceed at all. For instance, Lévi-Strauss recalls how his career as an anthropologist started in 1934 when Celestin Bouglé, the head of École Normale Supérieur, offered him a teaching position in São Paolo, a place that according to Bouglé was a fine choice for an aspiring anthropologist as the "suburbs are full of Indians, whom you can study at the weekends" (Lévi-Strauss 1955 [1973]: 47). Such a thinly veiled pragmatic view of the research pursuit is rarely disclosed in the writing that is eventually produced in the scholar's study. Indians should be studied *in situ*, in their "natural habitat," the anthropological imagination stipulates, and not serve as some object of casual observations during some lecturer's spare-time and weekends. Nevertheless, Lévi-Strauss (1955 [1973]) accounts for what John Law (1994: 43–44) would four decades later refer to as "the ethnographer's anxiety," the lingering concern that the anthropologist or ethnographer misses out much of the action as he or she unfortunately fails to be at the right place at the right time. "Where the ethnographer is, the Action is not," Law (1994: 45) deduces.

In addition to portraying patience—almost super-human patience—as the principal virtue of the anthropologist, *Tristes Tropiques* also addresses the issue of *how* to represent a social community and the social world this community creates and maintains when the observer cannot fully apprehend the life world of these people being subject to scholarly inquiries. Werner von Herzog's movie *Where the Green Ants Dream* (1984) portrays a conflict between an Australian mining company and the Aboriginal community whose land the mining company in their view desecrates through its business operations. In one scene, one of the spokesmen of the Aboriginal community, following a considerably long explanation of the significance of the land for the tribe, exclaims that the mining company representative "does not understand!" The mining company interlocutor is the first to admit that this is undoubtedly true as he has no possibilities given his cultural background and, indeed, inherited cosmology, to fully understand the worldview of the Aboriginal community. At this point, Herzog suggests that there are things that are simply impossible to "understand" in the conventional sense of the term. The scene shows, as Ludwig Wittgenstein once remarked, that in order to have a dispute, many norms and beliefs need to be shared (perhaps this is why disputes in the realm of marriage can be both animated and prolonged, at times lasting for decades), or else the dispute dissolves into sheer misunderstanding as there is no shared common ground wherein the dispute can be staged and fuelled. In the end, this predicament instructs the anthropologist or ethnographer to be concerned with the representation of the other.

Perceived realities are indeed *social* (a truism, for sure), and to be able to account for the constitutive elements of such realities, the observer needs to be familiar with the norms and beliefs that render social realities meaningful and intelligible. This means that the ethnographer needs to maintain an open-ended attitude towards the object of study and abandon any misconceptions when there is limited empirical support for propositions stipulated *ex ante*. To better illustrate the virtue of critically assessing assumptions, the laboratory studies literature, being part of the wider science and technology studies scholarship, can be referenced. From afar, scientific research work may appear authoritative, conclusive, and credible: The end result *is what it is*, and there are few other outcomes that appear plausible for the reader of the final article that, say, convey the laboratory research data and theoretical implications derived therefrom. At the same time, to assume that the laboratory research work that precedes this contribution is equally well ordered is mistaken. Instead, for example, laboratory studies reveal that the day-to-day work in the laboratory is more open-ended, messier, more confusing, and more difficult to overlook for the outside observer than a common sense view would assume. Knorr Cetina (1983: 123) accounts for such experiences on the basis of her fieldwork:

> If ethnographers of science had hoped to come up with a set of parameters which neatly specify this process they were quickly disappointed. A day in the laboratory will usually suffice to impress upon the observer a sense of the disorder within which scientists operate, and a month in the lab with confirm that most laboratory work is concerned with counteracting and remedying this disorder. (Knorr Cetina 1983: 123)

Also Jordan and Lynch (1992: 84) testify to such insights: "[W]e are alerted to the conditions of instability and fragmentation in routine laboratory practice." Does this struggle against "disorder" and the "instability" of the laboratory work in any way compromise the authority of the research community? If the messiness of things *per se* is regarded as an evidence of poor practices, that may be the case, but such lay beliefs do not contain the detailed expertise needed to pass such judgement with credibility. A more reasonable assumption is that the perceived messiness of the procedures and day-to-day routine is either derived from the external observers' inability to detect and account for the intricate order of the laboratory work, or, alternatively and plausibly, that the complexity or the empirical issues at hand *demand* the work procedures to operate outside of the pedant's preference for order and structure. Under all conditions, the laboratory researcher's capacity to navigate within complex experimental systems and theoretical frameworks is admirable and is arguably not everybody's business. In the end, the example of laboratory research studies indicates that it is very easy for the external observer to project beliefs and/or preferences onto the object of study and to inscribe qualities, norms, preferences, and so on into equally humans and the machines and tools they use in their day-to-day work. Common sense thinking is one component to consider when seeking to avoid such projections. Preference is another issue, being more difficult to handle as individuals are not always aware of their preferences, and because preferences shift over time as novel conditions and opportunities emerge (March 1978). Consequently, what scholars may learn from Lévi-Strauss and others who are concerned with the challenge to portray specific communities is that this is a lingering concern, with few ready-made off-the-shelf solutions.

A considerable scholarly literature calls for reflexivity as a remedy to this predicament (Holmes 2010; Mauthner and Doucet 2003; Cunliffe 2003; Pels 2000; Bourdieu and Wacquant 1992), but for most part, reflexivity is conceived in voluntarism terms, that is, it is assumed that individual scholars can *choose* to be reflexive whenever it suits their interests (Lynch 2000). An alternative view portrays reflexivity in determinist terms, being a "gift"—or, perhaps better, a "curse"—that cannot be escaped or simply ignored at will. Reflexivity may also be considered in more fatalist terms, being something that surfaces during episodes of clear-sighted revelations and epiphanies, which make the scholar capable of suddenly overseeing their entire field of inquiry in a broad daylight. In the end, to refer to reflexivity is little more than a threadbare argument that renders interpretative skills to both the cause and effect of scholarly inquiry, simply reasserting that the scholar by experience, training, or sheer authority has a capacity to transcend his or her own cognitive and affective dispositions. That is, to simply invoke reflexivity as an epistemological *ad hoc* hypothesis of sorts does not solve anything but only introduces additional epistemological issues.

To cut to the chase, the ethnographer's anxiety does not simply refer to the sense of wasting one's career in places where not much is happening, but also denotes the more epistemological question regarding the authority to portray communities not being your own. This is not exclusively a scholar's predicament but is part of a variety of social activities and economic and administrative functions: Can adults write books for children, when they no longer are children themselves, for instance? Children are not likely to write their own books, so children's books as a genre may be permitted on the basis of factual conditions and practical limitations. How can the upper crust of political parties represent the working people, when they themselves have chosen to leave this career path (e.g., Carnes 2013)? The democratic system is far from perfect, but the political system demands skilled and experienced actors which unfortunately make careers as professional politicians a necessary evil in the eyes of sceptical voters. The list goes on. In this case, how can a non-gamer gain insight into the everyday life world of a community of individuals committed to video game development? Is this person stuck in the same position as Werner von Herzog's mining industry site manager, of necessity unable to "understand" the concerns of the other as he does not share their life world nor the norms, beliefs, and aspirations derived therefrom. One may answer this question non-affirmatively if "understanding" is treated as a complete and unified whole, unable to be compromised. If "understanding" is treated as what can be permitted to be partial, sketchy, and incomplete, and yet carrying some meaning that benefits an outside observer or an audience, then this specific community may be explored under such premises. Just like the adult author writing for juvenile audiences, the uninformed or uncommitted scholar may try his or her best to understand what is at the fringe of his or her own social worlds. Yet, the predicament of representation remains, and this is the primary reason why insightful writers such as Claude Lévi-Strauss should be read by every new generation of scholars. In the end, this is what this volume intends to do, to account for what indie developers do, but under the influence of the all-too-human cognitive and affective limitations that befalls all scholarly writers. Indeed, all real work is hard work.

The Ethnographer's Assignment: To Unveil Everyday Practices and Their Meaning

Watson (2011: 205. Original emphasis omitted) defines an ethnographic study as a "style of social science writing which draws upon the writer's close observation of and involvement with people in a particular social setting and relates the words spoken and the practices observed or experienced to the overall cultural framework within which they occurred." Barley and Kunda (2004: 19), in turn, offer the following definition: "An ethnography is a study of a group of people in which the data are collected by some combination of participant observation and interviews. The ethnographer's objective is usually to describe and depict 'the native's point of view', the perspective of the people studied." It is precisely what Watson (2011: 205) refers to as "the overall cultural framework," and Barley and Kunda (2004: 19) call "the native's point of view" that is vexing in the eyes of individual scholar, and that calls for the discussions addressed in the previous section. To make the claim that a certain study indubitably recognizes an "overall cultural framework," or that the observations made, or the quotes included in the volume, honour "the native's point of view" is a bold statement. More specifically, for the practicing scholar, spending time with "the other," these qualities mentioned in the passing in such definitions appear as sweeping formulations, still to be filled with meaning on the basis of example. Above all, such components of the ethnographic study assume some kind of heterogeneity in the community subject to empirical research. Several ethnographic scholars have called attention to the risk of overstating such heterogeneity. Clifford Geertz, for instance, speaks about the need to pay attention to the "soft facts" of any community being examined:

> No matter how much one train one's attention on the supposedly hard facts of social existence ... the supposedly soft facts of that existence, what do people imagine human life to be all about, how do they think one ought to live, what grounds belief, legitimizes punishment, sustains hope, or accounts for loss, crowd in to disturb simple pictures of might, desire, calculation, and interest. (Geertz 1995: 43)

What may appear to be the conventional wisdom or widely shared beliefs in a community may on closer inspection include a variety of norms and beliefs. Furthermore, the human preference for coherence, and the predictability such a coherence permits, is mirrored in scholarly research procedures and the accompanying reward system that compensates research that stipulates coherence and predictability. In addition, the conventional wisdom is that scholars can actively construct meaningful images of the whole on the basis of detailed understanding of the parts: "A major problem in any form of social research is reasoning from the parts we know something about the whole they and parts like them make up," Becker (1992: 213) writes. He continues: "We want to create an image of the entire organization or process, based on the parts we have been able to uncover." This assumption manifests itself in a variety of claims derived from a reductionist epistemology wherein the parts mirror the whole, wherein synergies are marginal, and the analysis can "zoom in and out" without ignoring any details or nuances in the empirical material. The belief that the analyst can already assume a certain coherence in the object of study oftentimes results in an overconfidence regarding the quality of the object of study, Becker (2009) says:

> Researchers usually don't know enough to formulate good hypotheses until they are well into their work, a fact which results from the iterative nature of qualitative social science. It follows that they should deliberately not accept the common understanding on which such theorizing would have to rest. (Becker 2009: 548)

For instance, rather than to build a study on neither what "everybody knows," or what representatives of the object of study tell the researcher, Becker (2009: 548) instructs scholars to build theories on "unexpected observations made in the field." As a matter of fact, scholars do for most parts know relatively little, and therefore they need to pursue an explorative research activity, designed to maximize the inflow of meaningful empirical data and observations. This predicament regarding the inability to anticipate outcomes is an unavoidable fact of ethnographic work, Van Maanen (2011: 220) argues, worth citing at length:

> Fieldwork my appear romantic and adventurous from the outside, but on the inside there is a good deal of child-like if now blind wandering about the field. Cultural oversight, misunderstandings, embarrassment, and ineptitudes are common. Relationships based on certain kind of rapport form only

> with time, patience, and luck. Choices of topics, frameworks, and substantive domains emerge only after considerable thought and experimentation ... In short, learning is (and out) of the field is uneven, usually unforeseen, and rests more on a logic of discovery and happenstance than a logic of verification and plan. (Van Maanen 2011: 220)

To claim to know what the outcome would be prior to the engagement in the field is not a flattering attitude, and in the worst case scenario, this overconfidence may block meaningful learnings or insights.

Based on these admonitions and concerns, the design of the study of unfamiliar communities and their business practices needs to recognize both practical concerns and epistemological fallacies. Agar (1996) instructs aspiring ethnographers to fashion a "professional stranger" identity for themselves. That is, the ethnographer is a stranger to the community being explored, an outsider or an uninformed visitor, but this visitor acts professionally to be able to learn as much as possible about the community he or she enters. Professionalism is here tangential to being "ambitious" inasmuch as the professional stranger actively seeks to overcome his or her lack of know-how and skill in the new domain. Agar's (1996) model offers the benefit of actively encouraging scholars to re-locate themselves to unfamiliar domains, and to actively take risks and to explore what is yet unchartered territories. In the current university governance regime, structured around algorithm governance on the basis of bibliometric publishing data (Wedlin 2006; Bok 2002; Espeland and Stevens 1998), scholarly liberties are no longer of necessity claimed as many academic researchers are more concerned with taking the shortest route to secure positions. In the current study, the professional stranger model was adhered to inasmuch as the indie video game development work is largely alien to the author's own life: having only limited experience from gaming in a fairly distant adolescent past, and being mildly informed about the cultural circuit of video gamers, and with few professional connections to the industry outside of the research activities, the indie video game development community appears to be remote from the author's everyday life.

The Study: Methodological Issues

Design of the Study

The Social Science Ethnography Literature

The ethnographic literature in the social sciences and in management studies is quite diverse and covers many areas. To structure this literature in terms of the socio-economic hierarchy of the object of study, the high-brow topics include ethnographic studies of business practices such as a breakfast meeting in New York City (Rosen 1985), Wall Street's (Ho 2009) or Shanghai's (Hertz 1998) finance institutions, advanced medical practice and research work such as reproductive medicine (Franklin and Roberts 2006) or work in medical visualization (Cohn 2004), professional design work such as architect work (Comi and Whyte 2018), or industry design (Stigliani and Ravasi 2018). All these studies explore professional communities, in many cases generously compensated and bestowed with extensive benefits such as annual bonuses, as in the case of financial traders. The middle-brow literature includes ethnographic studies of sales work (Leidner 1993), service workers such as doormen (Fine 1996), and a host of studies that are perhaps best characterized as industry sociology studies, including workplace studies either on the shop-floor (Korczynski 2011a, b; Delbridge 1998; Burawoy 1979; Roy 1952) or in the middle management ranks (Dalton 1959; Gouldner 1954; Jaques 1951). This category of studies also includes ethnographies wherein technologies and digital media are key components such as the studies of copy machines technicians (Orr 1996), video game users (Thornham 2011), and digital media work, such as the work to edit and negotiate Wikipedia entries (Jemielniak 2014). At the lower-end of the socio-economic hierarchy, there are studies of waitresses (Paules 1991), maids (Constable 1997), and homeless people (Spradley 1988), all leading an everyday life that tends to be precarious and fraught by difficulties. Finally, a small proportion of ethnographies address activities that are for most part "out of sight" as they are either illegal as in the case of the wholesale drug dealers studied by Adler (1985), or are located at the fringe of society as in the case of nightclub hostesses who work for free or are compensated by gifts such as meals or free drinks (Mears 2015). Taken together, this corpus of ethnographic texts reveals the remarkable complexity of the contemporary and highly differentiated society, and provides insight into the human condition, wherein issues such as economic compensation, authority, expertise, status, and so on are key analytical terms that serve to decode the unchartered territories visited by academic researchers.

Technology-Based Ethnographies

Of particular interest in this setting is the role of technology, and more specifically digital media played in indie video game development. Ingold (1999: 434) references the work of the French archaeologist André Leroi-Gourhan, who argued that technology is the "driving force" behind all progress, and that technology development is an "autonomous force that is effectively outside of human control." "The relationship between individual and social values in humans varies in direct proportion with the evolution of technoeconomic structures," Leroi-Gourhan (1993 [1964]: 146) writes. Ingold's (1999) view, technology is constitutive of human societies inasmuch as the invention of, for example, pottery to store food, and the capacity to prepare hot meals enabled better nutrition. Better nutrition in turn increased the intelligence of the population over time and released time for additional technological innovations as less time had to committed to collecting foodstuff. Technology considered in such terms is co-produced with human civilization—not its primary consequence. "In a sense," Georges Canguilhem (2008: 8) writes, "nothing is more human than a machine, if it is true that man distinguishes himself from animals through the construction of tools and machines."

When technologies are further developed, when the tool is combined with other devices and becomes a machine, or when machines are co-located into technological ensembles, technologies become more complicated to oversee and understand. The French philosopher Gilbert Simondon (2017 [1958]: 40) speaks about the "concretization of technical objects" as the process wherein the distance between science and technology becomes narrower and eventually merges in the materialization of the tool, machinery, or technological apparatus. Seen in this view, technologies do not fall from the sky, nor are they immediately invented by an act of genius, but rather tend to slowly materialize and stabilize over time, and on the basis of the numerous modifications and improvements made by its inventors and users. If technology is always already part of the social community and its way of functioning, technology is never self-enclosed or final; rather, technology is subject to ceaseless modifications and manipulations made by its users, practices that adjust and direct the technology towards practical utility in specific domains (Anderson and Robey 2017;

Denis and Pontille 2015; Faulkner and Runde 2009). Franz (2005) proposes the term *tinkering* as a concept that liberates technology from it more grandiose scientific connotations and inscribes agency into the users, now qualified to actively interact with and modify technology:

> The concept of tinkering is useful in scholarly terms because it acknowledges that small changes in the technology were important in challenging dominant ideas about who could access and have some power over new technologies and who could cross the boundaries between consumption and invention. (Franz 2005: 165)

This view serves to demystify technology and to re-locate it in *medias res*, in the middle of things, in its domain of practical use. "Technology is not about universality as most philosophy of technology misleadingly suggests. It is about functioning in concrete, complex situations," Brian Wynne says (cited in Downer 2007: 20). By implication, if technology is what gradually emerges from within human communities and societies, being simultaneously the cause and effect of socially differentiated orders, technology cannot be functionally separated from what is social; technology and society are always already co-produced in ways that make the two entities complicated to disentangle *ex post* (Rennstam 2012; Latour 1991; Barley 1986): "Technology is not reducible to politics. Nor is to claim that technological devices and artefacts are 'social constructions' or are 'socially shaped': for the social is not something which exists independently from technology," Barry (2001: 9) suggests.

The concept of tinkering is of particular interest in the domain of digital media, a specific form of technology that combines computer technology and digital technologies. Digital media is today a pervasive phenomenon, structuring and shaping everyday life as billions of people spend everyday life within the realm of digital media. "[T]oday's life is not only concerned with technology, it co-emerges with it," Boucher (2012: 92) remarks, and the philosopher of technology Paul Virilio remarks that "technology is our own nature" (cited in Virilio and Lotringer 1997: 28). At the same time as it is easy to be mesmerized by digital media and to overstate the similarities between different digital media, it is important, media theorists emphasize, to discriminate between classes and types of digital media. Aaseth (2001: 418) suggests that "some paper media had more in common with some digital media than certain digital media had with each other," and that the "analog/digital distinction" widely used in popular culture and in scholarly communities is "overrated," "uninformative," and "breaks down under scrutiny." Just like a pair of scissors are structurally and functionally different from a microwave oven, so do classes and types of digital media, say a smartphone application or an mp3 file, display diverse qualities that need to be recognized on closer inspection.

This snapshot overview of the literature on technology, digital media, and human society, beginning in the pre-historic period and ending in the current period of time, is important for the object of study as indie video game developers spend a considerable period of time within the technological frame[1] defined by digital media: video games are developed within digital media, distributed through the Internet, and played by the end-user, the gamer, on laptops and mobile devices such as smart phones or tablets, and the reviews and commentaries are posted on digital forums such as the digital distributor's (the "publisher") home pages or social media sites. In addition, indie developers are in many cases themselves gamers, spending at least certain periods browsing the supply of new games and checking out new gaming ideas and concepts. Based on these experiences, it would be adequate to claim that digital media are the indie developer's "own nature." Furthermore, the collapse of the distinction between technology and society advocated by technology philosophers and technology studies scholars is of relevance for indie developers as video games are cutting through the conventional categories that are constitutive of everyday life. "As a cultural product, a video game is a complex mix of technology, art, and interactive story," Cohendet and Simon (2007: 587) says. Furthermore, Jagoda (2018: 200–201) argues that the historical view of video games as commodities or entertainment product is now questioned as video games are more frequently associated with art and political advocacy. To better substantiate such claims, Jagoda (2018: 201) distinguishes between three discrete types of difficulties in video games. The first is the *mechanical difficulty* of the video game that includes the challenge the video game introduces and that is dependent on the gamer's

[1]The concept *technological frame* was introduced in science and technology studies and comprises, Bijker (1995: 123) writes, "all elements that influence the interactions within relevant social groups and lead to the attribution of meanings to technical artefacts." That is, the technological frame constitutes the technology as what it practically speaking is. In Pinch and Trocco's (2002: 309–310) more recent use of the term, a technological frame "captures the way a whole series of practices, ideas, and values get built around a technology." Importantly in this context, the technological frame "includes both the ways technologies are produced and the ways they are used and consumed."

performance and skills. The second challenge is *interpretive difficulty*, which denotes the aesthetic and design elements of the game that the user needs to decode and understand. Jagoda (2018) proposes that video games share this difficulty with, for example, poetry and visual arts, demanding interpretative skills from its readers and audience. Third and finally, Jagoda (2018) speaks about *affective difficulty* in the case wherein video games "[e]voke emotions and generate affects in players that include experiences of anger, boredom, curiosity, complicity, pleasure, and uncertainty." In this new analytical framework, Jagoda (2018) paves the way for a more comprehensive and affirmative view of video games as complex and manifold digital objects that simultaneously need to be understood as technological entities, artistic expressions, and meaning-generating devices to fully apprehend the video game developer's challenge and accomplishment.

In summary, ethnographic research work serves to unveil the intricate details and the expertise needed to handle these issues inherent to virtually all professional or occupational work, or any other activity that a common sense attitude would render insignificant and unworthy of more detailed investigation. To reach down to this sufficient scale of detail, various forms of tools, machines, technologies, and digital media need to be included and also understood as what are constitutive of the specific community being examined.

The Mode of Production: Indie Game Development and the Video Game Industry

The historical view. Media theorists such as Lev Manovich (2001: 20) argue persuasively that video games represent a convergence of two separate historical trajectories, that of *computing* and *media technologies*, respectively, both being developed in the middle of the first half of the nineteenth century. Many scholars and video game researchers in particular emphasize that video games constitute an entirely new species in the domain of digital media, in need of its own theories and analytical framework to be apprehended in their entire complexity. "Video games have introduced a new language and aesthetic field that is distinct from visual new media of the twentieth century such as film and television," Jagoda (2018: 133) writes. Following Manovich (2001: 132), video games are "cinematographic" in their interface, "digital" on the material level, and "computational" (i.e., "software driven") in their logic.

In terms of practical development, the history of video game development is quite recent, stretching back to the early 1950s, and being essentially a form of curiosity within the field of computer science development, intimately co-developed with the industrial-military complex. Whereas the development of the computer was the outcome from Big Government and Big Science joining hands to defeat the risk of being outmanoeuvred by political antagonists during the cold war period, the video game industry has its roots in a hobbyist tradition and an adolescent—primarily male—culture. Jørgensen, Sandqvist, and Sotamaa (2017: 458) examine the development of a video game industry in the proper sense of the term in the Three Nordic countries of Sweden, Norway, and Finland, and they remark that there were commercial games developed already in the mid-1980s, but the first companies were not established until the early 1900s. What was referred to as the *demoscene* in the 1980s, a hobbyist subculture that "had its origins in the earlier forms of home computer culture such as 1980s software piracy scene" (Jørgensen et al. 2017: 458), served as the first platform for video game development. Participants in the *demoscene* developed small games that they shared in the community, and which was further improved on the basis of suggestions from other gamers. This trade of games, ideas, and suggestions for improvements in the games resulted in what Jørgensen, Sandqvist, and Sotamaa (2017: 458) refer to as "an ambitious art form of its own," a new cultural expression derived from the creative use of computer technology and video game technologies.

The development of the first components of an emerging video game industry also differed between regions. In Japan, for instance, a highly urbanized society with 120 million people living in an area no larger than Great Britain, and being one of the world's most advanced economies, there was already a differentiated popular culture that included game arcades, an autochthonous toy and popular culture industry, and a consumer electronics industry that jointly supported the development of the regional video game industry (Aoyama and Izushi 2003). In contrast, the more rural societies of the Nordic countries essentially lacked this cultural and industrial infrastructure but had to seek other ways to integrate regional participants in video game development:

> A Nordic game company in the 1980s or early 1990s could not rely on much domestic support. There were no local publishers and few hardware manufacturers interested in games. Subsequently they had to turn to the international market from the very beginning. Game companies would simultaneously have to compete for employees with other more established industries. (Jørgensen et al. 2017: 460)

Instead of taking advantage of "cross-sectoral transfer of skills" (Jørgensen et al. 2017: 461), the competitive advantage of the Nordic countries included components such as "social policy systems" that provided "tax-financed healthcare and educational systems," wage synchronization that translated into low degrees of economic inequality, and "active political incentives towards the media and cultural sphere" (Jørgensen et al. 2017: 460). Above all, the Nordic countries are sparsely populated and thus lack a sizeable domestic market, which results in industry policies that emphasize innovation and export-oriented business policies. Furthermore, climatological conditions in the regions, with long and comparably cold winters, promote indoor activities, and computer skills were treated as one domain of technical expertise worthy of respect. In the end, Jørgensen, Sandqvist, and Sotamaa (2017: 461) summarize, "The development of the Nordic game industry does not follow the historical trajectory of the Anglo-American or Japanese regions."

Practices and industry structure. Aoyama and Izushi (2003: 426) argue that creative industries have traditionally been regarded as "craft-based, low-tech-oriented, and therefore labor-intensive" production activities. Video game development combines traditional creative industry skills and highly sophisticated computer science and digital media expertise, which include graphic design, computer programming, and expertise in Internet-based distribution channels. Such expertise includes "the development and integration of a scenario, design of interactivity, programming activities, graphic arts, sound design, music, integration and tests/quality assessment" (Cohendet and Simon 2007: 587). As an engineered digital object, video games are developed within fairly standardized production models and oftentimes include "agile" methods (O'Donnel 2014). Video game development is a project-based business, wherein video game developers participate in team-based project work, each having its own idiosyncratic qualities and conditions, including "work atmosphere, level of motivation, types of social relationships," Cohendet and Simon (2007: 598) argue.

Concerning the sub-set of video game development examined in this context, Cohendet, Grandadam, and Simon (2010: 92) make an important distinction between the *upper*, *middle*, and *underground* in creative industries, and the video game industry more specifically. The upperground segment includes formal institutions such as creative or cultural firms, "whose specific role is to bring creative ideas to the market" (Cohendet et al. 2010: 92). The underground segment is constituted by "creative individuals" such as artists or other skilled "creatives" who are not "[i]mmediately linked to the commercial and industrial world," Cohendet, Grandadam, and Simon (2010: 92) write. That is, they continue, the underground culture "lies outside the corporate logic of standardization." The intermediary level, the middle ground, is the segment of the local setting that serves as a trading zone wherein "knowledge transmission and learning" is enabled (Cohendet et al. 2010: 92). The upperground and the underground are thus connected and brought into conversation, hopefully with mutual benefits identified, within the middle ground segment. In more practical terms, the middle ground is constituted as physical places where people "can meet, wander, confront ideas, build daring assumptions and validate new creative forms" (Cohendet et al. 2010: 107). In Grandadam, Cohendet, and Simon's (2013: 1702) view, this three-partite structure is important for the local setting as it effectively absorbs the "creative externalities" generated in video game development. That is, the "new ideas, concepts or skills" generated through the interactions of various creative actors may be better exploited in either upperground or underground development activities.

The scholarly video game literature has been occupied with the concept of indie and relates it to a number of structural changes in the video game industry. Ruffino (2013: 106) suggests that the "rise of the indies" (with Crogan's 2018: 673, phrase) is indicative of "the democratization of the production process of a video game." Johns (2006) provides an overview of the video game industry in the console era, which ended when digital distribution channels were established, and games were no longer primarily sold "over the counter." Johns (2006: 176) predicted that digital distribution would affect the industry structure: "The online distribution of games will have an impact on the console manufacturers' sequential release windows across the three regional territories, essentially 'flattening' the global market" (Johns 2006: 176). The scholarly literature disputes whether the indie community represents a continuation of previous industry practices, or if the new development work activities represent a new way of developing and designing video games. Ruffino (2013: 115) is inclined to accept that the video game industry is essentially, as Planells (2017: 621) puts it, "an oligopolistic business," and that the indie development work can do little to change that situation:

> Independent gaming can be defined as a series of discourses in video game culture that changes the understanding of the values attributed to the production of a video game. These values, rather than indicating a radical separation from the practices of the industry, further embed video game culture within capitalist modes of production. (Ruffino 2013: 115)

That is, rather than representing a disruption in video game development, "[i]ndependence presents itself in the video game industry as a form of discursive justification of a series of changes in the production process of a video game," Ruffino (2013: 116) argues. Expressed differently, and as a matter of fact, the freedom that the term "independent" and its derived concept of indie imply is largely the claim to the "freedom to fail": "The freedom claimed by the designers of independent games often turns out to be a freedom to fail—the vast majority of independent games do not succeed" (Ruffino 2013: 116). The alternative view is that the re-emergence of indie developers represents a "[a] watershed moment in the history of video games as a medium" (Crogan 2018: 673). For Crogan (2018: 673), this represents "the passage away from a large studio profile of console games production toward a more variegated and diversified sector." Crogan (2018: 672) sketches how these changes affect video game development work: the new possibilities "for small and independent game developers and creatives ... include the diversification of video game forms; scope and content through the increase in the number and (potentially) variety of game makers; and the expanded options for funding, distribution, and player community engagement" (Crogan 2018: 672). Planells (2017) points at two interrelated changes in the industry that have benefitted video game development. The first change is that the cost of qualified technology has been reduced, which lowers the threshold for new market entrants:

> The rise of 'indie' game reflects the establishment of a digital culture that has reduced technological costs of major game engines [such as Unreal and Unity] ... and it has also allowed greater dissemination of content through the democratization of online distribution. (Planells 2017: 622)

Second, Planells (2017: 621–622) associates indie development with a cultural base and an "ideological framework," wherein "aesthetic and creative nostalgia" and "the fan phenomenon" are combined with ideas regarding "authenticity, innovation, and creativity." Seen in this view, the indie developer community is the outcome from both reduced production technology costs and a distinctive gamer culture that regards the video game either as an art in itself or as a means for artistic expression. The disruptive element in indie development derives from the ambition to develop games that matters for both the developer and the gamer community. In practical terms, Ruffino (2013: 116) adds, the indie life style choice is premised "on a peculiar form of intimacy between the producer and the final product," and one of the consequences is that the distinction between work and life is blurred.

Indie developers constitute the core agents of what Cohendet et al. (2010) refer to as the underground segment of the local creative industry. As Lipkin remarks, the concept indie not only denotes a relative distance from the market capitalization of creative ideas and output, as suggested by Cohendet, Grandadam, and Simon (2010: 92), but also assumes certain moral and ethical connotations inasmuch as indie developers represent a more "honest" and "independent" culture (Lipkin 2013: 9), which operates with an arm's-length distance from mainstream commercial activities. Indie developers are thus essentially defined negatively (see e.g., Elsbach and Bhattacharya 2001) insofar as they are ideologically and ethically—but not practically—separated from the mainstream. Dean (2015: 1246) defines indie developers on the basis of the distribution channel used, as "individuals or small studios, who self-publish their games rather than going through a major video game publisher." However, as will be discussed below, the indie developer concept is elusive inasmuch as it defies any attempts to define the term propositionally; almost any definition can be refuted on the basis of some specific case that violates the specific definition. In the end, the term "indie developer" is linguistically speaking a weak signifier that still has considerable practical value as it is widely used in day-to-day communication.

In practical terms, video game development includes a number of distinct competencies that need to be integrated and aligned, such as "the development and integration of a scenario, design of interactivity, programming activities, graphic arts, sound design, music, integration and tests/quality assessment" (Cohendet and Simon 2007: 587). Developing video games is a complex practice, and the industry structure includes a variety of actors such as "developers, publishers, distributors, retailers, costumers, consumers, IP-owners, platform owners, and hardware owners" (Zackariasson and Wilson 2012: 3). At the apex of the industry are the major Triple-A video game developers, which release video games that generate billions of dollars in revenues, and whose product releases are covered in detail, also in mainstream media. In Triple-A studios, all or a majority of these competencies are maintained in-house, while, for example, indie developers produce games in the absence of a full range of state-of-the-art expertise. This means that indie developers need to cobble together serviceable solutions to perceived game design problems, and that this work of necessity includes trade-offs to cut costs and development time.

The relationship between indie developers and Triple-A companies is commonly portrayed as being sceptical from the indies' perspective. Keogh (2015: 153) argues that Triple-A "blockbuster studios" are risk-averse and promote a "conservative design" in combination with technological innovations. In contrast, Keogh (2015: 153) continues, "the rise of 'indie' challenges many of the Triple-A industry's core values, with individual developers making names for themselves by refusing to look 'forward' but instead aiming to replicate a 'golden age' of video game nostalgia." The aesthetic ideal of Triple-A studio games is *realism*, Keogh (2015: 154) proposes, and as the targeted audiences—the hardcore gamer community—crave these features in the game, there is little room for creatively developing novel video game genres:

> A Triple-A arm of videogames is ... dominated by games that must fit into known thematic and mechanical genres (fantasy, sci-fi, military; first-person shooter, role-playing game, action game); must be 'difficult,' 'realistic,' and 'complex' in the conventional ways; must be appealing to a particular 'core' audience of young men; and must also be technologically innovative. (Keogh 2015: 155)

The indie community and indie developers can now take advantage of online distribution platforms and produce "cheaper and smaller games" (Keogh 2015: 155) that are more risky to develop but also more innovative than what Triple-A studios produce: "The rise of indie studios, with their lower overhead costs, has created new game genres and design directions (and resurrected old ones) outside of the central trajectory of technological upgrades culture that Triple-A publishers deem a safe investment"

(Keogh 2015: 156). The differences between Triple-A studio development work and indie development work are substantial. Occasionally, these practical, economic, and ideological differences translate into indie developers passing remarks on Triple-A developers that reveal their unwillingness to enrol on a career in a major studio.

Another issue worthy of consideration is the relative immaturity of the industry. One indication of this condition is the relatively low degree of copyright and intellectual property right law enforcement in the industry, which leaves the video game industry "rife with the copying, recycling, and redevelopment of other developers' ideas" (Dean 2015: 1249). The so-called cloning of a successful game (say, King's *Candy Crush Saga*) is thus a major concern for developers (Phillips 2015), but the practice remains subject to weak sanctions. Coleman and Dyer-Witheford (2007: 948) argue that the line of demarcation between "commons" and "commodities" remains "fluid, fertile and unresolved" in the industry, with ideas floating freely. At the same time, the growth of the industry cast a shadow of doubt over the value of intellectual property right and points at the risk of "over-propertisation" (see e.g., Pagano and Rossi 2009) as thin legal protection of intellectual property rights has not stopped the video game industry from "[e]xperiencing monumental growth and booming cultural importance" (Dean 2015: 1250).

Economic performance. The video game industry is a bona fide high-growth industry, characterized by enterprising and the integration of a variety of technical skills and artistic competencies, and being recognized by broad customer segments. In addition, the video game industry is an exemplary industry in an innovation-led economy, which demonstrates several traits of textbook style enterprising and innovative thinking. In the U.S., 59 per cent of the population play computer games today (Vesa et al. 2017: 274), and an estimate indicates that 144 million people—eight out of ten smartphone owners—played video games on their smartphones in 2016 (Dean 2015: 1244). Already in 2010, the global video game industry was worth more than "twice the size of the recorded-music industry" (Storz et al. 2014: 125). Regardless of this market penetration and the economic significance of the industry, the mainstream view of gaming and video games has been sceptical to condescending as gaming has been portrayed as "trivial and childish, or worse, damaging," Molesworth and Watkins (2014: 6) write. Furthermore, video games are commonly associated with "a realm of escapism and fantasy" (Molesworth and Watkins 2014: 2).

One industry characteristic, indicative of the immaturity of industry and its high growth expansion, is that video game genres are constantly invented, introduced, and further developed (Zhao et al. 2018; Clarke et al. 2017). Zhao et al.'s (2018) study, including a sample of 6544 games categorized into 78 so-called *proto-categories* (i.e., transient video game genres), shows that unlike in more mature markets, there are no penalties imposed on video game that transgress genre boundaries. This means that vaguely defined industry output is tolerated by the audience, affirmative of creative ideas and new thinking. O'Donnel (2014) emphasizes that the turnover of game developers is high, another indication of the changeable and flexible nature of the industry. "50 percent of the game developers leave the industry in fewer than ten years," O'Donnel (2014: 161) writes, and "nearly a third drop out before their fifth year."

The indie developer—performatively defined in accordance with a variety of categories in Chap. 4—is a key actor in the industry, but the indie developer position, outside of the commercial mainstream, yet depending on financing and revenues, underlines the immaturity of the industry. To offer a tentative definition of indie developers, an indie developer is an individual or a small studio that "self-publish their games" rather than using a major game publisher (e.g., Electronic Arts or Activision Blizzard) (Dean 2015: 1246). As will be explored in greater detail shortly, indie developers assume a key role in the video game industry as they for most part operate outside of the mainstream development activities, which to some extent constitute a form of laboratory or workshop for video game development work in the outskirts of the commercial domains of the industry.

Swedish video game industry performance and structure. The empirical material is collected on the basis of a case study methodology, wherein the case at hand is the Swedish video industry and more specifically indie developers. Over a ten-year period, the Swedish video game industry has grown considerably. In 2012–2017 period, the industry turnover grew by 296 per cent, which corresponds to a turnover per employee growth of 46 per cent (Video Game Industry Report 2018). In 2017 alone, job growth in the industry was 24 per cent, and the number of newly registered companies grew by 22 per cent. In 2018, job growth in the industry doubled to 48 per cent, and this despite the growth of new registered companies growing at a lower rate, at 12 per cent per annum, a ten percentage point lower rate than the year before (Swedish Games Industry 2019). Over the five-year period 2012–2017, aggregated job growth was 171 per cent in the industry, and the number of new registered firms grew by 137 per cent. In 2018, more than half of all registered Swedish video game companies were less than five years old, but over the same period, the turnover has tripled, and is now in the range of 1.84 billion euros for the entire industry. Out of that turnover, roughly half are reported as profits. Over the last ten-year period (2009–2018), the industry has reported a net profit every single year. This has also translated into increased market value of listed Nordic video game companies, the Swedish Games Industry reports. The market value of Nordic video game companies (listed in Sweden, Finland, Norway, or Denmark) grew from 0.24 billion euros in 2012 to 5 billion euros in four years (2015–2019), a more that 20-fold growth in market value (Swedish Games Industry 2019: 31).

Of the 383 active video game companies listed by the industry interest organization, 96 per cent are "solo companies," "micro companies," or small-sized companies. Yet, these three categories of companies employ only 19 per cent of all developers, which indicates that the industry is fragmented. Seven companies have a turnover in excess of SEK 1 billion, slightly less 100 million euros (Swedish Games Industry 2019: 6). Being in an expansive stage, the Swedish video game industry's largest challenge is the shortage of human resources, that is, qualified developers, especially in Sweden. "There is currently a substantial demand for co-workers in all professional categories. This dampens the companies' ability to further expand their business activities, not the least in terms of the ability to recruit in the Swedish labour market," the Swedish Games Industry (2019: 10) writes in its annual review. One specific challenge is how to recruit more female developers, and currently 21 per cent of the employees in the industry are women, a figure that has grown with one percentage point per annum over the last five years. The underrepresentation of female developers is particularly pronounced in start-ups and smaller studios, and in terms of the number of female entrepreneurs and developers that start their own studios. Despite making noticeable advancements in terms of gender equality, the Swedish Games Industry remarks in its annual report that women who play video games are three times as likely to choose a "technical profession" (Swedish Games Industry 2019: 14). As an increased proportion of female students in technical professions has been a long-term gender equality indication in policy-making communities, the Swedish Games Industry promotes video game as a pathway towards an increased interest in technical and scientific disciplines among children and adolescents.

Given the market penetration and global outreach—in the age group 11–14 years, 84 per cent play video games, the Interactive Software Federation of Europe (ISFE) reported in 2019—the production of appealing video games is a question of what political scientists and policy makers refer to as "soft power." Based on sales and downloading figures, video games developed in Sweden reach out to 1 billion people (Swedish Games Industry 2019: 6), and a popular game such as *Candy Crush Saga* is estimated to be played by 258 million people every month (Swedish Games Industry 2019: 7). Seen in such terms, the Swedish video game industry has implications and relevance beyond its mere job creation and tax-generation activities. Today, video games are a form of what political scientists call "soft power." Industry representatives have promoted video games not only as a form of light entertainment but as an art or artistic expression (Styhre et al. 2017), and the industry interest organization's annual report of 2019 lists art and culture institutions such as MoMA in New York, Smithsonian in Washington, The Barbican and the Victoria & Albert Museum in London, and NTT InterCommunication Center in Tokyo that recently have recognized video game development in such terms as part of their activities. After decades of advocacy, video game developers are increasingly recognized for their diverse portfolio of digital artefacts. On balance, industry data reported by the industry interest organization reveals that the Swedish video game industry is in a stage of expansion, which makes it a suitable industry for the study of the formation of new professional roles, professional identities, and professional ideologies and norms.

Data Collection

The primary data collection was interviews with industry representatives, and the use of industry reports and various web-based materials (e.g., indie developers and video game incubators homepages). The sample of interviewees included a variety of actors including indie developers, incubator directors, video game development education programmes on the tertiary education level, industry interest organizations representatives, and academic scholars specializing in video game studies (the "ludologists"). Interviews with innovation system agents (e.g., incubator directors, business counsellor, and education program directors) are justified by the central role of what Vedula and Kim (2019: 844) refer to as the "regional entrepreneurial ecosystem," in supporting new ventures and what Schoar (2010) calls *transformational entrepreneurs*. On the basis of U.S. data, Vedula and Kim (2019: 844) found that ventures that operate in the highest quality entrepreneurial ecosystem "have a 29-percentage point higher probability of survival relative to a comparable venture in the lowest quality entrepreneurial ecosystem." Expressed in statistical terms, one standard deviation increase in the quality of the regional entrepreneurial ecosystem increases "the likelihood of survival by 4% percentage points" (Vedula and Kim 2019: 844). Such data has not been examined in the case of Sweden, and nor more specifically for the video game industry, but Vedula and Kim's (2019) study justifies a more inclusive selection of interview subjects.

All interviews were structured on the basis of an interview guide, combining both questions derived from the scholarly literature and more practically oriented questions regarding, for example, day-to-day work routines and questions about the nature of the work and the subject's aspirations and ambitions. Most of the interviews were conducted *in situ*, in the offices or workspaces of the interviewees, but a smaller number of interviews were conducted over the telephone. The interview data was collected in two research projects. In the first research project, conducted in the 2014–2017 period, 51 persons were interviewed, whereof at least 21 were categorized as indie developers. In the second study, conducted in the 2018–2020 period, 24 persons were included in the sample. Interviewees were informed about the research question and the scope of the study prior to the interviews, and interviewees who requested the interview guide prior to the interviews were sent the questions.

Data Analysis

All interviews were digitally recorded and transcribed by a professional writing bureau. The interview transcripts were thereafter coded in three steps by a senior researcher, a full professor. In the first step, each interview was coded on the basis of primarily empirical categories, structuring each interview into sections that addressed specific issues. In the second stage, such sections were collected from each interview document, thus creating broader and more inclusive categories that structured the empirical data into theoretical categories. In the third round of coding, these intermediary categories, being part empirical, part theoretical categories were structured into distinctively theoretical classes, which were related to the overall research question stipulating that industry-specific classification systems are a function of industry growth and the degree of industry maturity. Through this step-wise coding of the interview data, interview excerpts were restructured into a theoretically informed structure, more easily lending itself to theoretical analysis.

Connecting the Ethnographic Data to Theoretical Frameworks

In the conventional research design process, methodologies tend to follow theory, and the choice of theory therefore precedes the choice of methodology and the data collection approach of choice. This volume is structured differently, opening with a discussion about the ethnographer's predicament regarding how to accurately depict the object of study, and only thereafter constructing the methodological framework that applies to the study of indie video game developers, being the purpose of this volume. So, given a certain amount of ethnographic data is being collected, how can this empirical material be connected to a theoretical framework within the discipline of management studies? Any inquiry into the life world of a specific community needs to address two issues: First, how is net economic value generated in the community, and if that is not the situation or even the intention, how do the actors convince financiers (e.g., the state, patrons, a dispersed community of financiers as in the case of crowdfunding) that the activities need to be maintained? This is an economic and not the least a financial issue, pertaining to all entrepreneurial and enterprising activities that not yet generate the cash-flow needed to self-finance the development activities whose outcome would, if successful, eventually generate such cash-flow. Second, only partially coinciding with the first issue, how do actors participating in a specific industry, trade, or domain of professional or occupational work justify their career choice for themselves and vis-à-vis others, for example, family members, spouses, and friends? One specific industry, especially in a growth phase as the Swedish indie video game development industry, may create net economic welfare, but the revenues may be distributed so that only certain industry participants benefit unproportionally (e.g., the employees in the Triple-A companies). A certain proportion of the industry participants may then work in companies that generate its own cash-flow and can take advantage of stable and predictable work contracts and economic compensation, whereas other industry participants are employed in companies that are financed by venture capital, are self-employed, or work for free. The industry participants that are employed by profitable corporations face no needs for justification of their career choice beyond those of any salaried worker in other industries or sectors of the economy. In contrast, the venture workers employed by thinly capitalized firms share this predicament with a variety of workers in other entrepreneurial companies or freelance workers, which include life science start-ups, software companies, consultancy firms, freelance journalists, freelance workers in the culture sector (e.g., actors working on the basis of short-term contracts), and so forth. In this case, it is reasonable to assume that there are intangible benefits or rewards associated with a line of work that does not compensate, at least not fully, for the higher degree of economic insecurity in the current employment contract. Workers are quite simply assumed to take calculated risks to pursue a line of professional work that they regard as meaningful, self-fulfilling, or otherwise rewarding, regardless of the economic insecurity associated with this career choice.

The former issue is addressed in the second chapter of the volume, introducing economic and financial theory to explain how enterprising work is thinly capitalized at the same time as it is the primary driver of capitalist economies. The second chapter of the volume shifts attention to the career choice issue, that is, how do professional workers make informed choices and take calculated risks in the labour market and decide to pursue a career that appears to be more uncertain and includes a higher degree of economic insecurity than to make a safe bet? These two chapters thus address the question of how to actively promote innovation-led economic growth from two perspectives. The first chapter of the volume stresses the role of economic policy and an integrated economic theory for examining the nature of economic growth, and the dynamic capacity to generate innovations in an economy. The second chapter addresses the behavioural and motivational aspects of enterprising and entrepreneurship, and points at the more fuzzy and ambiguous elements of career choices, rendering, for example, self-fulfilment and meaningful work as key analytical categories when studying innovation-led growth.

Summary and Conclusion

To embark on an ethnographer's research project may appear as an adventure inasmuch as new and previously unchartered territories are now to be discovered and mapped. At the same time, if the ambition extends beyond the sheer adventure as such, the penetration of unknown lands may also induce a sense of insufficiency and inability to be able to sift out what matters and what is worthy of further attention from what is insignificant, or only marginally interesting. Claude Lévi-Strauss captures the *ennui* of the anthropologist exploring foreign land, struggling to understand a culture that is not his own, yet carrying the burden of ambition to learn about these societies and their participants. The contemporary explorer of more geographically close domains faces similar challenges inasmuch as it is complicated to fully apprehend the life world of a community with its own idiosyncratic norms and beliefs, practices, technologies, rituals, and mythologies. The digital media-based communities of the indie video game developers are not necessarily less complicated to map and survey than any Amazonian people, studied by e.g., Claude Lévi-Strauss. At the same time, the ethnographer's foremost virtue is hope, the willingness to surrender to the uncertainty that any genuine research work activity entails. To fail to withstand the burden of uncertainty does not solve anything but only leaves the practicing scholar in a limbo: to desire exploration while failing to endure the conditions this work would entail. Like in the domain of love, as the saying goes, it is better to try one's best and to fail than to not try at all. After all, failure is a matter of fact in any reasonable risky venture, whereas the failure to tolerate risk is an entirely different matter. Overconfidence has caused many epic failures over the course of human history, but under some conditions, it is a blessing that is conducive to risk-taking that generates returns whose value can only be assessed in hindsight. That is, the ethnographer should carry his or her overconfidence like a shield against the worries and concerns—the ethnographer's anxiety—that sooner or later surface when being in the field. Based on these premises, this volume will examine the life world of video indie game developers, the creators and crafters of life worlds and gaming experiences in digital media.

References

Aaseth, E. (2001 [2003]). We all want to change the world: The ideology of innovation in digital media. In G. Liestøl, A. Morrison, & T. Rasmussen (Eds.), *Digital media revisited* (pp. 415–439). Cambridge and London: MIT Press.

Adler, P. A. (1985). *Wheeling and dealing: An ethnography of an upper-level drug dealing and smuggling community.* New York: Columbia University Press.

Agar, M. H. (1996). *The professional stranger: An informal introduction to ethnography* (2nd ed.). San Diego: Academic Press.
Anderson, C., & Robey, D. (2017). Affordance potency: Explaining the actualization of technology affordances. *Information and Organization, 27*(2), 100–115.
Aoyama, Y., & Izushi, H. (2003). Hardware gimmick or cultural innovation? Technological, cultural, and social foundations of the Japanese video game industry. *Research Policy, 32*(3), 423–444.
Barley, S. R. (1986). Technology as an occasion of structuring: Evidence from observations of CT scanners and the social order of radiology departments. *Administrative Science Quarterly, 31*, 78–108.
Barley, S. S., & Kunda, G. (2004). *Gurus, warm bodies and hired guns: Itinerant experts in the knowledge economy*. Princeton: Princeton University Press.
Barry, A. (2001). *Political machines: Governing a technological society*. London: Athlone.
Becker, H. S. (1992). Cases, causes, conjunctures, stories, and imagery. In C. C. Ragin & H. S. Becker (Eds.), *What is a case?: Rexploring the foundations of social inquiry*. Cambridge: Cambridge University Press.
Becker, H. S. (2009). How to find out how to do qualitative research. *International Journal of Communication, 3*, 545–553.
Bijker, W. E. (1995). *Of bicycles, bakelites, and bulbs: Toward a theory of sociotechnical change*. Cambridge and London: The MIT Press.
Bok, D. (2002). *Universities in the marketplace: The commercialization of higher education*. Princeton: Princeton University Press.
Boucher, M.-P. (2012). Infra-psychic individualization: Transductive connections and the genesis of living techniques. In A. De Boever, A. Murray, J. Roffe, & A. Woodward (Eds.), *Gilbert Simondon: Being and technology* (pp. 93–109). Edinburgh: Edinburgh University Press.
Bourdieu, P., & Wacquant, L. J. D. (1992). *An invitation to reflexive sociology*. Chicago and London: The University of Chicago Press.
Burawoy, M. (1979). *Manufacturing consent: Changes in the labour process under monopoly capitalism*. Chicago: University of Chicago Press.
Canguilhem, G. (2008). *Knowledge of life* (S. Geroulanos & D. Ginsburg, Trans.). New York: Fordham University Press.
Carnes, N. (2013). *White-collar government: The hidden role of class in economic policy making*. Chicago and London: The University of Chicago Press.
Clarke, R. I., Lee, J. H., & Clark, N. (2017). Why video game genres fail: A classificatory analysis. *Games and Culture, 12*(5), 445–465.
Cohendet, P., & Simon, L. (2007). Playing across the playground: Paradoxes of knowledge creation in the video game industry. *Journal of Organizational Behavior, 28*(5), 587–605.
Cohendet, P., Grandadam, D., & Simon, L. (2010). The anatomy of the creative city. *Industry and Innovation, 7*(1), 91–111.

Cohn, S. (2004). Increasing resolution, intensifying ambiguity: An ethnographic account of seeing life in brain scans. *Economy and Society, 33*(1), 52–76.
Coleman, S., & Dyer-Witheford, N. (2007). Playing on the digital commons: Collectivities, capital and contestation in videogame culture. *Media, Culture & Society, 29*(6), 934–953.
Comi, A., & Whyte, J. (2018). Future making and visual artefacts: An ethnographic study of a design project. *Organization Studies, 39*(8), 1055–1083.
Constable, N. (1997). *Maid to order in Hong Kong: Stories of Filippina workers.* Ithaca and London: Cornell University Press.
Crogan, P. (2018). Indie dreams: Video games, creative economy, and the hyperindustrial epoch. *Games and Culture, 13*(7), 671–689.
Cunliffe, A. L. (2003). Reflexive inquiry in organizational research: Questions and possibilities. *Human Relations, 56*(8), 983–1003.
Dalton, M. (1959). *Men who manage: Fusion of feeling and theory in administration.* New York: Wiley.
Dean, D. S. (2015). Hitting reset: Devising a new video game copyright regime. *University of Pennsylvania Law Review, 164*, 1239–1280.
Delbridge, R. (1998). *Life on the line in contemporary manufacturing: The workplace experience of lean production and the 'Japanese model'.* Oxford and New York: Oxford University Press.
Denis, J., & Pontille, D. (2015). Material ordering and the care of things. *Science, Technology, & Human Values, 40*(3), 338–367.
Downer, J. (2007). When the chick hits the fan: Representativeness and reproducibility in technological tests. *Social Studies of Science, 37*(1), 7–26.
Duras, M. (2011 [1993]). *Writing* (M. Polizzotti, Trans.). Minneapolis and London: The University of Minnesota Press.
Elsbach, K. D., & Bhattacharya, C. B. (2001). Defining what you are by at you're not: Organizational disidentifiation and the National Rifle Association. *Organization Science, 12*, 393–413.
Espeland, W. N., & Stevens, M. L. (1998). Commensuration as a social process. *Annual Review of Sociology, 24*, 13–24.
Faulkner, P., & Runde, J. (2009). On the identity of technological objects and user innovation in function. *Academy of Management Review, 34*(3), 442–462.
Fine, G.-A. (1996). Reputational entrepreneurs and the memory of incompetence: Melting supporters, partisan warriors, and images of President Harding. *American Journal of Sociology, 101*, 159–1193.
Franklin, S., & Roberts, C. (2006). *Born and made: An ethnography of preimplantation genetic diagnosis.* Princeton and London: Princeton University Press.
Franz, K. (2005). *Tinkering: Customers invent the early automobile.* Philadelphia: University of Pennsylvania Press.
Geertz, C. (1995). *After the fact: Two countries, four decades, one anthropologist.* Cambridge: Harvard University Press.

Gouldner, A. W. (1954). *Patterns of industrial bureaucracy*. Glencoe: The Free Press.

Grandadam, D., Cohendet, P., & Simon, L. (2013). Places, spaces and the dynamics of creativity: The video game industry in Montreal. *Regional Studies, 47*(10), 1701–1714.

Hertz, E. (1998). *The trading crowd: An ethnography of the Shanghai Stock market*. Cambridge: Cambridge University Press.

Ho, K. (2009). *Liquidated. An ethnography of Wall Street*. Durham and London: Duke University Press.

Holmes, M. (2010). The emotionalization of reflexivity. *Sociology, 44*(1), 139–154.

Ingold, T. (1999). 'Tools for the hand, language for the face': An appreciation of Leroi-Gourhan's *Gesture and Speech. Studies in the History and Philosophy of the Biological & Biomedical Sciences, 30*(4), 411–453.

Jagoda, P. (2018). On difficulty in video games: Mechanics, interpretation, affect. *Critical Inquiry, 45*, 199–233.

Jaques, E. (1951). *The changing culture of a factory*. London: Tavistock Publications.

Jemielniak, D. (2014). *Common knowledge: An ethnography of Wikipedia*. Stanford University: Press.

Johns, J. (2006). Video games production networks: Value capture, power relations and embeddedness. *Journal of Economic Geography, 6*(2), 151–180.

Jordan, K., & Lynch, M. (1992). The sociology of a genetic engineering technique: Ritual and rationality in the performance of the "plasmic prep". In A. E. Clarke & J. H. Fujimura (Eds.), *The right tools for the job. At work in Twentieth-century life sciences* (pp. 77–114). Princeton: Princeton University Press.

Jørgensen, K., Sandqvist, U., & Sotamaa, O. (2017). From hobbyists to entrepreneurs: On the formation of the Nordic game industry. *Convergence, 23*(5), 457–476.

Keogh, B. (2014). Across worlds and bodies: Criticism in the age of video games. *Journal of Games Criticism, 1*(1), 1–26.

Keogh, B. (2015). Between Triple-A, indie, casual, and DIY. In K. Oakley & J. O'Connor (Eds.), *The Routledge companion to the cultural industries* (pp. 152–162). Abingdon: Routledge.

Knorr Cetina, K. D. (1983). The ethnographic study of scientific work: Towards a constructivist interpretation of science. In K. Cetina, D. Karin, & M. Mulkay (Eds.), *Science observed: Perspectives on the social study of science* (pp. 115–140). London, Beverly Hills, and New Delhi: Sage.

Korczynski, M. (2011a). The dialectical sense of humour: Routine joking in a Taylorized factory. *Organization Studies, 32*(10), 1421–1439.

Korczynski, M. (2011b). Stayin' alive on the shop-floor: An ethnography of the dialectics of music use in the workplace. *Poetics, 39*, 87–106.

Latour, B. (1991). Technology is society made durable. In J. Law (Ed.), *A sociology of monsters: Essays on power, technology and domination*. London and New York: Routledge.
Law, J. (1994). *Organizing modernity*. Oxford and Cambridge: Blackwell.
Leidner, R. (1993). *Fast food, fast talk: Service work and the routinization of everyday life*. Berkeley: University of California Press.
Leroi-Gourhan, A. (1993 [1964]). *Gesture and speech*. Cambridge and London: The MIT Press.
Lévi-Strauss, C. (1955 [1973]). *Tristes tropiques*. London: Penguin.
Lipkin, N. (2013). Examining. *Indie's independence: The meaning of "Indie" games, the politics of production, and mainstream co-optation, Loading... The Journal of the Canadian Game Studies Association, 7*(11), 8–24.
Lynch, M. (2000). Against reflexivity as an academic virture and source of privileged knowledge, *Theory. Culture and Society, 17*(3), 26–54.
Manovich, L. (2001). *The language of new media*. Cambridge and London: The MIT Press.
March, J. G. (1978). Bounded rationality, ambiguity, and the engineering of choice. *Bell Journal of Economics, 9*(2), 587–608.
Mauthner, N. S., & Doucet, A. (2003). Reflexive accounts and accounts of reflexivity in qualitative data analysis. *Sociology, 37*(3), 413–431.
Mears, A. (2015). Working for free in the VIP: Relational work and the production of consent. *American Sociological Review, 80*(6), 1099–1122.
Molesworth, M., & Watkins, R. D. (2014). Adult videogame consumption as individualised, episodic progress. *Journal of Consumer Culture, 16*(2), 510–530.
O'Donnel, C. (2014). *Developer's dilemma: The secret world of videogame creators*. Cambridge: The MIT Press.
Orr, J. E. (1996). *Talking about machines: An ethnography of a modern job*. Ithaca and London: Cornell University Press.
Pagano, U., & Rossi, M. A. (2009). The crash of the knowledge economy. *Cambridge Journal of Economics, 33*(4), 665–683.
Paules, G. F. (1991). *Dishing it out; Power and resistance among waitresses in a New Jersey Restaurant*. Philadelphia: Temple University Press.
Pels, D. (2000). Reflexiviy: One step up, *Theory. Culture and Society, 17*(3), 1–25.
Phillips, T. (2015). "Don't clone my indie game, bro": Informal cultures of videogame regulation in the independent sector. *Cultural Trends, 24*(2), 143–153.
Pinch, T., & Trocco, F. (2002). *Analog days: The invention and impact of the Moog synthesizer*. Cambridge and London: Harvard University Press.
Planells, J. A. (2017). Video games and the crowdfunding ideology: From the gamer-buyer to the prosumer-investor. *Journal of Consumer Culture, 17*(3), 620–638.
Rennstam, J. (2012). Object-control: A study of technologically dense knowledge work. *Organization Studies, 33*(8), 1071–1090.

Rosen, M. (1985). Breakfast at Spiro's: Dramaturgy and dominance. *Journal of Management, 11*(2), 31–48.

Roth, P. (2017). *Why write?: Collected nonfiction 1960–2013*. New York: Library of America.

Roy, D. (1952). Quota restriction and goldbricking in a machine shop. *American Journal of Sociology, 57*(5), 427–442.

Ruffino, P. (2013). Narratives of independent production in video game culture. *Loading, 7*(11), 106–121.

Schoar, A. (2010). The divide between subsistence and transformational entrepreneurship. *Innovation Policy and the Economy, 10*(1), 57–81.

Simondon, G. (2017 [1958]). *On the mode of existence of technical objects* (C. Malaspina & J. Rogove, Trans.). Minneapolis: Univocal.

Spradley, J. P. (1988). *You owe yourself a drunk: An ethnography of urban nomads*. Lanham, New York, and London: The University Press of America.

Stigliani, I., & Ravasi, D. (2018). The shaping of form: Exploring designers' use of aesthetic knowledge. *Organization Studies, 39*(5), 747–784.

Storz, C., Riboldazzi, F., & Moritz, J. (2014). Mobility and innovation: A cross-country comparison in the videogames industry. *Research Policy, 44*(1), 121–137.

Styhre, A., Remneland-Wikhamn, B., & Szczepanska, A. M. (2017). Consecrating video games as cultural artifacts: Intellectual legitimation as a source of industry renewal. *Scandinavian Journal of Management, 34*(1), 22–28.

Swedish Games Industry. (2019). *Game development index 2019*, Stockholm. Retrieved September 30, 2019, from https://static1.squarespace.com/static/5a61edb7a803bb7a65252b2d/t/5d8a30a5c6a41508c50d8e6c/1569337529201/Spelutvecklarindex_digital_20190924.pdf

Thornham, H. (2011). *Ethnographies of the videogame: Gender, narrative and praxis*. Farnham: Ashgate.

Van Maanen, J. (2011). Ethnography as work: Some rules of engagement. *Journal of Management Studies, 48*, 218–234.

Vedula, S., & Kim, P. H. (2019). Gimme shelter or fade away: The impact of regional entrepreneurial ecosystem quality on venture survival. *Industrial and Corporate Change, 28*(4), 827–854.

Vesa, M., Hamari, J., & Harviainen, J. T. (2017). Computer games and organization studies. *Organization Studies, 38*(2), 273–284.

Video Game Industry Report. (2018).

Virilio, P., & Lotringer, S. (1997). *Pure War*. New York: Semiotext[e].

Watson, T. J. (2011). Ethnography, reality, and truth: The vital need for studies of how things work organizations and management. *Journal of Management Studies, 48*, 202–217.

Wedlin, L. (2006). *Ranking Business Schools: Forming fields, identities and boundaries in internationla management education*. Cheltenham and Northampton: Edward Elgar.

Zackariasson, P., & Wilson, T. L. (Eds.). (2012). *The video game industry: Formation, present state, and future*. New York: Routledge.
Zhao, E. Y., Ishihara, M., Jennings, P. D., & Lounsbury, M. (2018). Optimal distinctiveness in the console video game industry: An exemplar-based model of proto-category evolution. *Organization Science, 29*(4), 588–611.

PART I

Theoretical Perspectives

CHAPTER 2

Governing Innovation-Led Economies: The Role of Business Creation and Creativity

Introduction: Problem, Purpose, and Research Question

"[E]conomic progress' means essentially putting productive resources to uses hitherto untried in practice, and withdrawing them from the uses they have served so far," Schumpeter (1928: 378) writes: "This is what we call 'innovation.'" This statement captures the essence of economic policy, how to incentivize finance capital owners to commit their resources to forward-oriented and productive activities that ensure further economic growth despite risks and uncertainties of varying kinds. Schumpeter's (1928) economic theory renders competitive capitalism a dynamic and inherently changeable economic system, wherein the flow of finance capital from mature industries to potential high-growth sectors of the economy is the principal mechanism conducive to economic growth and welfare. While large and mature industries of necessity also innovate and change, Schumpeter associates innovation with entrepreneurship and new business ventures, and finance capital ("credit") is the resource that enables such potential to materialize: "[As] innovation, being discontinuous and involving considerable change and being, in competitive capitalism, typically embodied in new firms, requires large expenditure previous to the emergence of any revenue, credit becomes an essential element of the process" (Schumpeter 1928: 381).

Schumpeter's (1928) seminal contribution to economic theory is the foundation for most entrepreneurship research and economic policy

A. Styhre, *Indie Video Game Development Work*,
https://doi.org/10.1007/978-3-030-45545-3_2

intended to support and finance entrepreneurial activities. At the same time, economic growth is not singlehandedly explained on the basis of entrepreneurial initiatives and activities. If the supply of credit is a key mechanism that supports entrepreneurial activities and economic growth in the second instant, then the wider macroeconomic system matters when explaining how new businesses are created and financed, and how presumptive entrepreneurs are incentivized to create new ventures. In this broader outlook on economic growth, and innovation-led growth in particular (Aghion and Roulet 2014), the financial crisis and the great recession that lingered on for several years have made economists and policy makers revise their assumptions regarding the relationship between the finance industry and macroeconomic conditions. The Harvard economist Larry Summers (2014: 67), one of the world's most experienced and respected economists and with credentials from the World Bank and the Obama Administration, argues that changes in industrial countries "over the last 15 years" indicate that the prospect of "maintaining substantial growth with financial stability" looks unpromising. More specifically, Summers (2014: 67) is concerned that changes in the structure of the economy have led to "a significant shift in the natural balance between savings and investment," which in turn has pushed down the "normal real rate of interest." For instance, since the finance crisis of 2008, the group of 25-to-54-year-old men, a group subject to the social norms of being expected to work to support themselves and their families, and therefore being indicative of the aggregated participation in the economy, has reduced their total number of hours worked considerably: during the period following the financial crisis, the employment/population ratio in this group "declined sharply." Unlike previous episodes of economic turbulence, wherein the labour market participation of this group has restored quickly, in this case, "only a small portion of that decrease has been recovered" (Summers 2014: 66). This is also part of a broader tendency towards a lower degree of labour market participation in this group. In the late 1960s, around 95 per cent of the group 25-to-54-year-old men worked, while in 2014, the figure was 83.5 per cent (Summers 2014: 67. Figure 3).

As economic security and public sector welfare insurances have not been markedly strengthened in the U.S. in the period, and with shrinking relative economic compensation on the basis of minimal income wage (in July 2007, "the real value of the US federal minimum wage fell to its lowest point in over three decades," Autor et al. 2016: 64, write), the partial withdrawal of this group from the labour market is not explained on the basis of weakened incentives to work. Instead, Summers (2014) argues that the shift in the balance between savings and investment, expressed as a lowered natural interest rate, is the underlying cause of labour market retractions. This change is only to a minor extent explained on the basis of slower Total Factor Productivity (TFP)—Summers says this estimate explains only around 10 per cent of the reduced natural interest rate—whereas "reduced capital investment" accounts for roughly half of the reduction in interest rate, followed by "reduced labor input," that explains the remaining 40 per cent (Summers 2014: 66). Given that economic theory stipulates that investment in production capital is the driver of labour demand and job growth, it is plausible that reduced capital investment is the primary cause for the current natural interest rate equilibrium. In Summers' view, this new macroeconomic situation calls for resolute economic policies that "raise the level of demand at any given rate of interest" so that the economic system can be pushed out of the stalemate, and, for example, increase the demand for "debt-financed investment" (Summers 2014: 69), that is, what Schumpeter (1928) described as entrepreneurial activities and investment in innovation.

In Summers' (2014) account, speaking from the apex of the global economic system and as a respected figure in the community of economists and economic advisors, being the entrusted economic advisors during the last four decades, policy makers and analysts are now facing an entirely new situation wherein the economic system of competitive capitalism needs to be assisted by initiatives by the sovereign state to be pushed out of its deadlock. Needless to say, this is a far from trivial assignment, especially since the low-inflation, de-regulatory economic policy persistently advocated by leading economists since the mid-1970s is arguably the foremost cause of the current situation (Eichengreen 2015; Blinder 2013; Stiglitz 2010). Given the difficulties involved in discarding old and antiquated doctrines in the face of novel challenges (Cerulo 2006), economic advisers and policy makers are presented with substantial behavioural challenges in addition to the cognitive difficulties involved when formulating economic policies that may remedy the current situation. The contemporary finance-led economic regime faces considerable difficulties in terms of how to restore the incentives to transfer finance capital from mature industries to new ventures, that is, how to supply finance capital to the entrepreneurial function of competitive capitalism.

Purpose and Research Question

The scenario sketched above serves as a vignette for the purpose of this volume. The economic system of competitive capitalism is praised by its proponents for two reasons: First, it is allegedly the most efficient economic system in terms of maximizing net economic output, and simultaneously reducing the return on opportunistic behaviour on the basis of a combination of legislation, regulatory control, and social norms. This does not suggest that high net-efficiency in economic production means that the capitalist economic system is superior in terms of allocating the economic resources generated equally or fairly, but as the economic system of competitive capitalism is in many cases accompanied by the political system of democratic parliamentarism, the state can redistribute economic resources on the basis of fiscal policy and economic transfer systems. Second, competitive capitalism is widely treated as a *dynamic* economic system, that is, an economic regime that promotes risk-taking and enterprising both normatively and practically as self-interested finance capital owners are incentivized to expand their capital holdings by investing in both mature industries and emerging, potential high-growth sectors of the economy. These two propositions have been supported by empirical evidence, but these benefits of the capitalist economic system are not facts of nature but social accomplishments that may work less effectively whenever market participants cease to act in ways that make these propositions become factually true. That is, if opportunistic behaviour such as fraud or illicit behaviour is revealed, sudden shocks of distrust such as in the case of episodes of corporate scandals compromise the trust in the economic system. In addition, if finance capital owners are only weakly incentivized to commit their resources to new business ventures as stipulated by the second proposition, the dynamics of the economic system is reduced. In Schumpeter's (1942) view, the economic system of competitive capitalism is considerably more protean and unstable than observers may think, and evidence of recurrent and occasionally deeper financial crises over the last four decades (see, e.g., Calomiris and Haber 2014) indicates the accuracy of this observation. The economic system may be a viable economic system that is upheld by the majority of the actors complying with legislation, regulatory statutes, and social norms, but in the case when imprudent or illicit behaviour threats the stability of the economic system (i.e., through state officials' rent seeking, or widespread corruption), the economic system may no longer serve as predicted by the ideal case scenario.

Against this background, this volume examines how professionals who work in thinly capitalized firms and start-ups, and more specifically so-called indie developers in the video game industry, are making sense out of the situation. On the one hand, indie developers contribute to the expansion and institutionalization of a bona fide high-growth and highly innovative industry, that of the Swedish video game industry, while, on the other hand, they feel that there is a shortage of finance capital supply and only limited support from policy makers and the political system. This predicament to both serve as the exemplary case of an industry or sector of the economy that generates innovation-led growth and to be in the fringe of the financial and political system that is otherwise ready to support and assist such economic activities apprehends the overall predicament of competitive capitalism that Schumpeter examined in great detail: At the same time as economic growth is a function of risk-taking and a tolerance of uncertainty, there is a shortage of incentives for finance capital owners to commit their assets to high-risk ventures whenever there are alternative investment opportunities, say, in the finance industry's derivative instruments trade market (see, e.g., Weiss and Huault 2016; Lynch 2011; Lépinay 2011; Omarova 2009). In this analytical model, simplified to make a point, the rentier economy is in opposition to the entrepreneurial economy, and the one side's loss is the other side's win. Expressed in Summers' (2014) terms, the new and considerably lower equilibrium for the natural interest rate is indicative of how the renter interests trump the entrepreneurial demand for capital, which results in companies also in high-growth industries being thinly capitalized or starved on capital as rentiers invest their finance capital elsewhere, in, for example, hedge funds and other forms of exotic financial innovations that promise high returns on the basis of nominally high risks taken. In this analytical framework, the empirical section of this volume will examine four idiosyncratic responses to this predicament:

- In Chap. 4, indie video game development is discussed as a form of professional work that is complicated to define in terms of the regular industry classification system inasmuch as it includes technical, aesthetic, narrative, and commercial skills and capacities. In this view, indie developers participate in an entrepreneurial business activity that is yet to be defined in more specific terms.
- In Chap. 5, indie video game development is examined as a form of capitalist production that regards, for example, the profit motive as a

"necessary evil" that must not compromise the developers' work and commitment to the video game as cultural expression and art form. In this view, video game developers simultaneously contain the profit motive in a capitalist mode of production, yet depart from the profit motive when making it a secondary concern vis-à-vis the commitment to the video game *per se*.

- Chapter 6 discusses how indie developers raise funds to finance their development work. As the venture capital market for video game development is comparably thin, indie developers make use of all sources, including crowdfunding, to attract finance capital. By and large, the thin venture capital market is regarded as a predicament for indie developers, who at times call for the state to provide pre-seed and seed funding initiatives to better support the industry.
- Chapter 7 examines how indie developers are committed to the idea to further develop video game genres as both a form of entertainment and as an art form. Historically, the video game has served as a form of entertainment, but the indie community has started to regard the video game as a platform for artistic, aesthetic, and political initiatives and projects. In this view, the indie community can contribute to fruitful development of the video game medium so it can serve other ends than to merely entertain the gamers.
- Chapter 8 is the final chapter of the volume and includes two sections. The first section of the chapter addresses the idiosyncratic culture of the video game industry wherein team production capacities and joint efforts are highly valued. That is, the visionary ideas and leadership of individual developers of leaders play only a marginal role in the development work, or are for most part not advertised to outsiders. The team production orientation of the video game industry is a specific cultural trait that would deserve more detailed scholarly attention as it runs counter to a visual media logic that consecrates individuals on a regular basis as part of the business activities. The second section of the chapter summarizes the principal arguments made in the volume and lists some implications for managerial practice and policy making.

These four cultural traits and industry-specific practices underline that indie video game developers operate in what they and finance capital investors regard as the fringe of the capitalist economic system. At the same time, when making innovation-led growth a central economic policy objective, the video game development industry, with its annual growth figures in the range of 13–17 per cent, and an industry-wide expansion for more than a decade, is no marginal phenomenon. Instead, it is reasonable to assume that the video game development industry is at the very core of the economic system and is an exemplary industry in terms of being a market-based economic venture that has expanded outside of the active support of the state and various subsidies and exemptions. Seen in this way, scholarly inquiries into high-growth segments of the economy may reveal new ways to generate economic growth, and new ideas and attitudes that only partially recognize and reproduce previous norms and beliefs. Ultimately, such scholarly inquiries examine how the economic system of competitive capitalism is reproduced in real-life economies.

The remainder of this chapter is structured accordingly: First, the concept of innovation-led growth is discussed as a central component in the economic policy directing advanced economies. The second section explores how well the contemporary finance-led economy is transferring finance capital from mature but capital-rich industries to potential high-growth industries. This includes an analysis of the supply of venture capital to this section, the entrepreneurial function of the economy. Thereafter, the creation of the venture capital market is discussed, being a form of professional finance capital investment activity that only supports a miniscule proportion of all businesses. In the face of thin or receding venture capital markets, business promoters and entrepreneurs may need to supply capital to the venture through Initial Public Offerings (IPOs) and being listed on junior stock markets, or to rely on research grants provided by state-controlled agencies, a theme being discussed in the final section of the chapter.

Innovation-Led Growth in a Finance-Led Economy

Aghion and Roulet (2014) discuss what they refer to as "innovation-led growth" as the mark of the advanced national economic system. According to Aghion and Roulet (2014: 914), innovation-led growth is based on three pillars: (1) a "top-down industrial policy" in which the central government would make the calls, "partly through the (often large) public sector and partly through subsidies directed toward national champions"; (2) a Keynesian macroeconomic regulation in which the government actively responds to a recession by fostering demand through increased public spending, financed either by public debt or through taxation; and

(3) a social policy that subsidizes education and health, and supplements small wages through subsidy schemes (e.g., family subsidies) to reduce economic inequality (Aghion and Roulet 2014: 914). In practical terms, Aghion and Roulet (2014: 915) list Canada, Germany, the Netherlands, and Scandinavian countries as exemplary in developing the "smart state institutions and practices" that promote innovation-led growth. In contrast to innovation-led growth, *imitation-led growth* denotes an economic system wherein previous technologies and products are re-produced by exploiting lower production factor costs to catch up with leading economies. In Aghion and Roulet's (2014: 916) account, China is a primary example of an imitation-led growth economy, lifting hundreds of millions out of poverty on the basis of the centrally planned campaign to imitate Western economies and their production activities.

As opposed to imitation-led growth, the capacity to innovate demands an active state that supports "high-quality universities, particularly at the graduate school level," Aghion and Roulet (2014: 917) write. In addition, as indicated by the name, innovation demands more investment in R&D, and to be able to reap the benefits from such investment, the state needs to support product market competition and labour market flexibility. The ability to innovate demands that corporations can acquire the new skills and expertise needed to exploit new technologies (e.g., digital media) and new market conditions. A flexible labour market, including various insurances provided by the state that benefit equally corporations and individuals, is thus conducive to innovation-led growth. However, Aghion and Roulet (2014: 917) argue that such policy making and active support of innovation-led growth initiatives demand high-quality services in public sector agencies and regulatory organizations: "instead of fostering growth through indiscriminate public spending, become selective as to where public funds should be invested." Furthermore, to actively support promising ventures, state-controlled agencies cannot invest on the basis of an equality principle preference as that would overcompensate low-quality entrepreneurs and less promising ventures vis-à-vis high-growth potential ventures and sectors of the economy: "Public investments should be targeted to a limited number of growth-enhancing areas and sectors" (Aghion and Roulet 2014: 917). Third and finally, Aghion and Roulet (2014: 917) argue that increased public spending should be accompanied by "appropriate governance to ensure that public funds are efficiently used," that is, tax-money cannot simply be spread out on the basis of the justification that such investment will result in economic growth. Regulatory agencies need to ensure that public funds are used wisely to curb opportunistic behaviour and/or ineffective investments.

Aghion and Roulet (2014) policy recommendations may sound persuasive, but politically speaking, the active sovereign state that they propose has been subject to severe and consistent critique since the early 1980s. Industry policy has come under disrepute as what prevents competition inasmuch as governments and their defined agencies claim the authority to pick winners and losers in a discretionary fashion, and consequently, critics claim, increase the "scope for capture of governments by local vested interests" (Aghion and Roulet 2014: 918). Aghion and Roulet (2014: 924) admit that their policy recommendations may be criticized for being too "Pigovian" (after the British economists Arthur Pigou) inasmuch as they treat the state as a legitimate social planner rather than "as the representative of an elite with strongly vested interests." In the end, the recipe for innovation-led growth proposed easily opens up for the so-called crony capitalism framework wherein policy makers collaborate with business interests to ensure benefits for themselves and their allies, eventually resulting in economic growth but unaccompanied by economic welfare that benefits actors outside of such decision-making communities. In such economic regimes, the economic resources generated on the basis of resolute economic policy are accumulating in certain communities and income groups, which undermine the legitimacy and long-term viability of the economic policy on the basis of democratic deficits.

Another issue to address within the regime of innovation-led growth is the shortage of financial capital and "thin" venture capital markets benefitting high-growth potential industries. "Credit constraints," Aghion and Roulet (2014: 918) write, "may further limit or slow down the reallocation of firms toward new (more growth-enhancing) sectors." One further complication is that in certain industries, and typically in high-tech sectors, including the video game industry, there are "knowledge spillovers"—*positive externalities* in the economics vocabulary—that benefit the rest of the economy. Unfortunately, current risk management models that finance market investors use cannot accommodate such uncertainties in meaningful ways. In such cases, for example, the spillover effects derived from assets which are highly intangible make it more difficult for finance market investors to commit their capital to such industries as a high-tech firm's investment in R&D benefits also other market actors. However, such cases of market failure—market actors seek productive investment opportunities, but their calculative models prevent them from investing, either as a policy matter or as a personal conviction—may justify state interventions in the form of subsidies or research grants to actively promote innovation-led growth.

Aghion and Roulet (2014) outline an ambitious policy programme for economies that wants to move beyond imitation-led growth. In their account, such pursuits cannot be left to the market or industry itself, and the state needs to actively build institutions conducive to economic growth and, in the case of market failure, supply finance capital to promising industry sectors. In this view, the sovereign state is an active co-creator of the economic systems and practices that generate economic welfare on the basis of novels means (Vogel 2018), and to navigate within this framework, orchestrate the policy-making changes, and provide the subsidies and economic support needed are way more complicated assignments than to advocate a more strictly market-based model. Free-market theorists are also considerably more sceptical towards such economic policies, and anticipate how the policy-making process is biased by forms of regulatory capture and other undesirable consequences of policy making. At the end of the day, the demand for finance capital to support the entrepreneurial function of competitive capitalism needs to be handled one way or another, and in the case wherein enterprising and innovation-oriented activities remain unassisted by professional finance market traders, unable to calculate discounted revenues on the basis of existing risk management models, then entrepreneurial firms in an expansive stage are either starved on finance capital, or the state steps in and acts through its defined agencies. As a fact of the matter, the supply of finance capital to entrepreneurial activities is lending itself to empirical analyses, and in the following section, the recent literature on the topic is reviewed to examine how well the inflated finance industry can support emerging industry sectors and start-up companies.

The State of Venturing and Entrepreneurialism

Lee (2018: 1439) argues that new technologies are "notoriously difficult to specify with precision," which results in contacts being written in new technology development areas being characterized by "a certain degree of incompleteness." Despite these concerns, small firms tend to be "disproportionately innovative relative to large firms," an empirical fact that is explained by what Lee refers to as "their nimble management structures" and their "proximity to high-powered market incentives." In contrast, large, bureaucratic companies offer few incentives for its co-workers to actively respond to market signals as they instead rely on a hierarchical and bureaucratic structure to accommodate such opportunities. This makes the species of start-up firms and companies in a development phase the primary devices for generating and refining new ideas in the economy. Schoar (2010) here makes the important distinction between subsistence entrepreneurs and transformational entrepreneurs. The former category, the subsistence entrepreneurs, participate in entrepreneurial activities "as a means of providing subsistence income," whereas the latter category, transformational entrepreneurs, are attracted to business venturing on the ground that their ambition is to "create large, vibrant businesses that grow much beyond the scope of an individual's subsistence needs and provide jobs and income for others" (Schoar 2010: 58). As an empirical matter, it is only transformational entrepreneurs that provide the more substantial economic benefits that policy makers value, including industry growth and job creation. In contrast, subsistence entrepreneurs tend to "run tiny operations that do not grow into larger firms but merely provide an alternative employment opportunity to the entrepreneur and potentially their family members," Schoar (2010: 59) says. Furthermore, transformational entrepreneurs are "much rarer in an economy and more difficult to identify for investors and policy makers," Schoar (2010: 59) adds. At the same time, if policy makers and investors establish mechanisms wherein this class of entrepreneurs is detected and supported, transformational entrepreneurs "build larger businesses that will achieve rapid growth if put in the right circumstances" (Schoar 2010: 59). As a consequence of this distinction, it is only transformational entrepreneurs that "can be seen as the true engines of growth in an economy" (Schoar 2010: 59). In this context, indie developers, who start their video development studios to make a contribution to a cultural expression and digital media that hold in esteem, are regarded as transformational entrepreneurs; for indie developers, the development work is more than a job—it is a way of life. Unfortunately, policy makers (and to a lower extent investors, who use their due diligence procedures to separate subsistence and transformational entrepreneurs) may confuse the two categories, and with tax-money spent in projects with limited prospects for economic returns and net economic welfare.

To better substantiate the claim that different classes of entrepreneurs contribute to economic growth and job creation to a varying degree, the work of Decker and colleagues is reviewed. Decker, Haltiwanger, Jarmin, and Miranda (2014) use data from the Business Dynamics Statistics and the Longitudinal Business Database, collected by the U.S. Census Bureau, for the 1976–2011 period. The analysis of the material reveals that most businesses exit within their first ten years of operation, and that most surviving young businesses do not grow in size (measured in terms of turnover and their capacity to create new jobs). At the same time, "a small fraction" of young firms exhibit "very high growth and contribute substantially to job creation" (Decker et al. 2014: 4). More importantly, these high-growth firms make up for nearly all the job losses "associated with shrinking and exiting firms within their cohort" (Decker et al. 2014: 4). In short, in the cohort of newly registered businesses in a specific year, the majority disappear within ten years, and those who remain do not grow for most part, whereas small proportion of the firms in the cohort demonstrates the capacity to generate economic value and to create jobs so that the net effect of each cohort does basically break even. Such results indicate that while entrepreneurial activities do actively contribute to the renewal of the economy, it would be overoptimistic to regard new ventures as the primary provider of new jobs. Between 1980 and 2010, the gross number of jobs created by all corporations averaged about 18 per cent of the workforce, and in this pool of new jobs, only one-sixth, approximately 2.7 per cent, were traced to new firms (Decker et al. 2014: 5–6). In contrast, roughly 50 per cent of the employment in the U.S. private sector is accounted for by the 1 per cent of the U.S. corporations, with more than 500 employees. This means that large corporations do play a significantly larger role for job growth than small businesses do. For policy makers, who tend to regard high or even full employment as a key political objective as it is associated with other positive consequences for the economy (and not the least a larger stock of taxable income), to attend to the needs of start-up firms are arguably less effective than to cater for the 1 per cent of the corporations that employ many co-workers.

Another issue is that the annual cohort of new businesses tends to shrink in the U.S. economy, which indicates some faults in the current industry policy: "[T]he share of US employment accounted for by young firms has declined by almost 30 percent over the last 30 years" (Decker et al. 2014: 4). Furthermore, firms aged five years or less provided on average 18.9 per cent of the employment in the late 1980s, but only 13.4 per cent just before the Great Recession that began in 2008. The principal explanation for this decline is the exodus of U.S. manufacturing firms. In 1980, manufacturing accounted for 28 per cent of all U.S. jobs, while retail and services accounted for 24 per cent (Decker et al. 2014: 17). By 2011, 31 years later, manufacturing accounted for only 11 per cent of all jobs, while retail and services now accounted for 43 per cent. Reasonably well compensated and stable jobs in manufacturing were thus displaced by less generously compensated and more uncertain and short-term employment in retailing and services over the course of three decades. Interestingly, this economic transformation was applauded by economic policy makers, treating the decline of manufacturing as indicative of the U.S. economy transforming into the innovation-led growth regime. Needless to say, this economic idea and policy recommendation failed to account for the central role of innovation in the manufacturing industry, being a bona fide knowledge-intensive and innovation-oriented sector of the economy. Second, these economic advisors either failed to recognize or ignored the macroeconomic consequences of their proposals, wherein the so-called Baumol effect, which suggests that low productivity growth sectors such as retail and services (for most part) cannot have as high real wage growth as sectors with high degrees of productively growth unless imbalances are generated in the economy, would push American salaried workers towards work associated with lower economic compensations. In other words, the offshoring and downsizing of the American manufacturing industry, the foremost economic trait of the Reagan era, was the shareholders' gain at the blue-collar worker community's loss. Such events provided the grist-for-the mill for social affairs-minded artists active in the period, such as Bruce Springsteen, who wrote songs about the state of communities such as Mahwah, New Jersey, or Youngstown, Ohio, that lost their manufacturing industry and with few positive consequences following. In the place of the large-scale oligopolies of manufacturing industry, gargantuan retail companies such as Wal-Mart and Costco emerged, and a steady supply of thinly capitalized start-up firms, whereof a handful in every cohort grew in size and economic turnover, and therefore by default convinced economic commentators and advisors that their economic theories and policies were sound and correct.

In a more recent paper, Decker, Haltiwanger, Jarmin, and Miranda (2016) further explore the secular decline in new firm growth in the American economy after year 2000. In 1999, the difference between the 90th percentile and 50th percentile in the employment-weighted firm growth-rate distribution was 31 percentage points. That means that the top 10 per cent of the fastest growing firms report significant higher economic growth than the near-median growth firm. By 2007, at the verge of the finance crisis, the 90–50 differential was considerably lower, and this tendency has continued until 2011. Decker, Haltiwanger, Jarmin, and Miranda (2016: 11) repeat their previous research finding that young American firms exhibit an "'up or out' dynamic." That is, they exhibit a high failure rate in each cohort, but also exhibit "a much higher mean net growth rate than their more mature counterparts" (Decker et al. 2016: 11). The macroeconomic consequence is that high-growth young firms generate both job growth and productivity growth despite their significant failure rate. Unfortunately, in the more recent period, the American economy no longer displays these patterns as there is a lower number of start-ups, and those business that are created "are less likely to be high-growth firms" (Decker et al. 2016: 21). Decker, Haltiwanger, Jarmin, and Miranda (2017: 322) argue that these patterns are "particularly notable in the high-tech sector," which was highly dynamic in the 1990s and thereafter declined sharply after 2000.

Gordon (2015: 54) measures economic growth in terms of Total Factor Productivity (TFP), a measure calculated on the basis of labour productivity growth minus the effects of production capital investment and improved educational attainment, and being what Gordon portrays as "the best available measure of the underlying pace of innovation and technological change." In the U.S., the annual average TPF growth was 0.70 per cent in the 1972–2014 period. In comparison, between 1920 and 1972, the growth rate was 2.01 per cent, three times as high as in the succeeding period (Gordon 2015: 54–55). The only period that was close to the 1920–1972 average was in 1996–2004 when the TFP growth was 1.43 per cent, which Gordon explains as a "delayed effect" of previous investment in digital technology and the development of the Internet: "Productivity analysts have credited the dot.com revolution, which married the computer with communications and developed e-commerce and search engines, for the productivity growth revival of 1996–2004" (Gordon 2015: 55). This period of high-tech industry growth is also the period that Decker et al. (2014, 2016, 2017) use as a reference point when they conclude that American venturing is in a state of decline. At the same time, Gordon (2015) argues that there are many worrying tendencies in the U.S. economy that justify Decker et al.'s (2014, 2016, 2017) concerns regarding declining job and productivity growth. For instance, the cost of tertiary education, which is treated as a decision to invest in human resources made on the household level and by individual students, has risen three times faster than the overall inflation during the period

1972–2015 (Gordon 2015: 57). In some societies and economies, such as in Scandinavia, the cost of education is carried by the state to incentivize younger people to invest time and effort in educating themselves, and student loans do instead cover living costs only. This results in the student loan pool being significantly reduced in comparison to the tuition-based American education system, which is maintained only on the basis of what Gordon (2015: 57) refers to as "a dramatic rise in student borrowing." In 2015, Americans owe $1.2 trillion in college debt, and the coming generation may choose to not invest in tertiary education unless they are convinced they will be sufficiently compensated by their future employers to be able to cover student loan costs and acquire a premium on education attainment. Unfortunately, lower compensation and stagnant or even declining real wages in middle-class professions and occupations do not support sceptical presumptive student populations that taking on massive student loan debt would be a reasonable decision. In this situation, the access to higher education, which historically has been a primary driver for productivity growth, becomes a privilege or entitlement for students from medium to high net-worth households, which not only slows down productivity growth, but also biases the distribution of economic resources so that already well-to-do households can benefit even more from their original advantages.

Gordon (2015) also points at the adverse effects of the decline of educational attainment at the lower end, among high school dropouts, being another indication of the risks of failing school systems. A study referenced by Gordon (2015: 57) showed that between 1979 and 2009, the percentage of "white male high-school dropouts" who had been in prison rose from 3.8 to 28.0 per cent. For black men in the same situation over the same period, the figure rose from 14.7 per cent in 1979 to 68 per cent in 2009. If criminality is a function of economic hardship and economic inequality, such figures are deeply worrying. "According to the FBI no less than one-third of all adult Americans have criminal records" (Gordon 2015: 58). In addition to the direct social and individual costs associated with the U.S. incarceration rate, which is substantially higher than that in comparable developed economies—Prasad (2012: 8. Table 1.1) shows that the rate of incarceration in the U.S. is roughly seven times as high as in other industrialized countries—the reliance on prisons as a principal punitive practice also transfers costs onto future generations. In 1963, 95 per cent of mothers aged 40 lived with their husbands and children, while in 2004, only 34 per cent did (Gordon 2015: 57). So-called "broken homes" may be a condescending term that ignores the efforts made by single mothers or fathers to care for their children, but in fact the loss of contact between fathers and their children has been proposed as a mechanism that explains various socio-economic concerns, such as the comparably lower educational attainment among children with absent parents.

All these factor add to declining Total Factor Productivity growth, but the ultimate factor explaining the largest share of the variance is a matter of how finance capital and other resources are allocated in the economy, being the neoclassical economist's "iron law of resource allocation" of sorts. "Aggregate productivity growth depends not only on innovations and technology investments within firms but also on the economy's ability to reallocate resources from businesses with lower productivity to businesses with higher productivity," Decker, Haltiwanger, Jarmin, and Miranda (2016: 21) argue. They (2016: 21) continue: "Evidence suggests that young firms devote disproportionately more resources to innovation, so the high growth of young firms is particularly important for aggregate productivity growth." At the same time, Gordon (2015: 58) remarks, "secular stagnation is not about just demand or supply but also about the interaction between demand and supply." That is, slower growth on the supply side, an effect of not only declining productivity growth but also slower population growth and declining labour-force participation, reduces the need for finance capital, and this decline in demand serves to push down productivity growth further, which results in a downward spiral of declining economic growth. Eventually, investment also in what historically has been high-growth/high-risk industries appears unattractive, especially as the finance industry itself provides many new financial innovations such as complex and highly illiquid derivative instruments, that is, high-growth/high-risk assets. In the end, the entrepreneurial function of the capitalist economic system is starved of the finance capital that would enable the development of new businesses. Based on these mechanisms and processes, Decker, Haltiwanger, Jarmin, and Miranda (2017: 322) predict that "declining business dynamism since 2000 is likely a drag on American living standards."

The Supply of Venture Capital

As indicated by the literature review above, enterprising and entrepreneurial activities are in decline in the U.S., a tendency towards lower industry dynamics, partially explained by the shortage of finance capital committed to the creation and development of new business ventures. Taking the mature non-financial industry as a proxy for the overall appetite for investment in production capital in the economy, the shortage of venture capital is unsurprising as numerous studies reveal that the finance industry extracts large shares of the aggregated value created in industry. This results in a smaller proportion of the aggregated residual cash being committed to production capital investment. Using data from the U.K., Tori and Onaran (2018: 1402) show that between 1985 and 2008, the financial payment as a ratio to total fixed capital increased from 16 per cent to 42 per cent in "Non-Financial Corporations" (NFC). Consequently, Tori and Onaran (2018: 1401) continue, there has been a "clear decline" of the operating income devoted to the "enlargement of NFCs' core activities" in the period. In the 1980s, 80 to 90 per cent of the operating income was reinvested to generate future revenues, whereas, in the period 2008–2017, this figure was in the 40–50 per cent range, roughly half the proportion. These tendencies towards increased payout policies are consistent with the shareholder primacy government model, which prescribes maximal shareholder welfare as the only legitimate corporate objective for public firms, and the expansion of the finance industry derived therefrom. Furthermore, this is a tendency that is accentuated in the manufacturing sector. Expressed differently, if finance capital owners such as fund managers are unwilling to reinvest the residual cash even in mature and profitable industries, how likely are they to commit their finance capital to the new potential high-growth industries and ventures? If risk aversion is a concern (as the work of Decker et al. 2014, 2016, 2017, indicates is the case), and finance capital owners are anxious to extract residual cash at the earliest possible point, then they may be reluctant to transfer this finance capital to more risky ventures managed by less experienced, yet entrepreneurial management teams?

While this new governance practice, to favour short-term shareholder interest, is highly disputed and for most part regarded as what is harmful for long-term economic growth, it may be that this extraction of finance capital in the form of dividends or stock repurchase programmes benefits the build-up of a stock of venture capital that, as neoclassical economic theory prescribes, is transferred to high-growth sectors of the economy. This represents the more "positive" scenario, enacting the shareholders as enlightened investors incentivized to be concerned with economic long-term growth and stability, and consequently investing a significant proportion of their residual cash in start-up firms and new ventures. The "negative" case would instead predict that the increased payout ratio is indicative of finance capital owners' withdrawal from an investor role, treating, for example, manufacturing firms as a vehicle for inflating the value of their asset portfolio and the stock of finance capital they manage, and who are not particularly interested in identifying nor supporting start-ups and new ventures. Fortunately, the adequacy and substance of the two scenarios are lending themselves to empirical investigation. One study design to determine how finance capital is committed to high-growth industries is to examine how the pool of venture capital correlates with the expansion of the monetary base, the stock of capital available in a defined economy. A shrinking relative size of the pool of venture capital vis-à-vis the monetary base would indicate a faltering risk appetite among finance capital owners. Another study would examine how, for example, high-risk funds and investment in illiquid financial assets (i.e., complex derivative instruments such as collateralized-debt obligations, CDOs, complicated to price and to trade) grow in size and in proportion. As it is outside of the scope of this volume to substantiate either the positive or the negative scenario, the focus in the coming sections is instead to examine the supply of venture capital in the current regime of finance-led economic growth and to explore how venture capital investors shape and inform high-growth industries.

The Creation and Operation of Private Venture Capital Markets

There is a conventional wisdom among entrepreneurship scholars that the capacity to attract venture capital investment, and private venture capital investment in particular, is the defining mark of a new business venture. Prior to that point, the business venture is more of a hobbyist activity, fuelled by the passionate business promoter and financed by private savings and helpful families and friends (the "three F model" conventionally also includes "fools," individuals with considerable risk appetite, and thus willing to commit their savings on high-risk ventures). The correlation between finance capital investment and future success is stronger than a random sample, but this accomplishment hardly merits a universal acclaim of all venture capital investment activities.

Gilson (2003) examines the formation of the U.S. venture capital market and argues that a public sector venture capital investor is an oxymoron inasmuch as state-controlled financiers cannot be reasonably assumed to be able to reconcile their economic and political objectives. For starters, Gilson (2003: 1070) claims that the U.S. venture capital market developed "organically" and "largely without government assistance," and certainly without "government design." Furthermore, as the U.S. has the largest venture capital market, policy makers in other jurisdictions are likely to mimic the U.S. model, but being exposed to different institutional structures and histories, it is complicated to reproduce this idiosyncratic model elsewhere. In many cases, this ambition to replicate the U.S. model results in a variety of state-controlled initiatives. For most part, Gilson argues, these initiatives fail in their ambition as they confuse the ends and the means, and on the basis of a misunderstanding of the nature of the business venture and start-up. As a matter of fact, venture capitalists invest in ventures to either make a future exit on the basis of an Initial Public Offering (IPO), wherein the company's stock is introduced on the stock exchange, oftentimes so-called junior stock exchanges, or through an acquisition by a larger or more mature firm, holding the funds demanded to acquire the focal company, and the resources needed to exploit the assets and know-how of the acquired company (Gilson 2003: 1075). In the latter case, the market price paid by the buying company hopefully exceeds the finance capital invested in the portfolio company, and preferably provides a return on investment for the venture capital investor so that the next fund can be raised for the coming ten-year period.

To invest in start-ups and business ventures is subject to professional expertise and experience, and Gilson (2003: 1076) argues that all contracts between investor and the business venture need to accommodate three central problems: "uncertainty," "information asymmetry," and "opportunism in the form of agency costs." Uncertainty is all finance capital investors' demon, representing the mathematical difficulty to calculate an expected return on investment on the basis of the non-parametric risk. At the same time as uncertainty is complicated to contain within current risk management models, it is simultaneously the capacity to select from a pool of investment objects that determines the venture capital investor's future success. That is, the capacity to navigate in domains beset by uncertainty is the venture capital investor's business. Second, information asymmetry is an information economics term that denotes that the entrepreneur and business promoter may at least initially know more than the presumptive investors do. Contracts written must therefore include various rules and statutes that regulate the relation between the entrepreneur/business promoter and the firm's investors (by tradition, venture capital investors work through syndicated investments to better pool the risks in their portfolios). Third and finally, like in all corporations wherein investor or shareholders confer the authority to make business decisions to salaried managers, the contract needs to specify how investors can execute control in the business venture. In most cases, venture capital investment includes a seat in the board of directors.

The U.S. venture capital investment model, especially in the Silicon Valley digital media cluster in the Bay Area in California, has served as the role model for policy makers in many different economies, but Gilson (2003: 1070) is sceptical regarding the viability of government initiatives as state-controlled agencies, granted the authority to serve as venture capital investors, simultaneously act as "financial intermediaries." Gilson (2003: 1100) lists a few reasons for why state-controlled initiatives are likely to reduce net economic welfare. First, the officers in agencies who make investments in business ventures typically "lack the incentives" to carefully monitor the portfolio companies as they are salaried state officials who can claim a limited proportion or none of the revenues on the basis of successful business investment. Furthermore, these officers are in many cases subject to "political pressure," including not the least the principal political objective to create jobs, and may therefore be reluctant to, or even prohibited from, making relevant business decisions that counteract such political objectives. Third, officers may lack the detailed expertise and know-how that is a *sine qua non* for venture capital investment, say, when investing in life science start-ups, which operate on the basis of state-of-the-art medicine research findings. Furthermore, in many cases being relatively inexperienced from practical entrepreneurial work, state-employed officers are unlikely to be able to provide what Gilson (2003: 1100) calls "the noncapital inputs" being of great importance for new businesses. Taken together, these conditions make state-controlled venture capital investment agencies relatively poorly equipped to serve in the role as venture capital investors and counsellors. In the end, the commitment of tax-money to entrepreneurial activities and new business ventures may become a mechanism that transfers resources from meaningful investments in, for example, health care and schooling, to low-performing entrepreneurs, which results in the destruction of economic resources and consequently a reduction of net economic welfare (Gilson 2003: 1100). In Gilson's (2003) account, venture capital investment is a risky business demanding considerable amounts of know-how and expertise, and the assignment to invest in new business ventures cannot be combined with a concern for additional policy issues and political objectives. Gilson (2003) clearly prefers a private venture capital market and regards state initiatives as being disadvantaged unless they mimic the private market model, that is, they are acting in accordance with current market standards.

One question following from Gilson's (2003) praise of private venture capital investment is to what extent even private investors are successful in detecting promising investment objects, and whether they nourish firm-specific resources over the investment period so that they can report a reasonable return on investment when the venture capital fund is terminated after approximately ten years of operation?

Private Venture Capital Investment Performance

Kerr et al. (2014) follow Gilson (2003) in portraying state-controlled agencies as being poor performers in venture capital markets. Even the most experienced venture capital firms "have substantial success" in only "one of every ten investments they pick," which Kerr, Nanda, and Rhodes-Kropf (2014: 43) regard as sufficient evidence to rule out state-controlled agencies as skilled investors: "We shouldn't expect inexperienced and possibly not-very-objective politicians to do better." This argument does unfortunately not follow logically consistently from evidence to proposition, as some intermediary lines of reasoning are eliminated (see, e.g., Gilson (2003), for a more detailed discussion). Kerr et al. (2014) still provide a meaningful role for the state in facilitating "effective entrepreneurship" through reducing the "costs of experimentation." This includes a careful analysis of labour laws to uphold or reform, the existing regulatory framework, and fiscal policy making, and to implement new innovation-led growth policies. Innovation-led growth is largely a matter of an active state that serves to assist market creation and market maintenance, despite proper venture capital investment not being its primary responsibility. At the same time, Kerr, Nanda, and Rhodes-Kropf (2014: 43) argue that "public equity markets" is critical for business venturing and "experimentation," and the state is therefore assigned the responsibility to ensure that equity markets are supported and properly regulated, preferably to reduce opportunistic behaviour and adverse market noise to a minimum. In this account, the active state is declared to be incompetent in investing venture capital, yet held responsible for the market creation and maintenance activities that are conductive to an abundant supply of finance capital.

Concerning the question regarding the effectiveness of venture capital investment conducted by private venture capital companies, Kerr, Nanda, and Rhodes-Kropf (2014: 30) use a data set collected from the Thompson Venture Economics database, covering the period 1985 to 2009. The data set reveals that around 55 per cent of the start-ups that received venture capital over the period were terminated at a loss, and only 6 per cent of these companies returned revenues in excess of five times of the amount originally invested. This may seem a meagre result, but the 6 per cent group was "extremely successful and together accounted for about 50 percent of the gross return generated over the period" (Kerr et al. 2014: 30). To address the wider net economic welfare effects of venture capital investment, for example, the creation of jobs and by implications taxable incomes, effects which benefit the interest and responsibility of the state, a data set including Census Bureau data for the 1986–1997 period indicates that venture capital-backed companies have a similar rate of failures in comparison to new businesses, not finance by venture capital. In addition, the group of venture capital-backed companies was considerably more successful than the reference group in creating new jobs: the former group grew with 364 per cent in employment rate on average, whereas the figure for the latter group was only 67 per cent. This result is consistent with Decker et al.'s (2014) finding that high-growth firms create new jobs but also eliminate jobs when they fail at a higher rate than mature industries.

Why Venture Capital Investors Commit Their Capital to High-Risk Ventures

As discussed in Chap. 1, innovation-led growth is dependent on the transfer of finance capital from mature industries with limited growth prospects, to enterprising activities in need for finance capital to further develop new goods and services. In fact, many commentators regard this mechanism as the primary motor of competitive capitalism, the ability to commit finance capital to more uncertain, yet high-growth potential ventures, currently in the fringe of the economy. Puri and Zarutskie (2012: 2247) account for how this stock of finance capital has grown over time in the U.S. In 1980, the total amount of money invested by venture capitalist was estimated to be $610 million. By 1990, a decade later, the venture capital stock was estimated to be $2.3 billion. In the 1990s, the venture capital market, propelled by advances in the computer science and digital media industry and in life science and biotech, expanded, and by 1998, the stock of venture capital reached nearly 20 billion. After the dot-com bubble of the 1999–2000 period, the capital stock accumulation slowed down, and before the 2008 finance industry crisis, American venture capitalists invested "around $28 billion" (Puri and Zarutskie 2012: 2247).

The literature enacts the role of the venture capitalist in largely functionalist terms inasmuch as investors are incentivized to develop the capacity to identify and sort out promising ventures to include in their current portfolios. For instance, Podolny (2001: 46) writes that a venture capital firm's "quality" is determined by "its ability to make superior investment decisions" in a context determined by uncertainty, that is, incalculable risk. Therefore, the venture capital firm must "learn to identify characteristics of an entrepreneurial firm that increase the likelihood that the start-up will emerge as a success" (Podolny 2001: 46). Daily et al. (2002: 400) speak more explicitly about venture capitalists as intermediaries that reduce the cost for connecting capital owners and entrepreneurs on the basis of their capacity to identify promising investment objects. Furthermore, the literature stresses that venture capitalists not only supply venture capital that finances salaried developed work, the procurement of critical technologies and instruments, and the outsourcing of specialist services (say, clinical research work in life science companies), but also actively connect the targeted firm within the venture capital investor's broader business network (Samila and Sorenson 2010). What is especially critical in many cases is the lack of commercial know-how in firms started by entrepreneurs with a technical or medicinal background, and primarily considering the scientific, technical, and practical consequences of the business operations, but oftentimes being less concerned with the business side of the activities. In such cases, venture capitalists, whom in most cases claim a seat on the board, recruit individuals with commercial know-how and leadership experience. In some cases, this increased focus on commercial aspects of the venture may create some tensions between, for example, the founding entrepreneur and the investors, but, in most cases, the entrepreneurs are aware of investors' expertise and skills and realize that they benefit if such concerns are handled by more experienced business partners. "Venture capitalists provide access to important networks which the start-up entrepreneurs would otherwise find difficult, if not impossible, to penetrate,"

Steier and Greenwood (1995: 348) argue. Expressed in terms of Granovetter's (1973) "weak ties" framework, the access to "information, resources, and market outlets," provided by the network that the venture capital investors open up, is "invaluable to the entrepreneurial firm," Steier and Greenwood (1995: 348) claim.

By and large, the literature on venture capital investment emphasizes a fairly straightforward relationship between the degree of venture capital invested in an economy and economic growth. First of all, venture capital investment is associated with a "substantial increase" on patenting (Kertum and Lerner 2000: 674). This legal protection of intellectual capital is critical for the venture capital investor's willingness to expose their funds to risk and uncertainty, and oftentimes the patenting of key entities and research findings is a qualifying criterion for even being considered for venture capital investment. In the next instant, the patenting activity in an economy is positively associated with economic growth (Howell 2017; Bronzini and Piselli 2016). However, it remains disputed whether it is the patenting *per se* that propels the degree of innovation and economic growth, or whether this is merely an intermediary function as, for example, the degree of differentiation of the finance industry may be the factual underlying cause of both economic growth and increased innovative activities, which would render patenting activity as merely a symptom of underlying structural and institutional conditions (Williams 2017; Safari 2017; Gittelman and Kogut 2003). Nevertheless, Kertum and Lerner (2000: 675) argue that venture capital investment does have "a strong positive impact on innovation," and that venture capital investment is comparably more effective in terms of promoting patenting than "traditional R&D": "[A] dollar of venture capital appears to be about three times more potent in stimulating patenting than a dollar of traditional R&D" (Kertum and Lerner 2000: 675).

Kogut, Urso, and Walker (2007), who examine the economic development of regions as a matter of the supply of venture capital, are less convinced of the close connections between venture capital supply, patenting, innovation, and the resulting economic growth. Instead, Kogut, Urso, and Walker (2007: 1197) argue that it is "premature" to conclude a causality between venture capital supply and "caused a high density of patenting." At the same time, Kogut, Urso, and Walker (2007: 1197) found evidence that venture capital investment and innovation co-vary, which potentially results in regional economic growth. In the end, it is plausible to assume that the infusion of venture capital in small and enterprising companies that create innovations and new businesses is beneficial for economic growth, at the same time as venture capital researchers fail to explain the growth of the stock of venture capital in the first place, and only insufficiently map the mechanisms and connections within a broader socio-economic and financial framework. Arguably, factors and conditions such as the degree of legal and regulatory protection of shareholders (i.e., the venture capital investors), political stability, governance quality, and the access to business-relevant services (e.g., legal and accounting services and other professional services expertise) matter when explaining innovation-led economic growth. This broader and systemic view of venture capital investor is justified on the basis of Kogut, Urso, and Walker's (2007: 1181) observation that "the market" for venture capital essentially consists of "a chain of investors and brokers who often do not know the start and the end of the chain, but who surely know their adjacent links." Fortunately, the efficient and financially successful venture capital investor may not need to maintain a comprehensive overview of the economic field, but the scholarly analyst, the policy makers, and regulator would benefit from such an oversight.

How Venture Capital Investors Commit Their Capital to High-Risk Ventures

A sizeable literature turns the perspective away from the systemic role of venture capital in the economic system of competitive capitalism and in an innovation-led growth regime more generally. In this view, venture capital investment is examined as a professional practice, based on a combination of calculative practices that process input data, and intuitive decision making that falls to the side of rational calculation and similar operations to estimate present and future market value of an investment object. The literature is largely consistent in terms of emphasizing this dual nature of the investment decision or due diligence process across the board. Kirsch, Goldfarb, and Gera (2009: 487) emphasize that as a practical matter, all investment decisions unfold within a temporal horizon, and therefore "time constraints" is a factual condition the venture capital investor or the investment team need to cope with. This means that each investment proposal cannot be examined in great detail. Instead, incoming proposals are screened on the basis of the analyst's various rules of thumb, or heuristics of choice, to increase the speed of the decision making. Furthermore,

Kirsch, Goldfarb, and Gera (2009: 487) argue that skilled and experienced venture capital investors are trained to "see beyond" the business promoter's formal presentations and future scenarios envisioned to better apprehend the actual market potential. This capacity to "look past the presentation of the plan and other strategic actions" (Kirsch et al. 2009: 488) is partially a necessity because the business promoter is likely to lack some of the commercial skills and market know-how, being the investor's business expertise, but also a way to outsmart competing venture capital investors (Ferrary 2010; Wright and Lockett 2003; Sorenson and Stuart 2001). At the same time, venture capital investors prefer to make syndicated investments, that is, co-invest in collaboration with other qualified venture capital investors to better pool the risks of their portfolio of companies. Regardless of such preferences, which result in collaborative activities further down the investment process, the capacity to detect and identify promising investment objects at an early stage is an operational and strategic advantage.

Zackarakis and Shepherd (2007: 177) identify five distinct phases in the investment process, which includes (1) deal origination, (2) deal screening, (3) deal evaluation, (4) deal structuring, and (5) post-investment. Such a linear and sequential investment process largely coincides with the "classic" view of decision making (see, e.g., Drucker 1955: 312). More recent theories of decision making underline that decisions unfold in a less well-ordered manner, wherein, for example, solutions may in fact precede problems (Cohen et al. 1972). In this view, the venture capital investment process may display a variety of patterns, only possible to map after the fact. More specifically, venture capital investors do not only need to assess future cash-flow and the market value of the company, or its critical assets (e.g., patents)—that is, to estimate the financial return on investment—but also need to carefully consider the human and social conditions that pertain to the capacity of the entrepreneurial team to realize the market potential. For instance, the corporate governance literature emphasizes that entrepreneurs are primarily concerned with raising funds to continue the development work that is their domain of expertise. As entrepreneurs are less skilled in and experienced from commercial activities, they may be less inclined to embrace the business side of their operations. This tension between the entrepreneur's love of the development work, and an entrepreneurial life style more widely—especially when being generously compensated to conduct such work—and the investor's demand for a return on equity investment over the ten-year investment horizon in the current portfolio generates agency costs. Agency costs are the investor's cost to monitor that the entrepreneur works in accordance with the investor's interests (see, e.g., Bratton and Wachter 2010). Therefore, by implication, agency costs are primarily reduced if there is a mutual trust between all participants so that the investors do not need to spend time and resources on monitoring the entrepreneur. "Venture capitalists and entrepreneurs alike think of accepting venture capital as equivalent to entering into a partnership," Gorman and Sahlman (1989: 241) propose.

To mitigate potential agency problems, Arthurs and Busenitz (2003: 153) write, the venture capital investor changes from being "a wary investor to a willing collaborator," that is, the investor encourages the entrepreneur to regard the investor as a business partner. In addition, as the entrepreneur reduces his or her ownership share of the corporation when new capital is committed to the development activities, the entrepreneur has rational reasons to tolerate and accept this novel business relationship. Regardless of the lower percentage of the ownership of the company, the pie is now ideally worth more through its recognition and certification in the venture capital investment process, and the entrepreneur is still intellectually and emotionally committed to the business venture and the development work being conducted. In functional terms, the new business partner model serves to reduce the risk of opportunistic behaviour (e.g., shirking or development activities that deviate from the strategic and tactic plans), which in the long run benefits all business partners, De Clercq and Manigart (2007: 203) argue. In addition to agency costs, uncertainty regarding the future needs to be contained within the investor-entrepreneur relation in meaningful ways (Sapienza and Gupta 1994: 1994). Whereas agency cost is essentially a matter of divergent interests (which can be monitored and re-aligned), opportunistic behaviour (which can be subject to sanctions such as shaming or penalties), or sheer incompetence or bad luck (which is minimized on the basis of effective executive work), task uncertainty is the residual factor that the venture capital investor needs to cope with in one way or another. In many cases, task uncertainty, which can derive from a variety of conditions including market risks derived from unpredictable consumer behaviour and shifting preferences, future legislative practices or regulatory reforms, or genuine uncertainty pertaining to, for example, clinical trials in new drug development projects that reveal the efficacy of a candidate drug only after significant investments have already been made, cannot be accommodated or tamed on the basis of, for example, risk assessment calculations. In fact, uncertainty is the primary reason for why venture capital investors choose to syndicate their investment, that is, they hold only a relatively smaller share of a potentially successful company rather than a larger share as a diversification of risk. The single most common way to reduce task uncertainty is to actively narrow down the development activities, and to make "safe bets" to reduce the uncertainty in the company and in the portfolio *per se*, Fochler (2016: 275), argues: "[V]enture capital tends to favour conservative strategies in developing a company's research direction and to stifle the type of 'outside-the-box' thinking."

At the same time, uncertainty cannot be entirely eliminated from venture capital investment, and as a consequence, a scholarly literature examines how intuitive thinking and "gut feel" remain key factors also in a period of time wherein actors widely embrace calculative reason and practices, and use various quanta and metrics to govern day-to-day business activities and civil society more largely (see, e.g., Dane and Pratt 2007; Sinclair and Ashkanasy 2005; Khatri and Ng 2000; Simon 1987). As indicated in Chap. 1, Huang and Pearce (2015: 648) argue that "venture capital investors do have "confidence in their own expert judgments." That is, they place "more weight on their own assessments of the entrepreneur when there were inconsistencies, and intuition trumped any business data they had" (Huang and Pearce 2015: 648). In the next section, this intuition-based investment work will be examined in more detail, being the residual factor in the skilled venture capital investor's toolbox that plays a role whenever "objective" data runs short.

Intuition-Based Venture Capital Investment Decisions

Huang (2018) studied business angels who invest in high-tech, high-growth start-ups at the earliest stages of development, that is, the so-called pre-seed and seed stages. These companies are complicated to invest in as they cannot already present a finished product or even a prototype, which makes the estimation of future cash-flow and the market value of the corporation complicated to calculate, especially in emerging market segments, or in the domain of new technology. Huang's empirical material, primarily based on interviews with business angels, reveals that investors tend to rely on two basic cognitive processes when making investment choices. First, they use economic or "algorithm-based" factors, that is, "objective and quantifiable information" such as financial statements, market information, and other categories of "hard data," as a "source of information to understand the risks" of the investment object (Huang 2018: 1824). In addition to the objective and quantifiable information, business angels recognize the uncertainty of a future unfolding and that informs every single investment decision. This means that business angels "integrate" their own personal beliefs and other forms of weak signals when they make the decision to invest. Huang (2018: 1824) refers to this process as the business angel's "gut feel." The process thus includes "[a] complex set of factors" that pertains to the investment process, complicated to assess as discrete and autonomous cognitive processes. Huang (2018: 1824) argues that previous scholarly literature would refer to such "gut feel" as a form of "rapid, emotional judgment," but in Huang's view, this is a misnomer as such a term underestimates how the gut feel is consistently directed towards resolving concerns regarding discordant information that pertains to the investment. To conflate the categories of "gut feel" and "emotional judgment" implies a failure "to consider how investor gut feel might integrate both emotional and cognitive factors in a processual fashion to produce what investors feel is an enduring, complete summary judgment about the investment opportunity that allows them to take action," Huang (2018: 1824) argues. Only by combining rational methods for calculating economic returns on investment, and the more fuzzy procedure to trust the "gut feel," business angels can conduct qualified investment decisions. The former procedure is protected against critique by the sheer authority conferred to calculative practices by the association with scientific pursuits, whereas the latter is complicated to vindicate: intuitive thinking by definition escapes rationalist modes of thinking (Daston 2019).

Huang (2018) cites extensively from her interview material, and business angels repeatedly referred to a relational view of the entities included in the investment object, being an important factor to consider when making a qualified investment decision: "It's not just 'the horse' (i.e., the venture) or the 'the jockey' (i.e., the founder), but also the 'fit' between the two [matters]—I evaluate them hand in hand," one business angel investor remarked (cited in Huang 2018: 1835). Another business angel explicitly referred to his "gut feel" as the final and comprehensive term that concluded the investment decision, and all the conditions that were considered: "I use my gut. After all is said and done, it's a gut feeling. It's really like the 'final score.' It summarizes the wins, losses, risks, rewards, all of it, into the 'final score'" (Business angel investor, cited in Huang 2018: 1839). Such statements are understood as being indicative of the business angel's acceptance of venture capital investment as a financial decision that straddles strictly rational calculation, and the use of additional information that is cognitively processed on the level of intuitive thinking. Furthermore, Huang (2018: 1839) argues that the narrative about the role of "gut feel" is also part of the emotional work of the business angels to better justify what they are doing on a daily, weekly, or monthly basis, but nonetheless may appear as riddled by inconsistencies or haphazard decision from the view of an external observer. That is, the concept of "gut feel" is introduced to avert potential criticism, and to establish investment behaviour as a credible and honest activity, carefully separated from, for example, gambling or sheer guess-work: "[I]nvestor gut feel seemed to include a consolidated narrative that helped them frame the investment decision to see past the extreme risk so that they could take action" (Huang 2018: 1839).

In summary, Huang (2018: 1840) argues that "early-stage investors" do not all "unilaterally invest in the same ways." There are considerable differences in how decisions are made. At the same time, the empirical data indicates that the cognitive process of intuitive thinking is located at the centre of relations. As rational calculation can only cover a sub-set of all relevant conditions, past, present, and future, which need to be considered, intuition and "gut feel" are indispensable cognitive and affective processes that need to be recognized by the business angel investor. Yet, the latter cognitive and affective processes still need to be better justified vis-à-vis external observers. Unfortunately, this reveals a weakness of Huang's study design: as business angels invest their own private wealth in ventures they believe will generate a net return, or deserve investment on the basis of other justifications (e.g., the business angel's preference for philanthropy), they may be less concerned about justifying their investment behaviour in rational (i.e., calculative) terms in comparison to, for example, venture capital fund investors, who invest "other people's money" to generate a net return. Rational investors who commit money to a venture capital fund may not share a preference for philanthropic investments, but expect a stipulated minimum return on investment, and therefore demand their agents, the fund manager, to be able to carefully account for how the capital was invested in a language shaped by calculative reason rather than more fuzzy or cuddly vocabularies about emotions and commitments. Under all conditions, the broader research finding of Huang's study, that financial investment is dependent on "extra-rational" conditions, is consistent with previous studies of the day-to-day work of, for example, fund managers (e.g., Taffler et al. 2017; Chong and Tuckett

2015; Zaloom 2006; Lo et al. 2005). In the end, venture capital investment shares the same predicament as investors who commit finance capital to uncertain activities, that is, the capacity to practically and emotionally cope with the uncertainty that renders rational calculations an incomplete basis for investment decision making.

The Return on Equity of Venture Capital Investment: Measuring Performance

As already indicated in Chap. 1 of this volume, only a very small proportion of all new incorporated businesses receive venture capital investment (Puri and Zarutskie 2012). Yet, the size of the stock of venture capital invested is regarded as an important indication of the health of the aggregated economy, even if roughly three fourths of the capital invested are written off as losses by the end of the investment period (in most cases, ten years). Kerr, Nanda, and Rhodes-Kropf (2014: 30) use data from the Thompson Venture Economics data base, collected for the 1985–2009 period, to measure the performance of venture capital investors. The data indicates that only a relatively small proportion of investments (approx. 6 per cent) is successful, and, more importantly, generates revenues so that the entire fund can make a net return on investment (Kerr et al. 2014: 30). To invest venture capital is therefore an uncertain business, wherein approximately 1 investment in 20 is successful enough to make the fund come out in black figures in the end. When venture capital investors for various reasons miss the opportunity to invest in firms that eventually prove to be high-growth businesses, they may end up in a dire situation when their funds report unsatisfactory results. This makes it difficult for the venture capitalist to raise another fund, which results in a high degree of exit in venture capital investment markets in an historical perspective. In fact, Rider and Swaminathan (2012: 178) remark, "[a] large percentage of venture capital firms raise only one fund." The large amount of exits in venture capital investment risk to mislead entrepreneurs and institutional investors to infer that the market for venture capital is "more munificent than it is actually is at any given point in time," Rider and Swaminathan (2012: 178) argue. Especially since venture capital investment is a prestigious activity, subject to news media attention and scholarly research, possibly out of proportion vis-à-vis its actual role in the economic system, the "thickness" of venture capital markets is easily overrated. There are fewer long-term investors than one may think, and fewer venture capital investors survive over time and can demonstrate a track record of above-normal returns on their high-risk, high-growth investments. In Europe, this situation is particularly salient, with lower returns on venture capital investment in comparison to the U.S. (Leleux 2007: 245).

Regardless of this condition, venture capital investors may fail in 75 per cent of the cases, but in the end, they nevertheless "do, in fact, add value" (Daily et al. 2002: 401). For instance, venture capital firms have served as "critical catalysts" in the development of new high-technology industries, Sorenson and Stuart (2001: 1549) argue. In addition, the shift from a sceptical attitude towards venturing and business creation in academic circles by the mid-1970s has been replaced by a new enterprising culture, wherein the formerly reluctant scholarly community has increasingly embraced business creation and start-ups as a vehicle for turning research findings into actual products, services, and therapies that make a difference in the clinical work and elsewhere. These changes have arguably been brought on the basis of venture capitalists' willingness to commit their stock of finance capital to risky and uncertain development work in new businesses. Despite all these contributions and benefits, venture capital investment remains a highly specialized professional domain of expertise, and there is an endemic shortage of skilled and resilient venture capital investors in all economies characterized by its ambition to promote innovation-led growth.

Other Ways of Financing Development Work: On the IPO Trail

As indicated above, only 0.11–0.22 of all new businesses acquire venture capital investment, which represents an insignificant proportion of all new businesses (Puri and Zarutskie 2012: 2248). For less successful firms, a stock market introduction through an Initial Public Offering (IPO) may be an alternative approach to finance the development work. To facilitate new business creation and to lower the threshold to capital markets, in the 1995–2008 period, many countries have opened junior stock markets such as AIM in the U.K., Neuer Markt in Germany, Nouveau Marché in France, Nuovo Mercato in Italy, and NASDAQ in the U.S. (Revest and Sapio 2012: 192). These junior stock markets are designed to assist thinly capitalized firms. A host of studies reveal that these junior stock markets may serve a certain role in connecting entrepreneurs and finance capital owners, but also indicate that there are some major concerns regarding the operation of these markets. For instance, the very term "junior stock market" suggests that these stock exchanges trade the stocks of new businesses being in a development phase, but studies of European new markets reveal that the listed companies commit only very limited resources to "innovative activities," approximately 1 per cent of its turnover (Revest and Sapio 2012: 193). Given this limited commitment to innovation, junior stock markets may list a variety of companies that are not potential high-growth ventures, which arguably compromise the founders' intention to supply finance capital to transformational entrepreneurs. "The European stock exchanges dedicated to high-tech companies have failed to deliver support to technology-based small firms," Revest and Sapio (2012: 194. Original emphasis omitted) summarize their findings.

Revest and Sapio (2013: 954) examine the performance of the U.K.-based AIM (Alternative Investment Market), which they believe has accomplished an "impressive growth in capitalization between 1993 and 2013." The analysis reveals that AIM-listed companies grow in size but not in performance in terms of "value added growth," which indicates that AIM-listed companies "underperform in productivity terms" (Revest and Sapio 2013: 955): "AIM companies are less likely to make acquisitions, they produce lower dividends, and they are more likely to be cancelled after an IPO than companies listed on the LSE [London Stock Exchange] main market," Revest and Sapio (2013: 958) write. Studies of actual companies listed on junior stock exchanges may explain why this meagre economic performance. Gleadle and Haslam (2010) studied Medco (a pseudonym), a medical diagnostics company and a university spin-out, listed on AIM. The study included data from the 2003–2007 period, that is, the period prior to the global finance industry crisis, characterized by a generous supply of venture capital. The life science hype in the dot.com bubble period in the late 1990s contributed to the favourable market evaluations of Medco's stock, but after March 2000, the situation changed. At the same time, being listed on AIM rather than being closely held by a syndicate of venture capital investors, meant that Medco had to comply with legally mandated market rules, and thinly capitalized firms such as Medco committed a significant proportion of their budgets to recruit qualified directors that signalled to market actors that Medco was an attractive investment object. "Directors fees and bonuses for this group accounted for one third of losses [of bio-pharma start-up firms] again suggesting that in small to medium start-up companies the emoluments and bonuses of directors constitute a substantial financial commitment out of profit and loss," Gleadle and Haslam (2010: 62) argue. These conditions indicate that companies like Medco, in need of venture capital infusions to further develop their products to make the firm qualified for a future acquisition, may not be supported by a junior stock exchange introduction. Birch (2017) reports that many life science ventures and start-ups have been de-listed as market actors express unreasonable expectations, or because mandatory roles for listed companies are too costly to attend to. Says one venture capital investor (cited in Birch 2017: 478): "Well, a lot [life science ventures] will delist because they're not raising the money, it might be finding the corporate governance and the reporting requirements too onerous, too restrictive, too difficult, and too threatening."

As a matter of policy implications, Revest and Sapio (2013: 969) argue that policy makers need to weigh the actual impact of junior markets, that is, the benefits they provide for the various actors, and the public costs the creation of such junior stock markets generates. Revest and Sapio (2013) thus call for a more comprehensive analysis of how various industry policy alternatives, for example, junior stock market introductions, contribute to net economic welfare: "If we accept the idea of a proactive state in the field of entrepreneurship and innovation, supporting measures should be effective and directed not only toward the most promising companies … but also towards the institutions that, unlike the AIM, are better suited to enhance the real performance of SMEs" (Revest and Sapio 2013: 969).

Audretsch and Elston (2006: 21) examine the performance of firms listed on the German junior market Neuer Markt, and find evidence that these listed firms grow faster than a comparable group of firms, but also learned that "nearly a third of the *Neuer Markt* firms have been voluntarily or non-voluntarily de-listed." Just like in the case of Revest and Sapio's (2013) policy recommendations to better combine a variety of policy initiatives, policy makers in Germany ponder that "new equity markets may not be the best solution for creating new firm growth and innovation" (Audretsch and Elston 2006: 21). Carpentier, L'Her, and Suret's (2010) study of TSXV, a junior stock exchange in Toronto, Canada, is slightly more positive as they found that "[t]he success rate of the TSXV is four times the estimated rate for traditional VCs [venture-backed firms]." At the same time, the "time to success" is longer for the public venture market than for the "conventional private VC market," Carpentier, L'Her, and Suret (2010: 404) remark. These positive results regarding

TSXV-listed companies are complemented by less assuring market data that reveals that in the June 1995–June 2005 period, the venture capital industry reported a "dismal net annual return of −3%" (Carpentier et al. 2010: 404), which one more time underlines the high degree of distribution in terms of investor performance. Apparently, high-quality venture capital investors are complemented by less skilled investors that reduce the aggregated performance.

In the end, junior stock exchanges may be beneficial for certain categories of companies, for example, companies with fewer challenges when communicating their business concept, and to explain the intricacies of the firm-specific assets to market actors. For other firms, especially firms demanding substantial venture capital infusions to materialize business ideas, may be less well served by junior stock markets. In such situations, de-listing may be an option: to rely on a smaller group of investors, more capable of advancing the business. In the case wherein both private venture capital markets fail, and when public stock exchanges are no attractive alternative, the sovereign state has to step in to serve as the financiers of ventures, regardless of, for example, Gilson's (2003) sceptical view of such "politicized" venture capital investments. A scholarly literature, reviewed in the section below, examines how, for example, research grants may have positive effects for start-ups and new businesses.

State-Funding Redux

Gilson (2003) and Lerner (2009) portray government venture capital investment initiatives as a squandering of tax-money as state officials seek to reconcile an investor function and an intermediary function, while they lack the incentives and the expertise to generate net economic welfare on the basis of such investment. In contrast, other studies point at the positive effects of, for example, state-controlled research grants. If the venture capital market can only support 2 out of 1000 new businesses, as shown by Puri and Zarutskie (2012: 2248), and junior stock markets are not serving the purpose the policy makers' intended they would, then there is still a meaningful role of the state in supplying venture capital through other channels and mechanisms. Howell (2017) points at four positive effects of R&D grants: First, firms that receive grants increase their patents registered by "at least 30 percent." Second, the so-called Phase 1 grant increases a firm's chances of receiving venture capital by 9 percentage point, from 10 to 19 per cent in Howell's sample. Third, a Phase 1 grant almost "doubles the probability of positive revenue," which generates the resources to continue the development work. Fourth and finally, Phase 1 grant increases "the probability of survival and successful exit (IPO or acquisition)" (Howell 2017: 1137). Furthermore, Howell (2017: 1137) argues that "on average," the early stage Phase 1 grants do not crowd out private capital. On the contrary, such grants enable new technologies to be further developed and to transform start-ups into investable ventures in the eyes of venture capital investors. In this way, state innovation agencies can issue grants that serve as catalysts for economic growth, setting off a positive spiral. Since 2000, the U.S. federal government has spent between "$130 and $150 billion per year on R&D," which represents about 30 per cent of total annual U.S. R&D investments (Howell 2017: 1162). As such investments are likely to be subject to detailed monitoring and regulatory control, and also being a bi-partisan interest, it is unlikely that this stock of tax-money is being squandered in predictable ways as indicated by critics of the state as an investor in private businesses. Instead, Howell (2017: 1162) finds evidence that "early-stage grants" have large, positive effects on "cite-weighted patents, finance, revenue, survival, and successful exit." In summary, therefore, "a grant is useful because it enables the firm to invest in reducing technological uncertainty, which makes the firm a more viable investment opportunity" (Howell 2017: 1162).

Summary and Conclusion

Innovation-led work not only demands novel and creative ideas and operable images of forthcoming products, services, and distribution systems, but also needs a finance capital supply and a governance system and a regulatory framework so that the rules of the game, not the least for venture capital investors, can be determined. This joint production of private business ventures and public regulation creates substantial challenges for industry actors, and not the least policy makers. The economics literature commonly portrays innovation-led work as being at the forefront of production, but the policy-making work demanded to make this economic regime operate as stipulated in textbook accounts is considerable. For instance, the question of how to finance innovation-oriented business ventures needs to include a discussion regarding how thin venture capital markets, with few qualified professional investors having the skills and the mandate to commit residual capital to high-growth potential ventures, can be complemented by other forms of financing and/or subsidies granted by the state. As private business ventures for most part cannot receive direct cash infusions from the sovereign state within, for example, current EU legislation and regulatory frameworks, and because such policies are widely questioned, the state needs to act through other mechanisms and channels. For most part, this results in the support of innovation-led work as operating in a secondary level and concentrating on incentives and regulatory models. While this is arguably the best possible model given the conditions at hand, it does not necessarily solve the question of how to attract venture capital to, for example, video game development studios. The long-term consequence of such industrial policy making is a patchwork of policies, initiatives, and projects, each making some kind of defined contribution in the support of innovative activities, but unfortunately creating a situation that is complicated to navigate in, especially for newcomers.

In the next chapter, passionate commitment to video game development is examined as what complements the more policy-oriented issues, addressed in the first chapter. That is, in order to accomplish innovation-led growth, there is a need for individuals that are animated by an ambition to make creative contributions, and such passionate commitment remains the principal asset in innovation-led growth regimes. Needless to say, the supply of such industry participants and entrants is complicated to promote through, for example, industrial policy making, and therefore the central role of human commitment needs to be examined in such terms.

References

Aghion, P., & Roulet, A. (2014). Growth and the smart state. *Annual Review of Economics, 6*, 913–926.

Arthurs, J. D., & Busenitz, L. W. (2003). The boundaries and limitations of agency theory and stewardship theory in the venture capitalist/entrepreneur relationship. *Entrepreneurship Theory and Practice, 28*(2), 145–162.

Audretsch, D. B., & Elston, J. A. (2006). Can institutional change impact high-technology firm growth?: Evidence from Germany's Neuer Markt. *Journal of Productivity Analalysis, 25*(1–2), 9–23.

Autor, D. H., Manning, A., & Smith, C. L. (2016). The contribution of the minimum wage to US wage inequality over three decades: A reassessment. *American Economic Journal: Applied Economics, 8*(1), 58–99.

Birch, K. (2017). Rethinking value in the bio-economy: Finance, assetization, and the management of value. *Science, Technology, & Human Values, 42*(3), 460–490.

Blinder, A. S. (2013). *When the music stopped: The financial crisis, the response, and the work ahead*. New York: Penguin.
Bratton, W. W., & Wachter, M. L. (2010). The case against shareholder empowerment. *Pennsylvania Law Review, 160*(1), 653–728.
Bronzini, R., & Piselli, P. (2016). The impact of R&D subsidies on firm innovation. *Research Policy, 45*(2), 442–457.
Calomiris, C. W., & Haber, S. H. (2014). *Fragile by design: The political origins of banking crises and scarce credit*. Princeton and Oxford: Princeton University Press.
Carpentier, C., L'Her, J.-F., & Suret, J.-M. (2010). Stock exchange markets for new ventures. *Journal of Business Venturing, 25*(4), 403–422.
Cerulo, K. A. (2006). *Never saw it coming: Cultural challenges to envisioning the worst*. Chicago: University of Chicago Press.
Chong, K., & Tuckett, D. (2015). Constructing conviction through action and narrative: How money managers manage uncertainty and the consequence for financial market functioning. *Socio-Economic Review, 13*(2), 309–330.
Cohen, M. D., March, J. G., & Olsen, J. P. (1972). A garbage can model of organizational choice. *Administrative Science Quarterly, 17*, 1–25.
Daily, C. M., McDougall, P. P., Covin, J. G., & Dalton, D. R. (2002). Governance and strategic leadership in entrepreneurial firms. *Journal of Management, 28*(3), 387–412.
Dane, E., & Pratt, M. G. (2007). Exploring intuition and its role in managerial decision making. *Academy of Management Review, 32*(1), 33–54.
Daston, L. (2019). The coup d'oeil: On a mode of understanding. *Critical Inquiry, 45*(2), 307–331.
De Clercq, D., & Manigart, S. (2007). The venture capital post-investment process: Opening the black box of involvement. In H. Landström (Ed.), *Handbook of research on venture capital* (pp. 193–1218). Cheltenham: Edward Elgar.
Decker, R., Haltiwanger, J., Jarmin, R., & Miranda, J. (2014). The role of entrepreneurship in US job creation and economic dynamism. *The Journal of Economic Perspectives, 28*(3), 3–24.
Decker, R. A., Haltiwanger, J., Jarmin, R. S., & Miranda, J. (2016). Where has all the skewness gone? The decline in high-growth (young) firms in the US. *European Economic Review, 86*, 4–23.
Decker, R. A., Haltiwanger, J., Jarmin, R. S., & Miranda, J. (2017). Declining dynamism, allocative efficiency, and the productivity slowdown. *American Economic Review, 107*(5), 322–326.
Drucker, P. F. (1955). *The practice of management*. Melbourne, London, and Toronto: Heineman.
Eichengreen, B. (2015). *Hall of mirrors: The great depression, the great recession, and the uses - and misuses - of history*. New York and Oxford: Oxford University Press.

Ferrary, M. (2010). Syndication of venture capital investment: The art of resource pooling. *Entrepreneurship: Theory & Practice, 34*(5), 885–907.

Fochler, M. (2016). Beyond and between academia and business: How Austrian biotechnology researchers describe high-tech startup companies as spaces of knowledge production. *Social Studies of Science, 46*(2), 259–281.

Gilson, R. J. (2003). Engineering the venture capital market. *Stanford Law Review, 55*(4), 1067–1103.

Gittelman, M., & Kogut, B. (2003). Does good science lead to valuable knowledge?: Biotechnology firms and the evolutionary logic of citation patterns. *Management Science, 49*(4), 366–382.

Gleadle, P., & Haslam, C. (2010). An exploratory study of an early stage R&D-intensive firm under financialization. *Accounting Forum., 34*(1), 54–65.

Gordon, R. J. (2015). Secular stagnation: A supply-side view. *The American Economic Review, 105*(5), 54–59.

Gorman, M., & Sahlman, W. A. (1989). What do venture capitalists do? *Journal of Business Venturing, 4*, 231–248.

Granovetter, M. S. (1973). The strength of weak ties. *American Journal of Sociology, 78*(6), 1360–1380.

Howell, S. T. (2017). Financing innovation: Evidence from R&D grants. *American Economic Review, 107*(4), 1136–1164.

Huang, L. (2018). The role of investor gut feel in managing complexity and extreme risk. *Academy of Management Journal, 61*(5), 1821–1847.

Huang, L., & Pearce, J. L. (2015). Managing the unknowable: The effectiveness of early-stage investor gut feel in entrepreneurial investment decisions. *Administrative Science Quarterly, 60*(4), 634–670.

Kerr, W. R., Nanda, R., & Rhodes-Kropf, M. (2014). Entrepreneurship as experimentation. *Journal of Economic Perspectives, 28*(3), 25–48.

Kertum, S., & Lerner, J. (2000). Assessing the contribution of venture capital to innovation. *RAND Journal of Economics, 31*, 674–692.

Khatri, N., & Ng, H. A. (2000). The role of intuition in strategic decion making. *Human Relations, 53*(1), 57–86.

Kirsch, D., Goldfarb, B., & Gera, A. (2009). Form or substance: The role of business plans in venture capital decision making. *Strategic Management Journal, 30*(5), 487–515.

Kogut, B., Urso, P., & Walker, G. (2007). Emergent properties of a new financial market: American venture capital syndication, 1960–2005. *Management Science, 53*, 181–198.

Lee, P. (2018). Innovation and the firm: A new synthesis. *Stanford Law Review, 70*, 1431–1501.

Leleux, B. F. (2007). The performance of venture capital investments. In H. Landström (Ed.), *Handbook of research on venture capital* (pp. 236–252). Cheltenham: Edward Elgar.

Lépinay, V. A. (2011). *Codes of finance: Engineering derivatives in a global bank*. Princeton: Princeton University Press.

Lerner, J. (2009). *Boulevard of broken dreams: Why public efforts to boost entrepreneurship and venture capital have failed and what to do about it*. Princeton and London: Princeton University Press.

Lo, A. W., Repin, D. V., & Steenbarger, B. N. (2005). Fear and greed in financial markets: A clinical study of day-traders. *American Economic Review, 95*, 352–359.

Lynch, T. E. (2011). Gambling by another name: The challenge of purely speculative derivatives. *Stanford Journal of Law, Business & Finance, 17*(1), 67–130.

Omarova, S. T. (2009). The quiet metamorphosis: How derivatives changed the 'business of banking'. *University Miami Law Review, 63*, 1041–1109.

Podolny, J. M. (2001). Networks as the pipes and prisms of the market. *American Journal of Sociology, 107*(1), 33–60.

Prasad, M. (2012). *The land of too much: American abundance and the paradox of poverty*. Cambridge and London: Harvard University Press.

Puri, M., & Zarutskie, R. (2012). On the life-cycle dynamics of venture-capital- and non-venture-capital-financed firms. *Journal of Finance, 67*(6), 2247–2293.

Revest, V., & Sapio, A. (2012). Financing technology-based small firms in Europe: What do we know? *Small Business Economics, 39*, 179–205.

Revest, V., & Sapio, A. (2013). Does the alternative investment market nurture firm growth? A comparison between listed and private companies. *Industrial & Corporate Change., 22*(4), 953–979.

Rider, C. I., & Swaminathan, A. (2012). They just fade away: Mortality in the US venture capital industry. *Industrial and Corporate Change, 21*(1), 151–185.

Safari, A. (2017). Worldwide venture capital, intellectual property rights, and innovation. *Industrial and Corporate Change, 26*(3), 485–515.

Samila, S., & Sorenson, O. (2010). Venture capital as a catalyst to commercialization. *Research Policy, 39*, 1348–1360.

Sapienza, H. J., & Gupta, A. K. (1994). Impact on agency risks and task uncertainty on venture capitalist-CEO interactions. *The Academy of Management Journal, 37*(6), 1618–1632.

Schoar, A. (2010). The divide between subsistence and transformational entrepreneurship. *Innovation Policy and the Economy, 10*(1), 57–81.

Schumpeter, J. A. (1928). The instability of capitalism. *Economic Journal, 38*, 361–386.

Schumpeter, J. A. (1942). *Capitalism, socialism, and democracy*. New York: Harper & Row.

Simon, H. A. (1987). Making management decisions: The role of intuition and emotion. *Academy of Management Executive, 1*(1), 57–64.

Sinclair, M., & Ashkanasy, N. M. (2005). Intuition: Myth or decision-making tool? *Management Learning, 36*(3), 353–370.

Sorenson, O., & Stuart, T. E. (2001). Syndication networks and the spatial distribution of venture capital investments. *American Journal of Sociology, 106*(6), 1546–1588.

Steier, L., & Greenwood, R. (1995). Venture capitalists relations in the deal structuring and post-investment stages in new firm creation. *Journal of Management Studies, 32*(3), 337–357.

Stiglitz, J. E. (2010). *Freefall: America, free markets, and the sinking of the world economy*. New York and London: WW. Norton.

Summers, L. H. (2014). US economic prospects: Secular stagnation, hysteresis, and the zero lower bound. *Business Economics, 49*(2), 65–73.

Taffler, R. J., Spence, C., & Eshraghi, A. (2017). Emotional economic man: Calculation and anxiety in fund management. *Accounting, Organizations, and Society, 61*, 53–67.

Tori, D., & Onaran, Ö. (2018). The effects of financialization on investment: Evidence from firm-level data for the UK. *Cambridge Journal of Economics, 42*(5), 1393–1416.

Vogel, S. K. (2018). *Marketcraft: How governments make markets work*. New York: Oxford University Press.

Weiss, H. R., & Huault, I. (2016). Business as usual in financial markets? The creation of incommensurables as institutional maintenance work. *Organization Studies, 37*(7), 991–1015.

Williams, H. L. (2017). How do patents affect research investments? *Annual Review in Eocnomics, 9*, 441–469.

Wright, M., & Lockett, A. (2003). The structure and management of alliances: Syndication in the venture capital industry. *Journal of Management Studies, 40*(8), 2073–2102.

Zackarakis, A., & Shepherd, D. A. (2007). The pre-investment process: Venture capitalists' decision process. In H. Landström (Ed.), *Handbook of research on venture capital* (pp. 177–192). Cheltenham: Edward Elgar.

Zaloom, C. (2006). *Out of the pits: Trading and technology from Chicago to London*. Durham and London: Duke University Press.

CHAPTER 3

The Passionate Worker and Deeply Meaningful Work

Introduction

In Chap. 1 of this volume, the "rise of the indies" was associated with what (Crogan 2018: 673) refers to as "democratization" of the production process of a video game, that is, lower technology costs and a larger and globalized market for video games provide venturing opportunities for small-scale development studios that honour certain aesthetics or game technology solutions that are held in esteem by the gamer community. Seen in this view, the indie developer is a passionate form of production, wherein certain ideologies and traditions pertaining to video gaming and video game production structure the work of indie studios (Planells 2017). This chapter complements the second chapter of the volume that examined the institutional framework supportive of innovation-led economic growth inasmuch as the human capacity to commit to certain practices and aesthetic and technological programs is being examined in some detail. To fully recognize the importance of what is here referred to as passionate work, a number of scholarly literatures are examined and included. In this chapter, the literature on games and gaming, affective capitalism and affective labour, and passionate work will be examined. The analytical framework is supportive of the empirical analysis of indie development work reported in Part II of the volume.

Recently, social and economic theory has increasingly recognized the role of affect and passion as social resources, not only playing a role in the fringes of the economy, for example, culture production and artistic

A. Styhre, *Indie Video Game Development Work*,
https://doi.org/10.1007/978-3-030-45545-3_3

circles, but now being a primary motivator for a variety of professional and occupational work activities in the post-industrial economy. This late-modern recognition of passionate work is of wider scholarly interest as it unearths the long-standing philosophical dispute regarding the relationship between the cognitive faculties and reason and the affects and emotions. For instance, the French nineteenth-century philosopher Félix Ravaisson (2008 [1838]: 43) argued that clear perception is "tightly bound to action," whereas passion "appears to consciousness merely as obscure *sensation*." For Ravaisson (2008 [1838]), passion obscures perception and leaves the individual with an incomplete and imprecise, perhaps even biased, image of the world. Similarly, writing nine decades later, Sigmund Freud's tripartite topology of the human psyche, including the *Ego*, The *Superego*, and the *Id*, distinguished between the Ego as what represents "what may be called reason and common sense," whereas the Id, not yet "modified by direct influence of the external world," contains "the passions" (Freud, *The ego and the id*, 1984 [1923]: 363–364. Cited in Homer 2005: 19). In the Freudian classification, the passions reside in the realm of the Id, the part of the human psyche that is not yet shaped by the individual's contact with an external world, which put pressure on the individual to not let the passions overtake the Ego and to fail to act in ways that are sanctioned by the social community. In these accounts, passion is a term that denotes what is partially in opposition to reason and rationality, yet being the pool of motivation and commitments, indeed drives, that propels the human ambition and imagination. One key challenge for any society is how to make productive uses of this passion, and to productively contain it (in Freudian terms) within the Ego. For instance, how should policy makers, social reformers, educators, and other social actors bestowed with decision-making authority translate, for example, the elementary sexuality of adolescents into meaningful practices and ultimately enshrined in the historically favoured bourgeoisie family structure, or how to discipline youthful aggressive behaviour to translate it into, for example, a willingness to compete over jobs and the resources in civil society and in the labour market, rather than being canalized into anti-social and dysfunctional behaviour? Such concerns are ultimately based on the idea that there are passionate drives in humans, and that such passions need to be subject to social and behavioural regulation, not the least self-discipline, the individual's commitment to master his or her impulses and to act in prudential ways as stipulated by social norms. At the same time, as is discussed in the contemporary social and economic literature, an overtly repressive view of the passions is potentially wasteful as it undermines a meaningful use of such emotional commitment. In what has been referred to as *affective capitalism* (Cockayne 2016), the current mode of production is not simply based on the capacity of corporations to exploit natural resources to produce commodities, but is also geared towards figuring out what humans tend to pay attention to, what their interests are, and how they commit time and resources to these interests. If nothing else, this is precisely what hugely successful companies such as Google have explored.

In this view, the contemporary mode of production is concerned with affects how the individual act in the market place as a consumer, as a citizen, and a member of a society more widely. Importantly, passionate interests and commitments are important qualities of the employee—the salaried worker. In this view, passion and passionate commitment are not only a source of interest for market analysts and trend spotting market gurus, but also pertain to the domain of work located at the hierarchical structure of the corporation, and the various networks of relations wherein the corporation is engaged.

Passion and Meaning in Day-to-Day Work

Affective Labour

Cockayne (2016) argues that competitive capitalism has shifted gears as it is increasingly fuelled by the capacity to use immaterial resources to generate immaterial products or digital objects such as public relation services, financial services, informational infrastructures, communication campaigns, patents, video games, and the like. In this new regime of economic production, wherein physical production capital accounts for a shrinking proportion of the corporation's assets (Haskel and Westlake 2017; Brynjolfsson and Saunders 2010), the beliefs, attitudes, and commitments of the co-workers become a key resource to manage effectively. "Affective labour" (in Gill and Pratt's 2008: 2, apt phrasing) is thus of key importance for the creation of economic value in the present regime of competitive capitalism. In order to sort out the various classes, sub-classes, and intersecting categories pertaining to theoretical constructs such as *affective capitalism,* it is important to discriminate between key terms. Thoits (1989: 318) distinguishes between *feelings, affects,* and *moods,* increasingly being separated from the perceiving subject. Thus, feelings include "the experience of physical drive states (e.g. hunger, pain, fatigue) as well as emotional states," whereas *affects* refer to "positive and negative evaluations (liking/disliking) of an object, behavior, or idea" (Thoits 1989:

318). In addition, Thoits (1989: 318) adds, affects have "intensity and activity dimensions," that is, can be understood as what motivates the subject to act under certain conditions, and with a varying degree of commitment. Adler and Obstfeld (2007: 23) similarly distinguish between affect and emotions, wherein affects are "characterized as the arousal of positive or negative evaluations," whereas emotions are "seen as more specific and transitory affective reactions to specific situations." Moods, finally, are more vaguely defined as being "more chronic, usually less intense, and less tightly tied to an eliciting situation" (Thoits 1989: 318). In order to understand how, for example, feelings and affect translate into actual day-to-day practices, relatively vague and indiscrete terms such as "passion" need to be deployed when studying affective labour.

The Passion of Everyday Work

In the management studies literature, the concept of affect and its role in economic value production are disputed. Cockayne (2016: 457) refers to affects as "the visceral configurations of habit and desire," which may "potentially blind and bind workers to dogmatic systems of governmentality by insecurity." In this account, affects are a means to pacify co-workers to tolerate or even embrace working conditions that are far from optimal from their own point of view. In contrast, the entrepreneurship studies literature addresses "the affective turn" in entrepreneurship research in more positive terms (Huang and Knight, 2017: 95) and makes a connection between affect as passion and commitment, and the development of the business venture. Chen, Yao, and Kotha (2009: 201) define "entrepreneurial passion" as an entrepreneur's "intense affective state," accompanied by "cognitive and behavioral manifestations of high personal value." The theoretical sub-set of entrepreneurial passion is thus consistent with Berg, Grant, and Johnson's (2010: 973) definition of passion, being "strong emotional inclinations toward work-related activities that individuals find interesting, important, and worthy of their time and energy."

Based on a study including 126 MBA students, Chen, Yao, and Kotha (2009: 209) offer a precise description of how passion is expressed by an individual. Chen et al. (2009) make an important distinction between the "affective aspects" of entrepreneurial commitment, a term that includes "passion," and "cognitive aspects," that is, the "preparedness" of the aspiring entrepreneur. Applying this distinction to their data set, Chen, Yao, and Kotha (2009: 209) propose that "passion is expressed through facial expressions, bodily movement tone of voice, and other nonverbal cues," whereas preparedness is "[m]anifested in the verbal content and substance of a presentation" (Chen et al. 2009: 209). Consistent with this analytical model, Cardon et al. (2017) introduce the term Team Entrepreneurial Passion (TEP) as being "the level of shared intense positive feelings for a collective team identity" (Cardon et al. 2017: 286. Original emphasis omitted). In this view, it is not only individuals that become passionately committed to enterprising activities, but also entire entrepreneurial teams share such affective commitment to joint projects. Passionate commitment is thus understood as a group phenomenon (see, e.g., Bartel and Saavedra 2000; Roy 1954; Homans 1951). Furthermore, the extant literature provides empirical evidence that such "entrepreneurial passion" is conducive to long-term entrepreneurial success (Baron 2008: 330). Similarly, affect has been positively related to creative work (Amabile et al. 2005) and work satisfaction more generally (Bunderson and Thompson 2009). At the same time, Cockayne (2016) insists, affect can also be manipulated to benefit specific interests, at times diverging from the individual co-worker's own preferences (see, e.g., Frenette 2013; Perlin 2011).

In contrast to affirmative accounts of entrepreneurial passion as a driver of entrepreneurial performance, Gielnik et al. (2015) argue that entrepreneurial passion is a side-effect rather than the cause of successful enterprising. Entrepreneurial passion is thus a myth that conceals the more material and not the least financial conditions under which entrepreneurial initiatives are formulated and materialized. Reporting statistical evidence from an empirical data set, Gielnik et al. (2015: 1017) propose that "entrepreneurial passion did not predict entrepreneurial effort," that is, informants may claim they are passionate, but this alleged passion does not of necessity translate into a *de facto* affective commitment to the venture. Gielnik et al. (2015) instead propose an analytical model wherein passion is an epiphenomenon of work efforts, that is, it is the work effort *per se* that generates a sense of passionate commitment to the venture, rather than a sense of passionate commitment being the primus motor of the activities. Gielnik et al. (2015) explicate this proposition:

> [T]here is substantial variance in entrepreneurial passion over time and changes in entrepreneurial passion are a consequence of entrepreneurs' efforts. Entrepreneurs increase their passion when they make significant progress in their venture and when they invest effort out of their own free choice. (Gielnik et al. 2015: 1017)

Seen in this view, passion might still be an important component of the entrepreneurial ethos, but its role is merely secondary to other activities, attitudes, and identifies. Passion is thus not a freestanding and independent variable, but is rather the effect of other behavioural and practical conditions, jointly constitutive of the situation wherein the subject expresses passionate commitment, but only after the fact, the work to promote the business venture.

Under all conditions, the individual needs to create a coherent and meaningful image of work life and career choices made, and affect is the primary human faculty being mobilized to accomplish such goals: a serviceable and operable enactment of the self within a horizon of meaning, co-produced by the institutions and practices of working life. Berg, Grant, and Johnson (2010: 978) here make an important distinction between *enjoyment* and *meaning*, wherein the former is associated with what Berg et al. (2010) call "hedonic well-being," which includes "happiness, a favorable balance of positive and negative affect, and satisfaction." In contrast, "eudaimonic well-being" includes a "sense of purpose and personal growth." In a taxonomy of human needs, enjoyment thus denotes the more elementary human demand for immediate recognition and a satisficing of basic needs, whereas meaning is a more subtle and differentiated sense of purpose and coherence that enjoyment *per se* can never fully accommodate nor fulfil. Expressed differently, when the demand for enjoyment is saturated, there can still be a sense of lack of meaning; meaning extends outside of the realm of enjoyment. This condition, defined in such terms, calls for a concept of *authenticity* to better apprehend the elementary mechanisms of affective capitalism.

The Authenticity Criterion in Creative Work

A further complication in passionate work is that participants consider such work as what demands an authentic and genuine commitment to the work and its underlying rules of the game. Neff (2013: 71), who studied digital media production in New York City's so-called "Silicon Alley" computer industry cluster, stresses that many of her interviewees "would often critique or denounce other kinds of people who worked in Silicon Alley as having an inauthentic or inappropriate stance toward work in the industry." "In their worldviews," Neff (2013: 71) continues, "there were right and wrong ways to be *in* Silicon Alley, modes of subjectivity that fit with how they valued work." In theoretical terms, the concept of authenticity is a complicated term that has been used in various philosophical frameworks and served various ends (Taylor 1991; Adorno 1973), but on closer inspection, in, for example, sociological research, authenticity is oftentimes portrayed as a form of fabrication to veil inconsistencies in the public gaze. For instance, Fine (2003: 164) argues that the culture industry, for example, the Nashville-based American country music industry, "fabricate authenticity" to make certain artists promoted and marketed better comply with the audiences' demand for "true grit" performers, deemed to have the first-hand experience from the hardship and struggles of everyday life that country music in many cases accounts for.

Another case wherein authenticity is a matter of social production is in studies of social status hierarchies, where laboratory research reveals that insecurities regarding authenticity result in behaviours that counteract a critique of specific privileges: "[S]uspicions of inconsiderateness and inauthenticity are inherent in the status attainment process unless there is credible evidence to override these suspicions … [T]hese concerns can be overridden by credible prosocial behavior," Hahl and Zuckerman (2014: 530) suggest. To unpack this statement, Hahl and Zuckerman (2014) demonstrate that situations wherein individuals are given a higher social status than the individual him or herself believe are justifiable, the individual acts in ways so that his or her authenticity is confirmed by the community. What Hahl and Zuckerman (2014: 543) refer to as "high-status insecurities" is thus mediated by activities that signal to audiences that the individual is authentic in, for example, his or her preferences or choices. Ultimately, sociological research indicates that authenticity does not so much denote some "natural" or "primordial" relations as it is a form of social fabrication of privilege. As Clifford (1988: 11) writes, "Intervening in an interconnected world, one is always, to varying degrees 'inauthentic'; caught between cultures, implicated in others."

In this view and under such conditions, authenticity is a conflicted term, which on the one hand is introduced to denote genuine commitment or qualities, while in fact being subject to various forms of manipulations. Fine (2003: 166) argues that authenticity is not so much a quality as it is an accomplishment, a form of license to operate under the banner of authentic commitment, defined by audiences who monitor the actor's capacity to honour these statutes. Consequently, Fine (2003) continues, "authenticity can be lost." For instance, well-established artists "too attuned to the market" are always at risk of being met with scorn from audiences who regard this market orientation as a violation of the rules jointly established (Fine 2003: 166). Pitts-Taylor (2007) adds that the authenticity criterion can be invoked in various marketing settings, for example, in the case of the cosmetic surgery industry. Pitts-Taylor (2007: 35) argues that the "dominant logic" of the contemporary cosmetic surgery is no longer to market itself on the basis of current beauty ideals, but instead the industry promotes "essentialist notions of authentic inner selves," wherein cosmetic surgery is portrayed as a legitimate vehicle for the unveiling of the authentic body of the subject, the "truer" surface of the body that more honestly represents the perceived genuine self. Needless to say, given, for example, the research results of Hahl and Zuckerman (2014), who show that a sense of authenticity is a social accomplishment that easily lends itself to external manipulations, the marketing of cosmetic surgery on such grounds induces social costs.

Kosmala and Herrbach (2006: 1400) propose that cynicism is the counterpoint of authenticity, being a "refusal to engage with the world as much as a disposition of antagonism towards it." The cynical marketing of, for example, cosmetic surgery (which naturally does not include *all* cosmetic surgery services) is veiled as a form of concern for the genuine, authentic self, and in such marketing activities the subject, the presumptive cosmetic surgery client, easily falls prey to what is in fact biased on contrived view of the self. The self is no longer recognized for what it is, regardless of the distinction made between surface and depth, as it is portrayed as what is to be "improved" on the basis of a re-sculpturing of the body's natural and given features. Much scholarly research and artistic work apprehend this sense of self-betrayal when the subject abandons his or her own ability to trust individual beliefs and convictions, and instead lays the authority to make choices in the hands of authorities. In the end, the concept of authenticity is two-sided as it can both encourage a recognition of the responsibilities of the self to live a life in full on the basis of one's hopes, dreams, and ambitions, while on the other hand, the ideological construct of the "authentic self" can serve to manipulate individuals to make decisions that deviate from their convictions and interests. Nevertheless, under all conditions, whenever the concept of passionate work is articulated, the idea of authenticity is not too far away, and this calls for an informed understanding of how this blending of passionate commitment and the quest for authenticity can generate unintended consequences and externalities. As, for example, Turner (1976: 1004) has emphasized, the subject's expectation regarding what institutions can accomplish for them may easily result in the waning of the subject's willingness to make self-sacrifices when individuals realize that such expectations cannot be fulfilled. In such situations, to continue to strive towards an authentic way of life easily results in a cynical view of society, or, alternatively, a sense of failure (as in the case of Mr Stevens) to practically anticipate how the subject's view of social life has been manipulated on the basis of promises and narratives that in the end proved to be inconsistent with the material and social conditions of human lives.

In the case of video game development, a passionate commitment to the games was not prescribed by the informants but was nevertheless assumed in most cases. Authenticity was for most part expressed in terms of the interest in the video game development work *per se* rather than the business activities and economic returns that a successful release of a game may result in. Neither passionate commitment nor an authentic relationship to gaming were mandatory, nor policed by the community, but to have a fair share of both qualities was widely regarded as supportive of being a qualified and credible video game developer. That is, it was not a shameful thing to be only moderately committed gamer, but marginal interests in video games demanded a credible story regarding the participation in the industry (Shaw 2011), not unlike the female engineers studied by Faulkner (2007: 334) who always had a ready-made story to tell about their career choice. In the end, passionate commitment and an authentic belief in the value of qualified video games were treated as industry-specific qualities.

Studies of Passionate Work

Bunderson and Thompson (2009: 32) examine what they refer to as "deeply meaningful work," work that "inspire a sense of significance, purpose, or transcendent meaning." To theorize this experience, Bunderson and Thompson (2009: 33) introduce the concept of *calling*, being a term originally reserved for work that "was created, designed, or destined to fill by virtue of God-given gifts and talents and the opportunities presented by one's station in life." A calling is thus simply more than a job or a career, but includes the individual's sense of destiny, a path that demands to be travelled to reach self-fulfilment, or an inspiration to fully recognize. In the contemporary period, the term calling has been gradually freed from its theological and faith-based connotations, and more recent conceptualizations tend to emphasize "self-actualization and personal passion" (Bunderson and Thompson 2009: 34). Furthermore, Bunderson and Thompson (2009: 32) argue that empirical research suggests that individuals "[w]ho view their work as a calling are more satisfied with their work and career."

To substantiate the sense of passionate commitment to a specific line of work, Bunderson and Thompson (2009) study zookeepers, individuals who work in zoos to care for the animals on display. In their empirical material, Bunderson and Thompson (2009: 52) found proof that zookeepers were willing to "sacrifice money, time, and physical comfort or well-being for their work," but also that this commitment to the calling was associated with "heightened expectations about management's moral duty related to the work." These high expectations on others, potentially individuals less animated by a calling, but potentially treating their day-to-day work as a salaried position with various benefits and disadvantages as any paid work is, could unfortunately result in the passionate worker being suspicious of colleagues not using all their capacities to care for the animals, whom the zookeepers regarded as their ultimate clients. This also resulted in a certain vigilance attitude among certain zookeepers, always eager to defend what they regarded was the best decision and policy. On balance, therefore, a calling is "a double-edged sword," Bunderson and Thompson (2009: 52) propose. On the one hand, the calling infuses a sense of passionate commitment to a specific line of work, conducive to meaning and a sense of solidarity with both colleagues and the animals being cared for; on the other hand, a zealous defence of what was treated as the only adequate way of organizing the work resulted in tensions and conflicts in employment relations. Bunderson and Thompson (2009: 52) speak about this condition as the "fundamental tension" inherent to deeply meaningful work: deep meaning is of necessity associated with "real responsibility," but the inability to fulfil high expectations can easily result in disappointment and cynicism among passionate workers.

Also Schabram and Maitlis (2017) examine passionate work and study individuals who believe they are subject to a calling. Schabram and Maitlis (2017: 584) argue that previous research on the topic tends to "emphasize the positive side of callings," but this one-sided understanding of passionate work easily misses some of the day-to-day concerns that a passionate commitment may entail. Passionate workers may respond to "workplace challenges" through various mechanisms, including a passive acceptance of less than optimal work conditions, withdrawal and disappointment, sabotage, or "job crafting" (i.e., the individuals make personal interpretations of what responsibilities and practices that should be included in the day-to-day work; Schabram and Maitlis 2017: 585). Studying animal-protection shelters, organizations that work to help animals find a new and hopefully more loving home, Schabram and Maitlis (2017) identify three distinct "calling paths"—strategies and tactics used by passionate workers to make sense out of their everyday life work experience. The first path is "identity-oriented" and describes how individuals who respond to challenges in their work continuously preserve and reinforce their sense of having "special gifts" in relation to animals (Schabram and Maitlis 2017: 592). This calling path thus stresses individual competencies and skills as what is structuring day-to-day work. The second calling path is "contribution-oriented," being an attitude that seeks to maximize the individual's positive and rewarding impact in the work no matter under what conditions this work is done. In this calling path, everyday work is a question of making a difference, no matter what resources that are committed to the purpose. Third and finally, Schabram and Maitlis (2017: 592) use the term "practice-oriented calling," which denotes the situation wherein the individual responded to challenges by learning new practices, and developing relationships with others that helped them become skilled practitioners in animal welfare. This third strategy did not take the skills and competences of the individual as given, but was rather treated as an original commitment that *per se* needs to be cultivated and further refined, and therefore also subject to meaningful managerial influence and organizational activities.

The empirical material reported by Schabram and Maitlis (2017) indicates that individuals on the identity-oriented path tended to react with "intense anger and sorrow" whenever managerial decisions violated their commitment to animal welfare, and over time such emotional responses resulted in "extreme disappointment" as the individuals were filled with a sense of failing in their ambition to protect the animals from unpleasant experiences. Individuals on the contribution-oriented path were less prone to respond with anger, but were equally enraged and frustrated by the obstacles they identified and that they believed prevented them from achieving their goals (Schabram and Maitlis 2017: 598). Also on this calling path, a passionate work ethic clashed with economic realities, budget constraints, and managerial decision-making procedures. Third and finally, workers on the practice-oriented path, who did not consider themselves as being uniquely gifted, were better equipped to strike a balance between making a contribution to animal welfare and to cope with everyday economic realities. Having more modest aspirations, the practice-oriented path workers did not turn potentially disappointing managerial decisions into a self-consuming sense of failure and betrayal of the beloved animals.

Based on these results, Schabram and Maitlis (2017) share Bunderson and Thompson's (2009) view that passionate inspiration is indeed two-sided. Individuals who follow a calling are often eager, hard-working, and dedicated, and therefore represent an attractive pool of job candidate to most organizations (in fact, the announcement of the belief in the value of "passionate commitment" and similar stock phrases is a cliché in labour market communication). Such employees oftentimes went beyond "the call of duty," invested unpaid hours and volunteered for difficult work tasks, and were diligent in their care, and yet this "overinvestment" in the work generated adverse effects. When these individuals felt their dedication to animal welfare was not fully shared by colleagues and/or management, there was a regressive tendency to engage in well-intentioned but often counterproductive behaviours to modify the situation. This resulted in conflicts with colleagues, disputes with management, and constant rumination, which lead to emotional and physical exhaustion (Schabram and Maitlis 2017: 606). The saying, "Being one's own worst enemy," certainly applied to the passionate workers on the identity-oriented and (to a lesser extent) contribution-oriented career paths.

Bozkurt and Cohen (2019) examine an entirely different but equally passion-driven business activity, that of classic car repairing and restoration. As Bozkurt and Cohen (2019: 1106) notice, cars are one of the few technical objects that are routinely repaired in advanced economies, and there is also a developed hobbyist culture based on the passionate interest for "classic cars," that is, car older than say 25 years (the legal definition of "antique cars" varies between jurisdictions). Furthermore, to be a skilled craftsman (a gender-neutral term in this context, yet being a domain that traditionally attracts more male than female entrants) demands "embodied knowledge"—at times referred to as "haptic skills"—and long-term practical experience (Bozkurt and Cohen 2019: 1107). At the same time as craftsmanship in mechanical engineering and related domains of expertise is widely respected, car repairing is associated with "dirty work," and the pay is low, as is its social status (Bozkurt and Cohen 2019: 1109).

Based on a study of a workshop course in classic car repairing work, Bozkurt and Cohen (2019) propose that the participants, whom for most part regarded the vocational training as a start of a new or more specialized career, regarded the occupational expertise as a species of "good work" inasmuch as it included both technical skills, recognized their love of cars, and classic cars in particular, and was consistent with recently established sustainability ideas wherein car repairing is regarded as a morally responsible and legitimate work (even though the car industry and automobility more widely is treated with scepticism among sustainability advocates). Furthermore, the participants were not only able to translate their love of cars, machines, and technical devices into an occupational identity and career opportunity, they were also able to reclaim "a more authentic working self," Bozkurt and Cohen (2019: 1119) propose. In summary, Bozkurt and Cohen (2019: 1123) argue that craft skills and love "were transformational" inasmuch as they elevate "mundane, dirty work" through interactions with the loved object, the classic car, "through the exercise of embodied skill." This process was in turn supported by the growing confidence and legitimacy acquired on the basis of "experiential learning" (Bozkurt and Cohen 2019: 1123).

As opposed to two cases of animal welfare work reported above, the car repair workers did not start within a domain that is widely respected (most people show at least some interest in animals, or at least for most part respect people who are passionate about their welfare), but rather started from within a "dirty work" setting, but just the same let their passionate commitment to technological systems, whose intricacies and (at times) quirkiness demand sophisticated and in many cases highly specialized skills and work experience, define and gradually encircle all of their day-to-day work. In this context, "good work" is defined on the basis of personal commitments, the respect for the expertise and skills involved in conducting the work, and a positive relation with wider societal ideologies, in this case pertaining to the need to repair and make better use of material resources that are costly to produce in terms of the energy and natural resources they demand. Ultimately, "good work" is therefore straddling personal passions and commitments and matters of joint concern, for example, how to wisely make use of available material resources in the face of diminishing possibilities for extracting natural resources. In addition, as opposed to the zookeepers and animal shelter workers, car repairing is to a lower extent bordering ethical and moral concerns, and the car repair workers were not agitated or alienated by how classic cars were treated by their owners, or otherwise imposed moral views of their work. By implications, the "good work" of car repairing arguably includes less risk of generating disappointed co-workers as their passionate commitment to classic cars was largely not challenged by competing societal interest or priorities (as in the case of shrinking budgets in zoos or in animal shelters).

In the end, the two empirical studies of animal welfare work show that passionate commitment in the domain of work can in fact be overstated, and that such cases can result in both individual costs in terms of deteriorating relations with colleagues and management and in emotional and physical consequences, and in social costs as continuous disputes regarding how economic resources are raised and committed to defined activities are counterproductive and reduce the overall efficiency of the activities. This "dark side of passionate work" is relatively limitedly recognized in everyday managerial practices, and a passionate commitment to work is widely treated as an attractive feature of the individual worker or job applicant. However, there is in fact a problem with also positive commitment inasmuch as this stated ambition can easily result in responses that are neither desirable nor free of costs. Passionate work induced by a perceived calling is therefore in many ways more complicated to manage than what may be recognized at first glance. The original and theological meaning of passion means *suffering*, and if the passionate individual is willing to suffer to, for example, fully exploit self-declared talents and skills, management needs to be able to identify and counteract such tendencies at an early stage so that the negative features of passionate work can be contained.

In contrast, the "good work" of car repairing is a more "positive" case of how passionate commitment can be a key resource to both motivate increased training and the acquiring of more advanced skills and experience and as a means to soften what some would regard as the stigma to work in low-pay, low-status jobs that are also regarded as being "dirty" or more widely unattractive. Furthermore, the leadership skills and qualities demanded to manage "good but dirty work" are arguably lower as car repairing is not commonly associated with moral sentiments. The epistemic line of demarcation between living biological systems such as animals and inert, non-vital matter as in the case of cars and other engineered objects precludes the introduction of moral categories in the domain of the latter type of objects. On balance, the car repairing workers have better possibilities for developing more sustainable and positive images of their work and their own skills over the career and the business cycle in comparison to animal welfare workers, it must be concluded.

On Gaming: A Sense of Being Alive

The substantive practice being studied and reported in this volume is video game development. In order to better understand the role of the games, play, and gaming in contemporary society, social theory that recognizes the functional role of games needs to be introduced. This theoretical review is thereafter assisted by the empirical material presented in the Chaps. 3 through 7 in the second part of this volume.

The Sacred and the Profane and the Rules of Conduct

In order to fully understand the commitment to video games and video games development, the passion that fuels the global video game industry, the experience of playing video games in a society beset by a combination of ambiguities and a thick texture of rules and norms needs to be explored. This survey of the field demands that social science and behavioural science concepts are introduced to better apprehend the emotional responses of the gamer. A starting point is to introduce the writings on the sociology of religion of Émile Durkheim, who makes a key distinction between the *sacred* and the *profane*. According to Durkheim (1995: 34–35), all "religious systems" display one common feature: they presuppose a classification of "the real" or "ideas" into "two distinct genera"—the sacred and the profane. The profane denotes all mundane, day-to-day life activities, and the practices, materials, and artefacts involved in such activities. The profane is devoid of "aura" or a "halo," and remains separated from the sacred. The sacred, in contrast, denotes all practices, materials, and artefacts that are qualitatively, and, in most cases, spatially or geographically separated from the profane, and that include or signify religious faith and worship. As Durkheim strongly emphasizes, the sacred does not need to denote extraordinary events or artefacts, but virtually any object can be treated as sacred in a specific culture:

> Sacred things are not simply those personal beings that are called gods or spirits. A rock, a tree, a spring, a pebble, a price of wood, a house, in a word anything, can be sacred. A rite can have sacredness; indeed there is no rite that does not have it to some degree. (Durkheim 1995: 34–35)

The line of demarcation introduced in all societies between the sacred and profane is significant and needs to be understood as a "social fact" in

Durkheim's (1938) vocabulary. The former category includes a variety of religious rituals, procedures, and taboos, whereas the profane domain is less strictly monitored and more widely regulated by social norms. Violating the rule of the sacred is associated with various punishment, sanctions, and shaming practices, whereas similar violations in profane domains are less strictly penalized. Durkheim (1995: 36) suggests that the line of demarcation between the sacred and the profane is "always and everywhere" maintained as separate genera in the human intellect, and the two domains must not be confused.

The value of Durkheim's analytical categories lies in their ability to apprehend how human societies and human culture are created on the basis of various classifications and distinctions, and how these classifications may appear arbitrary to external observers. More specifically, as Claude Lévi-Strauss (1985: 34) remarks, for Durkheim, culture is never neutral or artificial inasmuch as it is neither the product of "genetics" nor of "rational thought." Instead, human culture is essentially constituted as a set of "rules of conduct," whose history and function are not of necessity understood by the people who obey them. To make everyday life operable and to reduce social tensions and conflicts, which wield destructive effects on social cohesion, the members of a society are trained to accept the rules of conduct that society imposes upon them. By implication, Lévi-Strauss (1985: 34) deduces, reason is a product rather than the cause of "cultural evolution"; the ability to act reasonable in the eyes of a social community or members of a specific society means to adhere to, and to honour, rules of conduct, and therefore reason is a derived rather than original human virtue and capacity.

The distinction between the sacred and the profane, and the central role of rules of conduct in Durkheim's social theory, which emphasizes the various degrees of mechanical and organic solidarity as the "social glue" that maintains social cohesion, is important when understanding the role of games. Here, games and gaming as practice provide a socially sanctioned arena wherein the "rules of conduct" can be re-negotiated, and wherein certain social behaviour, penalized outside of the realm of the game, can be permitted (e.g., in the case of killing adversaries in so-called first-person shooter games and war games). "Games," Kear (2017: 354) writes, "are devices that, by creating a sense of distance between the individual and the role they play, allow for the performance of behaviours that might otherwise feel cruel, alien or meaningless."[1] It should be remarked, as video game industry representatives are the first to recognize, that not all commentators have been equally sanguine regarding, for example, the violence that a fair proportion of video games includes. A recurrent theme

[1]Elias ([1970] 1978: 153–154. Original emphasis omitted) suggests that the "task of sociological research" is to make "blind, uncontrolled [social] processes more accessible to human understanding by explaining them, and to enable people to orient themselves within the intervowen social web—which, though crated by their own needs and actions, is still opaque to them—and so better to control it." This is an ambitious scholarly programme, to both explain social processes and to educate an audience regarding their nature so they can better "control" their behaviour. Yet this programme is helpful when examining the nature of games and play in the differentiated society, at least if the interests for, for example, video games are to be explained in functionalist terms.

George Simmel (1955) argues that society does not only suffer the consequences of conflict, but also ascribe a social value to conflictual relations: "conflict contains something positive," Simmel (1955: 14) proposes. A society characterized by comfortable harmony and the lack of discordant views easily declines or fails to exploit its full potential, Simmel suggests, and therefore any society "needs to some quantitative ratio of harmony and disharmony, of association and competition, of favorable and unfavorable tendencies" (Simmel 1955: 15). In traditional society, such desire for conflict was frequently directed towards skirmishes and armed conflicts (see, e.g., Clastres 1994), in many cases with devastating consequences for, for example, European societies. In the era of de-traditionalization and rationalization in Max Weber's sense of the term, conflicts within as well as between societies are channelled into various sports activities, Elias and Dunning (1986: 46) argue: "[S]port is closely bound up with the conditions of civilization in society at large and thus with the interplay of civilizing and de-civilizing." In a society that increasingly relies on what Elias refers to as *Selbszwang*, self-control, rather than *Fremdzwang*, external disciplinary practices (Bijsterveld 2008: 250), the stress generated in society needs to be handled in one way or the other, Elias and Dunning (1986: 65) suggest:

> In advanced industrial societies, leisure activities form an enclave for socially approved arousal of moderate excitement behaviour in public. One cannot understand the specific character and the specific functions which leisure has in these societies if one is not aware that, in general, the public and even the private level of emotional control has become high in comparison with that of less highly differentiated societies. (Elias and Dunning 1986: 65)

Sports, and more recently, video games, are thus leisure activities that contemporary societies provide to offer "a type of excitements which does not disturb and endanger the relative orderliness of social life as the serious type of excitement is liable to do" (Elias and Dunning 1986: 71). In this way, Elias and Dunning (1986), assisted by Simmel's recognition of the social value of conflict, provide a functionalist justification for video gaming. In lieu of alternative justifications, this qualifies as a useful conjecture regarding the tolerance of games that depict and actively involve the gamer in violent acts that are otherwise subject to strict law enforcement and normative control in everyday life.

in the public discourse regarding video games has been the concern regarding the portrayal of and agency in violent acts in video games. For the time being, this debate seems to be at the trough but can easily flame up if certain events are reported.

Play Versus Games

The social theory literature makes an important distinction between *play* and *games*. Play is open-ended inasmuch as the participants can introduce and re-negotiate the rules of the play as they wish and *en route*. In this view, play trains, for example, children to both actively take the role of the other and actively understand that this identity and the social position of the imaged identity is dependent on rules of conduct which the individual needs to comply with. At the same time, to create dynamics and drama in the realm of play, new rules may be introduced and enforced, which results in new possibilities and scenarios that the participants must actively relate to. As the psychologist D.W. Winnicott (1971: 110) remarks, play leads to "the establishment of an autonomous self," a self that claims its own persona, yet is functionally capable of responding to exogenous changes in the realm of play. Play thus creates a sense of autonomy and mastery over a pre-defined, yet changeable, social situation.

In contrast, games, which older children start to appreciate, approximately from the age around seven, are based on pre-defined and non-negotiable rules of the game and rules of conduct (regarding expectations of "play fair," etc.). As opposed to the play situation, a game is defined by its specific rules, and mastery in the game derives from the capacity of the participant to both understand the rules of the games and their implications, and to outperform the other participants. Whereas play is relational and invites the participant to use their imagination to, for example, define alternative identities for themselves for the sake of amusement or intellectual stimulation, games introduce the elements of *rules* and *competition* that stipulate how the winner is defined. To participate in games is thus to tolerate, intellectually, socially, and emotionally, that there is commonly only one winner and that there is, by implication, a considerable risk that the individual participant will not win. Normally, to participate in the game is a sufficient reward for the individual, and winning the game comes as an additional benefit.

Several social theorists have remarked that in the era of a highly differentiated societies, characterized by detailed and continuous social control, games serve as a vehicle to release tensions, or to create gaming situations wherein the participants "feel alive" inasmuch as he or she either acquires a temporal sense of control over a defined situation, or are exposed to genuine choice. Walter Benjamin (1999: 199, D10a, 2) argues in his arcade project files that games were co-produced with the expansion of the administrative state apparatus and its inertia: "As life become more subject to administrative norms, people must learn to wait more. Games of chance possess the great charm of freeing people from having to wait." Similarly, Roger Caillois (2001: 159), the French social theorist associated with the *Collège de Sociologie* community, argues that games "[c]onstitutes a kind of haven in which one is master of destiny": In the realm of the game, "the player himself chooses his risks, which since they are determined in advance, cannot exceed what he has exactly agreed to put into play" (Caillois 2001: 159). Winnicott (1971: 65) even more strongly associates games with the growing demand for compliance in the highly differentiated administrative society, and suggests that games create experience that "makes the individual feel that life is worth living":

> Contrasted with this is a relationship to external reality which is one of compliance, the world and its details being recognized but only as something to be fitted in with or demanding adaptation. Compliance carries with it a sense of futility for the individual and is associated with the idea that nothing matters and that life is not worth living. In a tantalizing way many individuals have experienced just enough of creative living to recognize that for most of their time they are living uncreatively, as if caught up in the creativity of someone else, or of a machine. (Winnicott 1971: 65)

In this view, games are a functional mechanism within a society that otherwise imposes a strictly defined and dense texture of rules of conduct and social norms, which leave the individual with the predicament that there are few pockets of freedom or escape routes through which he or she may restore a sense of autonomy or even mastery. Games do, Caillois (2001) argues, mirror the underlying societies wherein they are created. Karl Marx formulated the proposition that certain technologies beget specific social relations and societies (e.g., feudalism, market capitalism), and Caillois (2001) continues this line of reasoning and suggests that specific social relations generate their own specific games.

A Taxonomy of Game

Caillois's (2001) theory of games is an idiosyncratic contribution to social theory, embedded in the *Collège de Sociologie* community's ambition to formulate a theory of society outside of academic quarters. Being strongly influenced by the work of Durkheim (Genosko 2003: 75), Caillois takes a somewhat self-contradictory view of play: on the one hand, Caillois (2001: 5–6) writes, "Play is an occasion of pure waste: waste of time, energy, ingenuity, skill, and often of money for the purchase of gambling equipment or eventually to pay for the establishment." The term "waste" arguably denotes the open-ended and non-functionalist nature of games, being located outside of the realm of industrial production, or other allegedly "rational" social practices. At the same time, gaming is far from wasteful inasmuch as it a "free activity" wherein a sense of uncertainty and suspense is maintained until the end of the game, its denouement (Caillois 2001: 7). To better distinguish between different game experiences, Caillois introduces a taxonomy of games: (1) *agôn* denotes any game based on competition, wherein the participant uses his or her abilities and strategic and tactic skills to outmanoeuvre the other contestants; (2) *alea* includes all games essentially structured around chance, say card or dice games wherein it is possible to a varying degree for the participants to a certain degree to calculate or estimate the risks involved, but otherwise essentially being exposed to non-parametric risks, that is, uncertainty; (3) *mimicry* involves all kinds of games or plays that include "simulation," for example, participants dress up or use their imagination to create new personas for themselves; (4) *ilinx* (from the Greek word for vertigo) denotes the last class of games in the taxonomy, being all sorts of games wherein the participants engage their bodies and their so-called proprioceptive sense to create a physical sensation, in, say, various forms of "dancing games" in folklore culture.

In Caillois's taxonomy, *agôn* and *alea* games are strongly associated with the differentiated administrative state, whereas *mimicry* and *ilinx* are more closely associated with "primitive" and agrarian societies. In Caillois (2001: 18) view, *agôn* games represent "the vindication of personal responsibility," the participant's acceptance of the rules of the games, and his or her ambition to compete and to compete fairly. In contrast, *alea* games represent "the negation of will, a surrender to destiny" (Caillois 2001: 18). This means that the participant is willing to submit to the seemingly random forces beyond the control of the otherwise accountable individual. Caillois (2001) implies that both these attitudes are highly acclaimed in the differentiated administrative state: *agôn* imposes a purified version of the enterprising and accountable subject that is the ideological foundation of, for example, societies based on competition, and *alea* denotes the other desirable quality of the citizen, the acceptance of the condition that each individual cannot determine the nature of society, or singlehandedly create one's own future (as prescribed by, e.g., the rugged individualism that Charles Wright Mills (1951, 1956) saw as the lingering myth of American culture, translated into a variety of norms, narratives, and symbols). Instead, *alea* encourages participants to recognize the fickle and uncertain nature of human existence, and provides an outlet for this sense of frustration, or even anger over the loss of autonomy and mastery.

In summary, differentiated societies create many benefits for the individual member, for example, the economic welfare generated on the basis of the division of labour, and institutions that protect the rights and interests of the individual. At the same time, the differentiated society may create a sense of loss of agency or autonomy, which may result in a loss of meaning. Games can serve as a social mechanism wherein the social rules of conduct are temporarily re-negotiated, even ignored, within the realm of the game. The game is a device that enables society to be maintained on the basis of other means, and serves a "carnival function" (Bakhtin 1968) as it provides a temporal relaxation of the strict enforcement of the mandatory social rules of conduct. Ultimately, games provide a refuge from the repetitious and predictable everyday life and its expectations imposed on the individual.

In a sociological or behavioural science perspective, games do play a key role in opening up for glimpses of the domain of the sacred (e.g., the taboo against killing humans) within the profane. Games constitute a domain wherein the lines of demarcation between the sacred and the profane are playfully transgressed, which creates a sense of "being alive" or releases tensions among the participants. Games and video games more specifically are thus social mechanisms that create a passionate engagement among users and developers. Yet, to fully understand this passionate commitment to video games and video game development, a more deep-seated theory of the social significance of the video game is demanded.

Summary and Conclusion

To be passionate about some interest is to some extent an elusive and evocative human condition. A passionate interest in video games may be examined on the basis of contemporary cognition science research, which proposes that the human mind, assisted by its perceptual (primarily visual) system, "produces its own content, i.e., the world" (Stafford 2009: 281). That is, cognition science reveals that what humans regard as reality is essentially the brain's construction (Luhmann 2000: 6). If this idea is tentatively accepted, the implication is that passion can be explained on the basis of how well cognitive and perceptual capacities motivate individuals to continue a specific activity, say, to play a video game. The limbic system, a section of the brain that processes sense impressions, "reinforces certain perceptual and cognitive constants of reality," Stafford (2009: 282) writes. That is, for example, vision operates as a "dynamic process in which the brain, largely automatically, filters, discards, selects and compares information to an individually stored record" (Stafford 2009: 277). Furthermore, gaming is a tactile experience wherein the ability to use devices such as joysticks or the computer keyboard is part of the gamer's skills, and the integration of visual and tactile sense impressions generates an image of reality that the gamer regards as engaging inasmuch as it involves a variety of cognitive and affective faculties.

In this view, both video gaming and art experiences are fundamentally embodied processes, wherein perceptual capacities, cognitive processes, and affects are triggered and reinforced, experiences that result in what is perceived as being meaningful.

If video games and art are considered in such terms, the implications are that creative work, including video game development, is understood in terms of the capacity to actively escape or ignore the regular, ready-made ways of seeing and experiencing the world to better generate new ideas (e.g., video game concepts) that have not yet materialized. If the cognitive and perceptual apparatus that constitutes the human mind and that generates images of reality as we experience it, this "autopoetic machinery" (Stafford 2009) must be transcended by the creative individual.

In Stafford's (2009) analytical model, visual perception is the key to creative and artistic work, and yet the perceptual apparatus is what needs to be distanced so that novel expressions can be generated. The creative individual needs to be able to look, and yet this gaze needs to be regarded as what is illusive and even treacherous as it already contains all the know-how and preconceived ideas that the seer has appropriated over the years (i.e., doctrines that dictate what is art proper or a plausible video game concept). That is, Stafford (2009: 290) says, "seeing, not seeing as, enables knowledge to grow." Creative work is therefore, in its essence, to struggle against the habits of the mind to think and perceive the world in certain ways, and to carve out a space wherein some reporting can be accomplished on the basis of artistic and technological means. The enterprising video game developer thus not only needs to convince the world regarding his or her venture and to raise funds to finance the development work, but he or she must also actively learn to distrust the sense impressions so that new ideas can be recognized and be exploited. That is no trivial challenge, to be fair.

The first part of this volume has introduced the economic and social and behavioural conditions that determine the possibilities for indie video game development. Video game development is a species of innovation-led economic development, and despite being thoroughly commercial from the outset, the industry is fuelled by the commitment of both developers and gamers. The second part of the volume will report empirical material that indicates how economic and social resources are deployed in the video game development activities, and how indie developers and other industry actors and commentators regard the possibilities for making fruitful contributions to what is today a global billion dollar industry, more or less exclusively embedded in the Internet communication system. The final chapter of the volume will examine the practical and theoretical implications of the study, and more specifically point at the implications for innovation-led growth policies, currently being a major issue in advanced economies.

References

Adler, P. S., & Obstfeld, D. (2007). The role of affect in creative projects and exploratory search. *Industrial and Corporate Change, 16*(1), 19–50.

Adorno, T. W. (1973). *The jargon of authenticity*. London and New York: Routledge.

Amabile, T. M., Barsade, S. G., Mueller, J. S., & Staw, B. M. (2005). Affect and creativity at work. *Administrative Science Quarterly, 50*, 367–403.

Bakhtin, M. (1968). *Rabelais and his world*. Bloomington: Indiana University Press.

Baron, R. A. (2008). The role of affect in the entrepreneurial process. *Academy of Management Review, 33*, 328–340.

Bartel, C. A., & Saavedra, R. (2000). The collective construction of work group moods. *Administrative Science Quarterly, 45*, 197–231.
Benjamin, W. (1999). *The arcades project* (H. Eiland & K. McLaughlin, Trans.). Cambridge: The Belknap Press.
Berg, J. M., Grant, A. M., & Johnson, V. (2010). When callings are calling: Crafting work and leisure in pursuit of unanswered occupational callings. *Organization Science, 21*, 973–994.
Bijsterveld, K. (2008). *Mechanical sound: technology, culture and public problems of noise in the twentieth century*. Cambridge and London: The MIT Press.
Bozkurt, Ö., & Cohen, R. L. (2019). Repair work as good work: Craft and love in classic car restoration training. *Human Relations, 72*(6), 1105–1128.
Brynjolfsson, E., & Saunders, A. (2010). *Wired for innovation: How information technology is reshaping the economy*. Cambridge and London: The MIT Press.
Bunderson, J. S., & Thompson, J. A. (2009). The call of the wild: Zookeepers, callings, and the double-edged sword of deeply meaningful work. *Administrative Science Quarterly, 54*(1), 32–57.
Caillois, R. (2001). *Man, play and games* (M. Barash, Trans.). Urbana and Chicago: University of Illinois Press.
Cardon, M. S., Post, C., & Forster, W. R. (2017). Team entrepreneurial passion: Its emergence and influence in new venture teams. *Academy of Management Review, 42*(1), 283–305.
Chen, X.-P., Yao, X., & Kotha, S. (2009). Entrepreneur passion and the preparedness in business plan presentations: A persuasion analysis of venture capitalists' finding decisions. *Academy of Management Journal, 52*(1), 199–214.
Clastres, P. (1994). *Archaeology of violence*. New York: Semiotext(e).
Clifford, J. (1988). *The predicament of culture: Twentieth-century ethnography, literature, and art*. Boston: Harvard University Press.
Cockayne, D. G. (2016). Entrepreneurial affect: Attachment to work practice in San Francisco's digital media sector. *Environment and Planning D: Society and Space, 34*(3), 456–473.
Crogan, P. (2018). Indie dreams: Video games, creative economy, and the hyperindustrial epoch. *Games and Culture, 13*(7), 671–689.
Durkheim, É. (1938 [1895]). *The rules of sociological method*. Glencoe: Free Press.
Durkheim, É. (1995 [1912]). *The elementary form of religious life*. New York: Free Press.
Elias, N. (1970). *What is sociology?* New York: Columbia University Press.
Elias, N., & Dunning, E. (1986). *Quest for excitement: Sport and leisure in the civilizing process*. Oxford: Blackwell.
Faulkner, W. (2007). 'Nuts and bolts and people': Gender-troubled engineering identities. *Social Studies of Science, 37*(3), 331–356.
Fine, G.-A. (2003). Crafting authenticity: The validation of identity in self-taught art. *Theory and Society, 32*(2), 153–180.

Frenette, A. (2013). Making the intern economy: Role and career challenges of the music industry intern. *Work and Occupations, 40*(4), 364–397.

Genosko, G. (2003). The bureaucratic beyond: Roger Caillois and the negation of the sacred in Hollywood cinema. *Economy and Society, 32*(1), 74–89.

Gielnik, M. M., Spitzmuller, M., Schmitt, A., Klemann, D. K., & Frese, M. (2015). "I put in effort, therefore I am passionate": Investigating the path from effort to passion in entrepreneurship. *Academy of Management Journal., 58*(4), 1012–1031.

Gill, R., & Pratt, A. (2008). In the social factory? : Immaterial labour, precariousness and cultural work, *Theory. Culture and Society, 25*(7–8), 1–30.

Hahl, O., & Zuckerman, E. W. (2014). The denigration of heroes? How the status attainment process shapes attributions of considerateness and authenticity. *American Journal of Sociology, 120*(2), 504–554.

Haskel, J., & Westlake, S. (2017). *Capitalism without capital: The rise of the intangible economy.* Princeton: Princeton University Press.

Homans, G. C. (1951). *The human group.* London: Routledge & Kegan Paul.

Homer, S. (2005). *Jacques Lacan.* London and New York: Routledge.

Huang, L., & Knight, A. P. (2017). Resources and relationships in entrepreneurship: An exchange theory of the development and effects of the entrepreneurs-investor relationship. *Academy of Management Review, 42*(1), 80–102.

Kear, M. (2017). Playing the credit score game: algorithms, 'positive' data and the personification of financial objects. *Economy and Society, 46*(3–4), 346–368.

Kosmala, K., & Herrbach, O. (2006). The ambivalence of professional identity: On cynicism and *jouissance* in audit firms. *Human Relations, 59*(10), 1393–1428.

Lévi-Strauss, C. (1985). *The view from afar* (J. Neugroshel & P. Hoss, Trans.). Oxford. Blackwell.

Luhmann, N. (2000). *Art as a social system* (E. M. Knodt, Trans.). Stanford: Stanford University Press.

Mills, C. W. (1951). *White Collars: The American Middle Class.* Oxford: Oxford University Press.

Mills, C. W. (1956). *The power elite.* Oxford and New York: Oxford University Press.

Neff, G. (2013). *Venture labor: Work and the burden of risk in innovative industries.* Cambridge and London: The MIT Press.

Perlin, R. (2011). *Intern nation: How to earn nothing and learn little in the brave new economy.* London and New York: Verso.

Pitts-Taylor, V. (2007). *Surgery junkies: Wellness and pathology in cosmetic culture.* New Brunswick: Rutgers University Press.

Planells, J. A. (2017). Video games and the crowdfunding ideology: From the gamer-buyer to the prosumer-investor. *Journal of Consumer Culture, 17*(3), 620–638.

Ravaisson, F. (2008). *Of habit.* London and New York: Continuum.

Roy, D. (1954). Efficiency and 'the fix': Informational intergroup relations in a piecework machine shop. *American Journal of Sociology, 60*(4), 255–266.
Schabram, K., & Maitlis, S. (2017). Negotiating the challenge of a calling: Sensemaking in animal shelter work. *Academy of Management Journal, 60*(2), 584–609.
Shaw, A. (2011). Do you identify as a gamer? Gender, race, sexuality, and gamer identity. *New Media Society, 14*(1), 28–44.
Simmel, G. (1955). *Conflict* (K. H. Wolff, Trans.). New York: Free Press.
Stafford, B. M. (2009). Thoughts not our own: Whatever happened to selective attention. *Theory, Culture and Society, 26*(2–3), 275–293.
Taylor, C. (1991). *The ethics of authenticity.* Cambridge: Harvard University Press.
Thoits, P. A. (1989). The sociology of emotions. *Annual Review of Sociology, 15*, 317–342.
Turner, R. H. (1976). The real self: From institution to impulse. *American Journal of Sociology, 81*(5), 989–1016.
Winnicott, D. W. (1971). *Playing and reality.* London: Tavistock.

PART II

The Empirical Material

CHAPTER 4

Who Is an Indie Developer? Sorting Out the Categories

Introduction

The video game industry is a relatively new industry, being at the intersection of computer science, entertainment, and the arts, and indie developers are to some extent both the cause and the effect of the establishment of a proper industry developing video games. The term *indie developer* is what linguistics scholars call a *retronym*, an original term that eventually becomes what needs to be explained in the face of new events. For instance, prior to the electric guitar being invented in the late 1940s and early 1950s, a guitar was by definition an acoustic guitar, but after decades of electric guitar playing, the prefix "acoustic" is added to the term guitar when this original version of the instrument is denoted. Similarly, an indie developer is today a person who contributes to the video game industry by working in a small studio or on his or her own, who accesses only rudimentary technology and resources and therefore needs to be inventive when designing the game and the graphic design of the game. These qualities and location in the fringe were quite much the original position of the pioneers of video game development: operating at the margins of the computer science cluster and being treated as a curiosity were the predicament and attraction of the first generation of video game developers.

This chapter will examine how video game industry participants discriminate between indie developers and other developer categories, and how the term "indie" is described in interview situations. Being indie is a short for "independent," but similar to the phrase "independent central

A. Styhre, *Indie Video Game Development Work*,
https://doi.org/10.1007/978-3-030-45545-3_4

banks" in the governance literature, the questions "independent from what?" and "independent in what way?" are relevant. As the empirical sections of this volume will indicate, there is a fair share of conditions and interest that no video game developer is independent from, say, the digital distribution channels that most video game developer distributors rely on. In addition, all video game developers are dependent on the gamer community and expert commentators to have their games recognized. Word of mouth marketing is the best way to promote a new game, and preferably some "buzz" regarding a game to be released shortly benefit the commercial success of the new game. Seen in this view, the terms "indie" and "independent" are to some extent misnomers as there are after all only limited possibilities for being genuinely independent in a technologically mediated industry that is based on shared norms and assessment criteria. Yet, the term "indie" prevails and is widely used, as will be discussed in the chapter.

Classification as Social Practice

The Argentinian author Jorge Luis Borges cites an ancient Chinese encyclopaedia to indicate how classificatory systems are arbitrary and culturally contingent (Borges 1999: 231. See also Foucault 1970: xv). This classification of animals into 14 seemingly randomly constructed categories appears unintelligible and inoperable to the contemporary (Western) reader. As, for example, Ludwig Wittgenstein (1974: 61) has remarked, classifications rest on definitions, and in order to understand definitions, one must already understand "a great deal of language." Classification systems are thus language-laden and therefore also cognition-dependent constructs. This in turn renders a classification system as what is mid-way between what Alfred North Whitehead (1929: 37) refers to as the "immediate concreteness of the individual thing" and an "abstraction"—an idea of what category-specific objects belong to. In other words, the epistemological basis for a classificatory system is far from self-explanatory or undisputed. In fact, social theorists show, classificatory systems are embedded in power relations and politics inasmuch as the epistemological fragility of the classificatory system is concealed to the outsider to render the act of classifying an object unproblematic (Panofsky and Bliss 2017; Power 2015). "Classifications are powerful technologies," Bowker and Star (1999: 319) argue: "Embedded in working infrastructures they become relatively invisible without losing any of that power."

In social theory and management studies, classificatory systems have been examined as an integral, for most part invisible, feature of everyday life in the advanced and differentiated contemporary society. "Our lives are hinged around with systems of classification, limned by standard formats, prescriptions, and objects," Bowker and Star (1999: 1) argue, pointing at the pervasive penetration of classificatory practices. At the same time, to practically include all species in a defined field of investigation, any classification system relies on reductionism, Chia (1999: 210) proposes: "Typologies, taxonomies and classification schemes are convenient but essentially reductionistic methods for abstracting, fixing and labelling what is an intrinsically changing, fluxing, and transforming social reality." Similarly, Waguespack and Sorenson (2011: 541) argue that the value of classification resides in a "reduction" of the available stock of information: "Many fewer categories exist than would result from a complete enumeration of all the possible combinations of characteristics." In fact, this reductionist epistemology is what renders classification systems useful tools in the hands of managers, administrators, and social reformers. By reducing the informational complexity through the practice to assign objects to categories, social reality including business activities appears to be both intelligible and manageable, that is, cognitive limitation and operational difficulties are simultaneously overcome, or at least reduced, by the introduction of a classificatory system.

Studies of classification practices include a variety of professional fields and industries, reported by management scholars, sociologists, and science and technology researchers. Carruthers and Espeland (1991: 55) examine accounting as a "classificatory" practice, wherein the accounting system (e.g., the original Italian double-entry book-keeping standard) is portrayed as a "cognitive device that sorts, orders, and names," and consequently "frame the economic reality in a particular way." In this view, the primary role of the accounting practice is to reduce uncertainty in the eyes of equally merchants, their clients, creditors, and the broader society. Fleischer (2009) examines the credit-rating industry on the basis of similar premises, wherein uncertainty is the money-lender's or loan-originator's demon, and consequently standardized assessment methods for the calculation of the presumptive borrower's creditworthiness are introduced. Regardless of the power imbalances in the finance industry, the credit-rating practice must "strike a careful balance among the interests of the rating organization, the producers of classified products, and the audience of the system," Fleischer (2009: 558) says.

In science and technology studies, the "epistemic ideal of exactness" (Sommerlund 2006: 917) dominates in scientific classification practices, but studies of, for example, embryology—the selection of embryos to be transplanted to the womb in *in-vitro* fertilization therapy—reveal that even when there are clearly defined standards for assessing the "quality" of the embryos (Svendsen and Koch 2008: 99), the classificatory system remains fluid inasmuch as there is "room for variation in practice to accommodate uncertainty, the rapidly shifting science and policy environment, and socially and ethically contested aspects of particular categories" (Ehrich et al. 2010: 2205). To select embryos is therefore not the unambiguous and straightforward activity that the *in-vitro* fertilization industry purports it is, but includes uncertainty derived from incomplete medical data and/or theories. A similar case is in psychiatry wherein classification systems such as the *Diagnostic and Statistical Manual of Mental Disorders* (DSM, now in its fifth edition, and consequently referred to as DSM-V), published by the American Psychiatric Association, represent a classificatory system that includes all widely documented psychiatric illnesses and disorders (Strand 2011). Strand (2011: 302) argues that DSM-V has the explicit purpose to impose a discrete classificatory system and that "ambiguous cases" are reinterpreted to fit into existing categories.

These empirical studies all indicate that despite the stated intentions of the classifier and the ambition to provide a conclusive taxonomy, classificatory systems tend to rest on incomplete scientific data and evidence, and that such systems are subject to prolonged debates and disputes. Seen in this view, classificatory systems are designed and introduced to reduce the undesirable effects of cognitive limitations and information costs, and they become social facts as soon as such classificatory systems serve to define and structure social reality. On these grounds, the authority to influence the design of, or the ongoing modification and upgrading of, a classificatory system is to execute significant political power. Unsurprisingly, classificatory systems are subject to much controversy and disputes. For instance, the growing literature on credit-rating practices, a key business in the U.S., which determines the individual's or households' access to credit (Kear 2017; Polillo 2011), suggests that credit rating is not the value-neutral and objective calculation of market data it purports to be, according to industry representatives. Instead, incomplete or biased input data, firm-specific algorithms that are subject to discretion, and inadequate inferences from statistical data are some conditions that may compromise the integrity and the accuracy of the credit-rating practice. In such cases, Fleischer (2009: 556) argues, organizations (e.g., credit-rating companies) can protect their own interest by imposing classificatory systems, operating behind closed doors, and yet fail to avert a lingering or growing critique that the "information value" of the classification scheme is "suspect."

In the end, classificatory systems are prevalent in all corners of contemporary society and in the economic system. Yet classificatory systems arguably rest on a more porous ground than official declarations, supportive of such devices, admit. Classificatory systems are epistemologically fragile, include various design and data input deficiencies, and easily mirror certain power imbalances and political interests in society. At the same time, as social theorists and management scholars have repeatedly demonstrated, also incomplete, biased, or inadequately designed classification systems generate social effects (Durkheim and Mauss 1963), whereof some are arguably unintended consequences from the vantage point of the promoters of a specific taxonomy. Such unintended consequences of intentional action are likely to surface whenever the secondary audiences, for example, local officers in the state administration, assigned the role to implement centrally developed classificatory systems, apply the taxonomy to local cases. The divergence, theoretical or actual, between classificatory systems as policy (i.e., as a written and politically determined framework) and as actual governance device justifies further empirical research. For instance, in high-growth industries or in emerging sectors (say, in the field of social entrepreneurship; Spicer et al. 2019) wherein classificatory systems are less institutionalized because the actors are busy making contributions, or wherein the economic growth *per se* does not yet result in a perceived need to make use of economic resources more effectively, classificatory systems are potentially less strictly defined, and consequently deviations from classificatory practices are not subject to penalties. In other words, to better understand how classificatory systems are institutionalized in industries or in specific socio-economic fields, high-growth industries offer primary possibilities for scholarly inquiries in this area. When industries are being formed or expanded, entrepreneurial and creative contributions are the primus motor of the activities, and therefore the structuring and ordering derived from the introduction of classificatory systems are less useful. By implications, classificatory systems play a more marginal role, and there are considerably more latitude for industry actors in terms of transgressing classificatory boundaries, leading to more "new combinations" and a more sanguine view of a more playful use of the current classificatory system.

To Classify the Indie Developer and the Indie Video Game

Indie developers constitute a specific class of developers in the video game industry, and yet this group is complicated to define in a straightforward manner, and alternative classifications apply in various contexts and situations. One of the analysts of the industry interest organization referred to a formal definition that was included in the annual industry report issued by the organization. This definition was inspired by the use of independent record labels in the music industry, widely associated with the creative capacity to detect and further refine the work of new artists and bands. "We write," the analyst read, "'From the English term *Independent*, i.e., autonomous, a prefix that characterizes free-standing developers. Oftentimes denoting development processes that include a limited number of actors'" (Analyst, Male, Swedish Video Game Interest Organization). Such formal definitions are helpful inasmuch as they performatively serve to fix an otherwise fluid and changeable term, which is supportive of the development of a joint vocabulary in an industry or sector of the economy. Interviews with industry representatives indicate that outside of this formal definition, there are at least four themes that are addressed when indie developers as a specific species of video game developers are discussed. Indie developers can be defined (1) on the basis of a certain attitude or identity, (2) as being a specific form of organization within the video game industry structure, (3) in terms of their position in the labour market, and (4) in terms of the output, the video game, that they produce. In this way, indie developers are portrayed as an inherently fluid and unstable category. This operational flexibility of the term is indicative of the high-growth nature of the video game industry, not yet being in the position wherein it needs to impose more strict taxonomies to reduce ambiguities and informational costs, but rather hold boundary transgressing activities in esteem. In more mature industries, more strict typologies and classification systems are arguably applied to accomplish certain benefits. In the following sections, the four classifications of the indie developer will be examined.

Indie as Attitude and Identity

Several of the interviewees argued that the essence of the indie developer credo was to be a gamer at heart, fully committed to the video games he or she loved to play as a child or adolescent, and actively translating such experiences into a professional identity and role. "Indie normally means a smaller team willing to take more artistic risks," the director of a video game development incubator argued: "They produce something that makes a difference, which is more niche-oriented, that deviates from the mainstream. And they are fueled by their passion." The term *passion* is indicative of the strong emotional commitment to the work in the indie community, and other interviewees referenced a variety of terms to apprehend this affect. "[An indie developer] is someone with a lot of attitude when it comes to doing your own thing: 'I am an artist,'" one video game industry entrepreneur said. Analyst #1 in the industry interest organization argued that even highly successful video game development companies, which report robust bottom-line results and reach large audiences, were prone to maintain an indie image. The analyst explicitly spoke about an "indie spirit" that was valued by also mature companies:

> Even world-class developers and their new companies they have started, they are referring to indie ... [One developer] said, 'We're an Indie developer, and there is an indie spirit in our work and in our company.' (Analyst, Male, Swedish Video Game Interest Organization)

The ambition to represent an artistic vision of video games is also a declaration of a specific identity. The analyst #2 in the industry interest organization addressed the identity of indie developers: "Above all, [the term "indie"] is a form of identity of certain video game developers. Then it matters what type of game you develop, and where you are located [in the country] when it comes the question of how important it is to be 'indie'" (Analyst #2, Female, Swedish Video Game Interest Organization). "It is more of a style than a question of independence," one indie developer and culture sector entrepreneur, organizing various events and game jams, stated. "I use the term indie because it is convenient. And I don't use it unless I really have to," he continued, to signal that he was aware of the term being somewhat threadbare at this stage.

As the term "indie" is never self-contained nor self-explanatory (as indicated by the empirical material), the use of the term "indie" was dependent on the context and situation, but for most interviewees, indie had positive connotations that captured the enthusiasm over the video game development that fuelled the industry. The artistic ambitions and the identity constructed on the basis of such ideas in many cases enacted the indie developer as a figure in the margins of the video game industry:

"[Indie developers] want to position themselves as more marginal to the rest, like a way of staying true to their ideas," a video game studies professor, working in a Canadian university, argued. This attitude was illustrated by a video game development educator, who half-jokingly addressed the preference for "casual looks" of developers as a manifestation of an attitude:

> A programmer that is neatly groomed and wears a suit, he looks for a job. If he looks like a homeless person, he's employed and does no longer have to care [about his attire]. (Video game development educator and Indie developer)

One of the indie developers testified to this ambition to maintain an "indie attitude" in the day-to-day development work:

> I regard [indie] as something positive. There is a certain pride in calling oneself an indie developer. There is this indie dream in all that you do. You can develop the next Minecraft. No one is our boss—we are our own bosses, That is the indie attitude. (Indie Developer #4, Video Game Company A)

This marginal position does not indicate any willingness to exclude oneself from the mainstream, but is better understood as a position that secures operational freedom, the autonomy needed to engage with experimental and creative video game development work. The analyst #1 in the industry interest organization emphasized that the indie community constituted a form of "laboratory" in the industry, a site wherein novel ideas were developed and tested:

> Indie represents the freedom to be a bit more artistic and to experiment with the expression. It is the laboratory of the video game industry, sort of… They have been able to produce some odd things that the major developers would not tolerate. (Analyst, Male, Swedish Video Game Interest Organization)

In this classification system, indie developer work is categorized as a specific form of affective labour, rooted in a passionate commitment to video games and video game development. One of the more experienced indie developer with a credible track record in video game development was concerned with how the original use of the term "indie" was abused: "Ever since, like ten years back, people have been using this like some kind [of slogan], 'We're indie.' But you know they are not indie in their hearts: they want to grow big" (Indie developer, Company K). For the developer, indie denotes specific qualities and attitudes that should be protected. Indie developers construct identities on the basis of images of themselves as artistic and creative professionals, endowed with the capacity to develop new video game ideas and even new video game genres. Under all conditions, this category primarily emphasizes the intellectual, cognitive, and artistic qualities of indie developers, and ignores, for example, industry and market conditions.

Industry Structure Conditions

The second category in the classification system applied by the interviewees emphasized how the video game industry is separated into various types of developers, publishers, and distributors (in many cases also being publishers). The interviewees stressed this autonomy vis-à-vis publishers as a formal mark of the indie developer. "If you are an Indie developer, you mustn't rely on a publisher. You should launch and distribute all by yourself," analyst #3 (Male, Swedish Video Game Interest Organization) argued. "Indie stands for independent. You are not owned by a publisher," the video game industry entrepreneur said. As video games are distributed digitally, through the Internet and for most part no longer sold over-the-counter, the central role of the publisher may appear somewhat confusing. As video game development has become a cottage industry and the Internet is today "a global village" (with Marshall McLuhan's memorable phrase), there is on the one hand a close connection between the indie developer and the end-user, the gamer, while the sheer supply of games on the market on the other hand creates a need for marketing skills to help a specific game become discovered by audiences. As there are thousands of new video games uploaded on publishers' sites such as Steam annually, "market noise" is a major concern. Publishers and distributors thus amplify market signals, which reduce the threshold for new industry entrants. In this industry context, publishers are the gatekeepers of the industry, being the gateway to the gamer community for video game development companies.

To further complicate the vocabulary, there is a distinction made in the industry between "indie" studios (denoting indie developers) and "independent" studios, wherein the latter term explicitly denotes the independence from publishers: "What makes things confusing is that 'Indie' comes from 'Independent.' Independent is another term being thrown around … Independent studios are not owned by any publisher," the director of the video game development incubator argued. To further explain the difference, the director provided an explanatory case, being one "independent studio" that "produce super-blockbusters with Hollywood action and stereotypes and violence and explosions and make multimillion dollars." According to the director, this studio is "still *independent* but not *indie*. No one would ever call them indie" (Director, Video Game Development Incubator #1). Another developer argued that, for example, Nintendo would to some extent qualify as an indie developer given the absence of publisher relations:

> [Indie] stands for 'Independent Developer.' That means that you have no publisher. But Nintendo has no publisher; they publish themselves. Is that Indie? No, it is not. But the general saying is that the firm size should be ten [developers to qualify as an indie studio]. (Indie developer, Company M)

In broader terms, indie can denote a situation wherein a video game developer studio operates without any finance capital investors who influence the development work, or more widely the size of the studio. For instance, one of the indie developers argued this was the case for them: "We do actually refer to ourselves as indie because it suits us in terms of the size of the company. In addition, we are independent for the time being" (Indie Developer #2, Video Game Company A). The CEO and one of the cofounder of Indie Company D also referred to size as a criterion for indie developers: "The lines of demarcation are fuzzy, but I'd say that indie denotes quite small [studios]." At the same time, the CEO argued that the term "indie" should be used with care, as the term was normally used quite strictly: "Officially, I never speak about us as an indie studio. I believe that the common view is that you need to be totally pure to qualify as an indie studio; untouched by the larger companies" (CEO and Founder, Indie Company D).

The distribution and marketing of video games are all indie developers' concern as it is a process where the word-of-mouth effects and quickly spreading reputation in the gamer community are in many cases hard to predict. The best safe bet for indie developers is therefore to rely on a major publisher—Steam being the publisher *par preference* among indie developers during the period—but this inevitably implied that the video game development process was geared towards certain genre conventions, some of the interviewees argued. Expressed differently, it is complicated to ensure absolute autonomy in an industry wherein the competition over the attention from the gamer community is fierce, and wherein the publishers serve a central curatorial function to classify and bundle games, in many cases on the basis of algorithms processing market data. Under all conditions, interviewees used industry structure categories to define indie developers, that is, objective market conditions served to position the indie developer vis-à-vis alternative categories.

Indie and Labour Market Structure

A third way to classify indie developers is in terms of their access to predictable and fully compensated work. As indicated in the first section, indie is a broad-sweeping term, and also highly commercially successful studios may refer to themselves as indie developers to signal their commitment to creative ideas and new thinking. This means that many self-declared indie developers are in fact employed by studios that offer regular employment as stipulated by industrial relations contracts and existing agreements. This group of indie developers still arguably represent a smaller share of the community. For many indie developers, the situation looks entirely different, especially as it takes time to figure out how to raise finance capital in an industry that the mainstream finance industry is relatively limitedly informed about. "Those who run indie companies, they are for most parts newcomers," the analyst #1 said: "Many of them have not worked in major companies, or have spent only a short time with such developers" (Analyst #1, Male, Swedish Video Game Interest Organization). The video game studies scholar argued that many indie developers had some experience from working in larger studios but that they have made an informed choice to leave such development activities to pursue a career in the fringes of the industry:

> The indies are the people outside of [the mainstream], and some of them are started out in Triple-A, and decided like, 'This isn't for me.' Some of them just never wanted to be in Triple-A in the first place. (Video Game Studies Professor, Canada)

What indie developers appreciated was the capacity to exploit one's own skills and artistic capacities, but it was also an active choice to escape undesirable work routines in the Triple-A firms, for example, the episodes of excessive overtime prior to the release of a new game, widely referred to as "crunch-time" or, more shortly, "the crunch" in the industry. "[Indie developers are] opposed to the corporate structure, 'the crunch' … Or they have ideas that they just feel are too marginal and would never be accepted," the video game studies professor argued. Also the indie developers addressed the use of excessive overtime during certain periods as a concern and an unattractive feature of the industry:

> What is referred to as 'the crunch' is a widespread practice, to work considerable amounts of overtime. That work is not fully compensated. You may get a few days off, or they offer you some food [when working overtime]. You are expected to work overtime since they have planned for it. (Indie Developer #4, Video Game Company A)

The indie developer in Company M told similar stories about alleged cases of mismanagement in Triple-A companies:

> I hear things from the Triple-A world when we did [a video game], that there were much crunch work and stories about people not getting paid and there was this dad who could not see his kids as he was forced to work instead. That is terrible! (Indie developer, Company M)

The video game development educator expressed the same concern regarding Triple-A studios based on his personal experience:

> The only place where I have crunched is at [multinational Triple-A studio]. Then the working days were ten hours rather than eights. I started to feel that 'these things wear you out' … My standpoint is that crunch is evil. (Video game development educator and Indie developer)

More generally speaking, indie developer was associated with work in absence of a very well-defined managerial structure. An indie developer in Company H argued that in the firm he worked, everybody was concerned with developing games, whereas nobody was interested in assuming managerial responsibilities:

> Everybody just wants to make games, by and large. There's nobody who likes managing people developing games. So we have tried to develop a model where nobody has to do that. As far as possible, we have tried to

> make people be self-managing and that they understand the totality of the activities. (Indie developer, Company H)

An indie developer in Company F, himself experienced from a major Triple-A company and being a renowned local indie developer, placed the ability to exploit creative skills as the primary purpose of the indie scene, a possibility that, for example, Triple-A companies cannot provide because of its functional specialization and managerial practices:

> The purpose of being an indie, if that's what I am, is to be creative, to be able to make decisions regarding creativity. To conduct the design that I like. Because if you get a job in the video game industry, you do not become lead designer right away, if you ever reach that position. You become a 'code-slave,' or the 'art-guy.' It's always been like that. (Indie developer, Company F)

These two interviewees defined indie development negatively, as *what is not* Triple-A development work. The choice to commit to a career in indie development was essentially a matter of choice on the basis of preferences:

> I definitely think that different things attract people. If you want structure and to be given specific assignments, like 'I am supposed to do this,' then Triple-A is much better. But If you appreciate to come and go as you like and to take initiatives, like 'What could possibly happen it I add this feature to the game?' then Indie developers is the right way to go. (Indie developer, Company H)

The developer in Company M emphasized that Triple-A companies are ultimately about making money, whereas indie development is allegedly driven by passionate commitment, at least in its ideal-typical forms:

> If you say 'Triple-A,' I think, 'they want to make all the money they can.' If you say Indie, I think that they are destitute but do it all out of the passion. That is the image people would get. (Indie developer, Company M)

"I didn't like the size of the [casino] company. It felt like a sweatshop," the indie developer in Company F bluntly stated. The Indie developer in Company K was equally sceptical regarding the Triple-A world—as a matter of fact, "it is an active choice you make all the time, to *not get* a regular job," he stated—but he still missed the opportunity to work on a team or in collaboration with others:

> I feel I would miss the freedom to do what I want [if being employed] … I'd rather develop my own ideas rather than someone else's … At the same time, it would be a source of learning to work with someone else. In the right company it would provide the possibilities for making something spectacular. (Indie developer, Company K)

Regardless of the benefits of operational freedom, the indie developers argued that economic insecurity was a concern for both the developers and the industry at large, especially as the industry grows quickly and the absolute majority of the Swedish video game companies are run at a profit. This economic insecurity was not only a concern in the fringes of the industry, among indie developers, but also in larger and financially robust companies, indie developer #4 (Video Game Company A) argued: "[Economic insecurity] is a factual matter also in Triple-A companies. By and large, the work conditions varies considerably depending on what industry you are working in." Unfortunately, there were limited prospects for things changing in the near future. For instance, as opposed to the rest of the Swedish economy, there was a relatively low degree of unionization in video game development, which indie developer #4 deplored: "I think it is pity that there is no trade unions in the video game industry. There is no economic security. It is a very insecure industry to work in." His colleagues shared this concern and addressed a recent upsurge in union membership registration that ended abruptly when video game developers learned that their union of choice was incapable of helping them:

> Like a year ago, there was this wave where people started to join a trade union, because they wanted to organize themselves. But apparently this particular union could not help them as they lacked the know-how and the authority to take action. (Indie Developer #2, Video Game Company A)

Such disappointing outcomes largely leave video game developers in a situation wherein they have to negotiate their work conditions on a one-on-one basis. Historically, such bilateral and individual negotiations have not benefitted labour interests (see, e.g., Brandl and Ibsen 2019). If the future of the industry will be unionized remains to be determined.

The labour market structure is an implicit classification of the indie developer as they for most part position themselves differently, mostly as either being a creative fringe or as a class of developers that maintain their autonomy vis-à-vis publishers and financiers. A closer inspection that penetrates the surface of the industry still indicates that indie developers are exposed to a higher degree of economic uncertainty as indie studios face challenges when they raise funds, and because the digital distribution and marketing include considerable uncertainty for all actors.

The Output: Indie Games

The fourth component of the classificatory system is to categorize indie developers on the basis of their actual output. A recurrent theme during the interviews was to portray indie developer as *bricoleurs* (with the anthropologist Claude Lévi-Strauss' [1966] term), as inventive and resourceful actors capable of accomplishing a lot on the basis of limited resources. "Indie is more closely associated with these small ideas, original and somewhat quirky and innovative stuff," analyst #3 (Swedish Video Game Interest Organization) argued. Being exposed to various shortages of resources (e.g., finance capital, technology, specialized skills, and know-how), the indie developer participates in a video game development process that evolves as a form of *bricolage*, using all available resources. "[Indie developers] are exposed to limitations: they cannot do the coolest 3D animation, or work with graphic design that take several years to accomplish. They need to work on a smaller scale," the video game industry entrepreneur said. This predicament in turn results in an output that is markedly different than the mainstream contributions, the director of the incubator argued:

> When people talk about indie and being interested in indie companies, it is oftentimes a matter of games that look different and that challenges standards. They may have a distinct aesthetic expression. (Director, Video Game Development Incubator)

Analyst #1 shared this view and argued that many indie games were held in esteem by the gamer community because of their novel game concepts, or their "minimalist design."

> There are new forms of narratives or [new] artistic expressions determining the interface. Indie games are not popular because of how their technical features, as there's no money for technology ... [The games] look better and has this minimalist design. (Analyst, Male, Swedish Video Game Interest Organization)

Interviews with indie developers indicate that they affirm this role as the inventors of limited means in the industry, and take pride in this capacity of householding: "Indie will always be at the bottom, those who do the odd things," Indie developer #4 (Video Game Company A) said. For instance, the indie developer and culture sector entrepreneur argued that "pixel-based graphics" was a typical indie video game design choice, "simply because it is quicker to develop": "That is the indie signature, to put it like that. And you need to appreciate chip music [the sound produced by rudimentary sound cards]," the informant said.

Needless to say, the indie community is marked by its heterogeneity, which includes a broad variety of preferences and artistic and aesthetic visions, but what unify all actors on equally the global and the local scale is the ambition to translate creative ideas into a materialized digital object that contains all such ideas and enables playability:

> What you consider as indie is this ambition to take the risk to develop a niche-game that offers a focused experience based on an artistic vision. It does not necessarily means a visual experience, but it can also be associated with a certain game design. There are indie games that takes the whole genre farther inasmuch as they skip the competition moment altogether, i.e., [your avatar] cannot 'die.' (Director, Video Game Development Incubator)

Interviewees frequently defended video games as an emerging cultural expression, worthy of the same recognition as other media-based culture, for example, film. Unfortunately, the interviewees argued that policy makers and administrative staff in various industry or culture agencies had only vague ideas about what video games are, and how they are developed, and that they for most part had inherited a sceptical view that portrayed video gaming as a primarily male adolescent pastime, associated with indolence, escapism, and, in many cases, excessive violence. Even policy makers and officials with a more informed and affirmative view had difficulties to understand the idiosyncrasies of the industry, the interviewees argued.

The director of the video game development incubator accounted for his communication with local government officials, and stressed these difficulties: "Officials in the public sector maintain their own image of reality. They try to categorize games within the existing taxonomy," he said. The director continued:

> Traditionally, we have been categorized as 'Film and Motion Pictures.' That is where games are located. But that is like putting a square peg into a round hole. It is the sum of all components that makes video games unique. It includes motion pictures and interaction, and it is art and high-tech, and it is a global and a digital [business]. (Director, Video Game Development Incubator)

Another faulty classification in the eyes of industry actors is to think more strictly of video game development as a digital technology industry branch, but that classification downplays the artistic and aesthetic qualities of video games: "We would prefer to be associated with culture rather than tech. In many cases, we have been sorted into some tech category that we are not really identifying ourselves with," analyst #3 argued (Male, Swedish Video Game Interest Organization). The recent focus on the consequences of digitalization and the penetration of digital media in all spheres of society in policy-making quarters, introduced as a major issue for the coming decades, left video game industry actors unimpressed. For them, digital media is the lifeblood of the industry and their everyday life world, and therefore such campaigns and policy making added little or nothing to what they already know about digital media: "The issue of 'digitalization is brought up,' but that is not a word or concept ever discussed in the video game industry … We have always been digital," the director argued. At the same time, the interviewees understood that they navigated in technically complex domains, for most part inaccessible to an uninformed audience. Consequently, video game industry representatives accepted the burden to inform and instruct policy makers, officials, and lay audiences regarding the possibilities and demands of the industry, but at times ignorant outsiders were an additional complication. A certain patience with uninformed audiences was thus a principal virtue for industry actors.

In summary, the indie developer is defined on the basis of shifting categories, all which captures some of the underlying complexity of the indie development activities. First of all, it is noteworthy that the term "indie developer" is an industry-specific term. In other industries, pre-seed or seed phase companies, thinly capitalized firms in the earliest stages of the development work, are oftentimes referred to as "start-ups" (or variations thereof, e.g., "spin-outs"). In the video game industry, that term is unpopular as it denotes a certain ready-made entrepreneurship identity that arguably violates the artistic and creative identity of indie developers. "I think the term 'indie' is used with more love than the term 'start-ups,'" analyst #2 (Female, Swedish Video Game Interest Organization) argued. At the same time, as soon as this industry-specific term is instituted, it is largely left to the industry participants to define the term as it suits their interests: "It's up to companies themselves to define whether they are indies or not," the video game industry entrepreneur argued. In the end, for good or for bad, the term "indie" is a floating signifier that is invoked in various conversations determined by context and situation.

Classification Systems and the Making of a Social Order

Classification systems matter in a variety of industries inasmuch as penalties are imposed on products that transgress categories (Waguespack and Sorenson 2011; Hsu 2006). In addition, classification systems constitute a bureaucratic and administrative system wherein certain benefits and possibilities can be negotiated for companies that fit into the current categories (Zuckerman 1999). At the same time, classification systems are arbitrary (Bowker and Star 1999) insofar as they are constructed to accomplish certain benefits such as a reduction of information costs and improved administrative transparency. In high-growth industries, classification systems are yet in the making as companies do not need to manage their resources more effectively. Consequently, market categories or administrative categories are more fluid, changeable, and overlapping (Zhao et al. 2018). Products and activities that include two or more categories are not subject to penalties to the same extent as in more mature industries.

The empirical material demonstrates that indie developers are defined on the basis of at least four distinct classifications, including (1) the identity of indie developers, (2) their position within the market structure, (3) existing labour market relations, and (4) the output indie developers produce. Indie developers constitute a specific class of video game developers, but their identity, attitude, market positions, and so on are highly heterogeneous and include a variety of activities and aspirations. In the vocabulary of Durkheim and Mauss (1963), the classification of indie developers is best characterized as a primitive classification system inasmuch as it is temporarily stabilized, but subject to ongoing modifications as the video game industry changes and evolves, and the role of indie developers is modified to respond to changing industry conditions. At the same time, also primitive classification system, regardless of their transient and protean qualities, imposes a hierarchical and taxonomic order that enables an industry or a community to cognitively apprehend the entities and practices that are constitutive of the social and economic activities. That is, primitive classification systems (or *proto-categories* in Zhao et al.'s 2018, phrasing), riddled by inconsistencies and ambiguities, are useful as they create a shared ground for communication, and impose hierarchies and meaning through their performative use. Durkheim and Mauss (1963: 8) propose that primitive classification systems are introduced by their protagonists as logically consistent analytical frameworks, but that the categories "have an extra-logical origin." As, for instance, Borges (1999) reminds us, historical or foreign classification systems do not of necessity appear logically consistent in hindsight, which suggests that context, situation, and interests determine the practical value of classification systems. Durkheim and Mauss (1963) thus suggest that all human societies demand tools and heuristics to cognitively apprehend and to help it members navigate within differentiated societies, a demand being partially satisfied by, for example, the introduction of classification systems.

More scholarly research is needed to better understand the formation of classification systems and their gradual institutionalization in markets, industries, and society more broadly. Especially in high-growth industries, characterized by a significant number of new entrants, which all suffer from what Stinchcombe (1965) referred to as "the liability of newness," the study of classification systems is welcome. For instance, as indicated by interviewees, industry policy is structured around historical data and classification systems derived therefrom. Industries such as the video game industry that integrate elements from a variety of previously compartmentalized industries and domains of expertise (e.g., computer science, digital media, and the film industry) easily become "the square peg" that does not fit into "a round hole" (as one interviewee put it), that is, boundary-spanning activities are penalized by current industry policy. For instance, in the film industry, Hsu (2006: 445) argues, by using the threat of "social and economic penalties," audiences pressure film producers to "conform to existing categories and serve to reproduce the existing structure of the market." Therefore, it is important to study both classification systems in mature industries and in high-growth industries. In the former case, for example, regulatory reforms may be advocated by industry actors to benefit their interests, that is, classification systems are negotiated en route. In the latter case, classification systems are to a large extent determined by ongoing changes in the market, that is, classification systems are constructed as an integral part of industry formation and change. At times, such classification systems lag behind factual conditions, as in the case of industry policy unable to fully apprehend the variety of businesses the policy is intended to include. A proposition lending itself to empirical testing is that classification systems evolve differently in mature versus high-growth industries. Such scholarly inquiries would shed further light on how classification systems are supportive of innovation-led growth, or if there are unintended consequences of such systems.

Summary and Conclusion

Social actors jointly construct the institutional environments within which they live and work. Social and economic lives, which include everyday work practices and routines, are constituted on the basis of material, symbolic, and legal conditions, and classificatory systems are part of the practico-cognitive institutional framework of any industry. In high-growth industries, characterized by quick economic growth and changes, taxonomies and classificatory systems are modified whenever new conditions and actors emerge. Seen in this view, the term *indie developer* has taken on a new meaning since the turn of the millennium. Some industry participants believe the term has limited denotative qualities (i.e., the term can mean basically anything) but still use it as it provides specific communicative qualities (primarily associative) that generate benefits. Others believe the term denotes important professional norms and values, and therefore advocates an indie lifestyle and an indie outlook on computer game development. Under all conditions, terms such as indie developer arguably serve a role in negotiating and enforcing certain professional norms that characterize an industry. Being indie denotes to be venturesome, innovative, creative, and to share a love for gaming and video games in particular. On the basis of such qualities and aspirations, the indie scene is constructed, arguably for the benefit of the industry. The indie community is the experimental workshop or the laboratory in an industry otherwise adopting more conventional business practices.

References

Borges, J. L. (1999). *John Wilkin's analytical language, in Selected non-fiction*. London: Penguin.

Bowker, G. C., & Star, S. L. (1999). *Sorting things out: Classification and its consequences*. Cambridge and London: The MIT Press.

Brandl, B., & Ibsen, C. L. (2019). Collective wage bargaining and the role of institutional stability: A cross-national comparison of macroeconomic performance. *Cambridge Journal of Economics, 43*, 677–694.

Carruthers, B., & Espeland, W. (1991). Accounting for rationality; Double-entry book-keeping and the rhetoric of economic rationality. *American Journal of Sociology, 97*(1), 31–69.

Chia, R. (1999). A 'Rhizomatic' model of organizational change and transformation: Perspective from a metaphysics of change. *British Journal of Management, 10*, 209–227.

Durkheim, É., & Mauss, M. (1963). *Primitive classification* (R. Needham, Trans.). Chicago: The University of Chicago Press.

Ehrich, K., Williams, C., & Farsides, B. (2010). Fresh or frozen? Classifying 'spare' embryos for donation to human embryonic stem cell research. *Social Science & Medicine, 71*(12), 2204–2211.

Fleischer, A. (2009). Ambiguity and the equity of rating systems: Unites States brokerage firms, 1995–2000. *Administrative Science Quarterly, 54*(4), 555–574.

Foucault, M. (1970). *The order of things*. London and New York: Routledge.

Hsu, G. (2006). Jacks of all trades and masters of none: Audiences' reactions to spanning genres in feature film production. *Administrative Science Quarterly, 51*(3), 420–450.

Kear, M. (2017). Playing the credit score game: algorithms, 'positive' data and the personification of financial objects. *Economy and Society, 46*(3–4), 346–368. https://doi.org/10.1080/03085147.2017.1412642.

Lévi-Strauss, C. (1966). *The savage mind*. Chicago and London: The University of Chicago Press.

Panofsky, A., & Bliss, C. (2017). Ambiguity and scientific authority: Population classification in genomic science. *American Sociological Review, 82*(1), 59–87.

Polillo, S. (2011). Money, moral authority, and the politics of creditworthiness. *American Sociological Review, 76*(3), 437–464.

Power, M. (2015). How accounting begins: Object formation and the accretion of infrastructure. *Accounting, Organizations, and Society, 47*, 43–55.

Sommerlund, J. (2006). Classifying microorganisms: The multiplicity of classifications and research practices in molecular microbial ecology. *Social Studies of Science, 36*(6), 909–928.

Spicer, J., Kay, T., & Ganz, M. (2019). Social entrepreneurship as field encroachment: How a neoliberal social movement constructed a new field. *Socio-Economic Review, 17*(1), 195–227.
Stinchcombe, A. L. (1965). Social structure and organization. In J. G. March (Ed.), *Handbook of Organizations* (pp. 142–155). Chicago: Rand Mcnally.
Strand, M. (2011). Where do classifications come from? The DSM-IIL, the transformation of American psychiatry, and the problem of origin in the sociology of knowledge. *Theory and Society, 40*, 273–231.
Svendsen, M. N., & Koch, L. (2008). Unpacking the 'spare embryo' facilitating stem cell research in a moral landscape. *Social Studies of Science, 38*(1), 93–110.
Waguespack, D. M., & Sorenson, O. (2011). The rating game: Asymmetry in classification. *Organization Science, 22*(3), 541–553.
Whitehead, A. N. (1929). *The aims of education*. New York: Mentor Books.
Wittgenstein, L. (1974). *Philosophical grammar* (R. Rhees, Ed.; A. Kenny, Trans.). Oxford: Blackwell.
Zhao, E. Y., Ishihara, M., Jennings, P. D., & Lounsbury, M. (2018). Optimal distinctiveness in the console video game industry: An exemplar-based model of proto-category evolution. *Organization Science, 29*(4), 588–611.
Zuckerman, E. W. (1999). The categorical imperative: Securities analysts and the illegitimacy discount. *American Journal of Sociology, 104*, 1398–1438.

CHAPTER 5

Social Norms in the Developer Community: The Ambiguity of Money-Making

Introduction

Making money is a virtue and a professional capacity in a capitalist economy, but it also matters *how* the money is being made as social norms interfere with strict economic incentives in many professional fields and industries (Bermiss and McDonald 2018; Turco 2012; Anteby 2010; Fine 2003). The purpose of this chapter is to examine how indie developers cope with monetary and pecuniary motives on the one hand, and social norms derived from the gamer community, on the other. In video game development, one of the fastest growing industries globally, video game developers express their concerns regarding monetary motives, Lipkin (2013) suggests. The so-called Triple-A companies, being at the apex of the industry structure and the producers of the most technically advanced video games, are at times criticized by indie developers for being "evil" as they "bluntly prioritize money over creative vision" (Lipkin 2013: 9). In contrast, the "indie culture" is treated as being more "authentic" and "creative" than the regular Triple-A companies. At the same time, this strictly dual model separating the commercially successful but creative company from its counterpart, the small but innovative indie studio, is not fully endorsed by indie developers themselves as they still recognize the creativity and skill needed to develop a blockbuster game such as *Grand Theft Auto* or *Assassins Creed*. Nevertheless, as Triple-A games are associated with certain ready-made game scripts, aesthetic expressions, and various project management development models, which demand strict

A. Styhre, *Indie Video Game Development Work*,
https://doi.org/10.1007/978-3-030-45545-3_5

timelines and detailed monitoring of the work process, indie developers tend to define themselves as what falls outside of this industry mainstream (Lipkin 2013: 10). Despite rejecting this industrial production of video games, indie developers need to pay attention to economic affairs to survive in a competitive business, operating strictly on the basis of digital technologies and digital distribution.

Empirical evidence indicates shrinking economic compensation for entrepreneurs (Dorner et al. 2017; Åstebro et al. 2013), which means that entrepreneurs and venture workers who work in thinly capitalized firms are not compensated for the market risks they are exposed to (Matsa 2018; Brown and Matsa 2016). "[W]ages must increase with leverage to compensate workers for the costs of financial distress that they suffer," Simintzi et al. (2015: 565) propose. Despite this condition, industry entrants are attracted to entrepreneurial careers, especially in high-growth industries. This is in turn indicative of entrepreneurial activities in many cases being shaped by professional ideologies and social norms that impose restrictions on how money is legitimately being made and how economic compensation is distributed. For instance, in certain professional communities, money-making is a necessary evil, easily compromising the integrity and autonomy of the professional worker (Turco 2012), whereas other professional communities may regard money-making and individual economic compensation as the principal motivator (see, e.g., Abolafia 2001: 30). Furthermore, in some communities, as in the community of folk artists (Fine 2003), money-making is more ambiguous inasmuch as the capacity to make money is a respectable, even honourable, objective, but only *ex post facto*, when the professional work is already completed and brought to an audience or a market. In contrast, these communities believe, being motivated by the objective to make money *ex ante* puts the professional competence at risk of being compromised by, for example, the willingness to appease targeted audiences, or to succumb to sheer greed (see also Resnik 2007). This indicates that *values*, which Bermiss and McDonald (2018: 2186) define as "beliefs held by individuals about the behaviors and end-states that they deem desirable," play a decisive role in both attracting industry entrants and in the day-to-day regulation of the work. Values are commonly understood as being the basis for *social norms*, that is, ideas and rules that determine behaviour in a social setting, Axelrod (1985: 1097. Original emphasis omitted) writes, "[t]o the extent that individuals usually act in a certain way and are often punished when seen not to be acting in this way." For instance, Neff (2013: 71) reports that computer industry workers advocated the social norm that industry participants should have an "authentic" and "appropriate" stance towards work, that is, they prescribed a certain normative degree of commitment to the industry they serve.

Social norms are part of the institutional set-up of industries and complement "incentives" and "rules" (Matten and Moon 2008: 406) inasmuch as they constitute a non-legal mechanism that coordinates behaviour. "A norm can be understood as a rule that distinguishes desirable and undesirable behavior and gives a third party the authority to punish a person who engages in the undesirable behavior," Posner (1996: 1699) writes: "Thus, a norm constrains attempts by people to satisfy their preferences." Eisenberg (1999) uses the term *obligational norms* to denote social norms that individuals both self-consciously adhere to and feel they are obliged to follow. As social norms, as opposed to legislation, by definition cannot be determined by some centrally located agency or legislator (Posner 1996: 1700), the scope of social norms is determined by "how many people are already following the norms and what other competing norms are available" (Katz 1996: 1750). In general, social norms have "positive externalities" inasmuch as they become more valuable as more people adhere to them (Katz 1996: 1750). In certain industries or in emerging industries undergoing quick changes, caused by, for example, economic growth, professional norms may be complementary or even competing. In the video game industry, having its roots in the hobbyist computer science culture that developed in the 1970s and 1980s, but today being an exemplary case of an entrepreneurial high-growth industry that engages a variety of technological and entrepreneurial competencies, the social norm to treat the video game as a form of cultural expression and a technological and artistic accomplishment is now complemented by the possibilities to generate considerable economic returns. This creates a tension between the social norms derived from the gamer community that most video game developers want to honour, and more regular industry-based social norms regarding the value of economic returns and compensation. The chapter examines how the community of indie developers, small and independent video game studios, at times even being "a company of one" (Lane 2010), copes with the situations wherein they adhere to the social norms of the gamer community, while they need to ensure an adequate compensation for their work efforts so they can finance future development projects.

To better substantiate the work done by indie developers to co-align and balance these social norms in their day-to-day work, the economic sociology literature that discriminates between different categories of money, that is, introduces what Viviana Zelizer (1989) refers to as "the social meaning of money," is referenced (for an overview, see, e.g., Bandelj et al. 2017; Dodd 2014; Zelizer 2011; Maurer 2006; Baker and Jimerson 1992). Zelizer (1989: 369–370) refers to *domestic money* as a variety of categories of monies and credit relations that all carry their distinct cultural and social connotations, and that regulate certain economic and social relations. In short, when the economic and financial definition of money, for example, as economic compensation for salaried work, is complemented by a social or cultural view of money, the role of money in the regulation of social and economic conditions becomes increasingly convoluted. Various culture industries, straddling the art world (Becker 1982) and the world of business to produce creative products that are subject to the same market assessment and transactions as any commodity or service, need to accommodate and cope with money-making ambiguities.

Based on theories of the social role of money, this chapter addresses how indie video game developers accommodate a view of economic compensation that simultaneously preserves their original ethos, to develop new and innovative games that acquire respect and even admiration among gamers and other video game developers, and provide a key motivator for exposing themselves to considerable market risks. Indie developers are aware that novel and creative ideas are valued by video game developers and the gamer community, but they are also cognizant of the enormous output of new games on everyday basis. This condition fosters a humble attitude towards the possibilities for producing a "hit," while at the same time there are a sufficient amount of "success stories" circulating in the community to entice aspiring indie developers to embark on a career in the fringes of the video game industry. Based on these possibilities for a global outreach through the digital sales and distribution channels, the ambiguity of money-making is an irreducible component of the indie developer culture and day-to-day activities. Making money is a desirable outcome at the same time as the production of novel video games cannot be predicated on economic and financial considerations as such motives risk to compromise creative ideas. In this view, money is both a motivator and deterrent, but to what extent and under what conditions is a question of situated action, social norms, and day-to-day practices, complicated to anticipate.

When shifting the focus from an economic theory of the compensation of enterprising to a social theory of money, the chapter contributes to a number of literatures. First, the study adds to the entrepreneurship literature inasmuch as the empirical data reveals that entrepreneurs may regard operational autonomy, the absence of managerial oversight, and so on as important qualities when they make career choices. Economic compensation is arguably a key motivator, but other factors should be recognized in scholarly research and policy making. Second, the chapter substantiates the theoretical proposition that monetary compensation is in many cases only secondary to other forms of compensation and credentials (e.g., Bandelj et al. 2017) on the basis of empirical data collected within the recently formed professional community of indie developers. Rather than being strictly a means of compensation for creative work, money also serves a role in the indie developer's storytelling as a metonym for a variety of undesirable conditions or dysfunctions associated with corporate activities and managerial practices, which indie developers for most part are eager to avoid and preferably escape altogether. Just as in the literature on the social meaning of money, money is not just *one* thing in the eyes of the spokesperson, but migrates from the desirable to the morally questionable and ambiguous depending on situation and context. Such research findings suggest that, for example, extant studies of the compensation of entrepreneurs can be complemented by research that accounts for more detailed justifications of career choices and the role of economic compensation.

The Ambiguous Nature of Money in Entrepreneurial Work

Various culture industries, straddling the art world (Becker 1982) and the world of business to produce creative products that are subject to the same market assessment and transactions as any commodity or service, need to accommodate and cope with money-making ambiguities. In the video game industry, Triple-A games are associated with certain ready-made scripts and aesthetic and various project work models, demanding strict timelines and detailed monitoring of the work process, whereas indie developers tend to define themselves as what falls outside this industry mainstream (Lipkin 2013: 10). These differences also translate into social norms that relate to economic compensation.

Money and Their Social Significance and Meaning

Money is a "legal invention" within the administrative state, supportive of the taxation of economic returns to finance the state administration (Desan 2005: 8). Goodhart (2009: 828) argues that the invention of money predated the development of markets, and that money facilitated the rise of markets rather than vice versa. That is, money was a measure of value before it became an exchange medium that lowers transaction costs. The category of money includes a number of classes, for example, *commodity money*, *fiat money*, and *managed money*, but such distinctions are primarily a matter of concern in macroeconomic theory and monetary policy. In everyday life, what Zelizer (1989) refers to as the "social meaning of money" is more practically relevant inasmuch as individuals participate in what the economist Richard Thaler (cited in Zelizer 2012: 158) refers to as "mental accounting," denoting a set of "[c]ognitive operations used by individuals and households to organize, evaluate, and keep track of financial activities."

Zelizer (1989: 369–370) introduces the term *domestic money* to describe how a certain class of money is not just a neutral medium for exchange, but is a "meaningful, socially constructed currency, shaped by the domestic sphere where it circulates, and by the gender and social class of its domestic 'money handlers.'" For instance, in the mental accounting associated with domestic money, *earmarked money* includes (1) "distinct categories of money" (e.g., a Christmas bonus, or money derived from the selling of a commodity, say, a piece of furniture no longer being used); (2) "new currencies," including frequent flyer credits and similar tokens issued by businesses and that operate as money-claims within certain settings; and (3) "monetary media," when, for example, physical objects serve as exchange media, for example, cigarettes assume the role of exchange medium in prison camps. In this view, the subject regards money differently depending on context and situation, with, for example, certain coins and banknotes carrying specific connotations as they signify meaningful social relations wherein the subject is included. For instance, a ten-year-old child receives a $10 bill from her grandmother as a reward for admirable accomplishments in school, and that $10 bill not only denotes the monetary value of the currency in the eyes of the recipient but also carries a wider significance that includes the honouring of family-ties, social norms regarding scholarly aptitude and accomplishments more widely, and a personal gratitude towards the older family member. An additional case is that an average person may allow herself to steal office supplies as social norms regard this as a minor offence, marginal to overall costs, or even part of the "informal rewards" (Dalton 1959) that many organizations tolerate or even encourage, while the same person would never steal the equivalent value of the items in cash (Amir and Lobel 2008: 2104). The illiquidity of the office supplies in comparison to cash justifies the act of stealing or pinching, and the social relations wherein the individual participates are not impaired by the petty crime. Domestic money thus shows "the limit of a purely instrumental, rationalized model of market money, which conceals qualitative distinctions among kinds of money in the modern world," Zelizer (1989: 369–370) argues.

Money is thus not one single and unified entity in the eyes of social actors, but money has a significant role in regulating and maintaining social relations. For instance, this is why economic compensation and wage setting is an emotionally charged domain; economic compensation is not only a matter of determining the individual's room for consumption on the basis of aggregated income, but has a commensuration effect by default inasmuch as individuals can construct hierarchical social orders on the basis of how, for example, individuals are compensated for their work (see, e.g., Kim et al. 2015). That is, the salary is not only a compensation for work *per se* but also treated as proof of the relative value of the individual or a specific professional community, gender category, and so on, within a broader socio-economic context. In addition, Vohs et al. (2006: 1154) report laboratory-based research that indicates that the access to money affects behaviour inasmuch it "[m]akes people feel self-sufficient and behave accordingly." "Self-sufficient behaviour" is here defined as "[a]n insulated state wherein people put forth effort to attain personal goals and prefer to be separate from others" (Vohs et al. 2006: 1154). When one group of experimental subjects was primed with money, whereas a second group was not, the former group of subjects was less helpful and put "more physical distance" between themselves and the other participants, that is, the moneyed subjects distanced themselves from less financially fortunate subjects: "Relative to people not reminded of money, people reminded of money reliably performed independent but socially insensitive actions" (Vohs et al. 2006: 1156). Operating through these behavioural mechanisms, money promotes individualism but also reduces "communal motivations," Vohs et al. (2006: 1156) say. Expressed differently, the individual bestowed with money faces more difficulties when contributing to communal affairs as he or she is more weakly incentivized to consider, or even recognize, the value of collectivist activities and accomplishments.

At the same time as access to pecuniary resources may have undesirable consequences, the risk of a downward shift in household income should also be recognized as a social issue. Meuris and Leana (2018: 408) show that economic hardship and financial worries have debilitating effects on, for example, employee performance: employees that constantly worry about how to make the ends meet display a lower ability to perform their jobs effectively as such concerns have detrimental effects on cognitive capacity. If money and the lack thereof are associated with wider social and cultural norms and beliefs, the failure to cover household expenses does not only result in lower financial autonomy, but also creates a sense of failure associated with shame and despair. Money is thus an abstract entity, yet deeply embedded in the wider social relations that money simultaneously serves to define, and from which it acquires its social significance.

Such research findings may also substantiate what Akerlof and Shiller (2009: 41) refer to as the "money illusion," the situation wherein, for example, policy makers assume that decisions are primarily, or even exclusively, determined by nominal dollars accounts, either as a penalty or as a reward. In the eyes of policy makers, citizens subject to legal or regulatory reform are singlehandedly motivated by economic rewards and penalties, and social norms and beliefs are at best secondary, possibly irrelevant altogether, to financial consequences of specific behaviours. The money illusion thus overstates the importance of economic incentives within social relations, and, say, the norm of not littering and non-monetary sanctions, for example, the shaming of the litterer, is possibly an equally strong predictor of the behaviour (Hausman and Welch 2010: 134). For instance, Hirsh (2009: 266) shows that direct economic sanctions to curb discrimination in work life are not associated with positive effects, but on the contrary result in organizations that pay fines "show *higher* levels of sex segregation in the following year." Such evidence cast a shadow of doubt over the role of economic incentives in policy making.

Furthermore, a failure to recognize the social components of money may result in secondary observers passing judgement on household economy decisions as being sub-optimal or even "irrational." For instance, Agarwal et al. (2017: 130) report that U.S. households tend to simultaneously hold significant credit card debt and "sizable liquid assets," which is technically speaking a sub-optimal allocation of resources as the return on liquid assets is typically lower than the interest charged on credit card debt. However, U.S. households hold liquid assets as an insurance against unanticipated situations wherein the credit card cannot be used, and whether the value of this insurance is worth the net difference between the return on liquid assets and the interest charged on credit card debt is a premised on details pertaining to the household economy and the priorities and trade-offs assessed by its members. In the end, what may look irrational from afar may be an informed choice to maintain financial autonomy in the event of an unforeseen situation that demands cash money.

In summary, money is a manifold and complex social invention, interpreted and used in a variety of ways depending on context and situation. The money being managed by a hedge fund manager is functionally and socially not the same money that a ten-year-old girl receives from her grandmother; both monies are part of the monetary economy, but their form, function, and social significance differ considerably. Similarly, in the eyes of indie video game developers, money made on the basis of a game design that strategically triggers a demand among the players for in-game purchases (e.g., tools, resources, "extra life," that benefit the performance of the gamer) is less honourable than money made on the basis of a new and innovative game design that carries a wider significance as an expression of artistic skill or technical prowess. In this view, indie developers recognize the distinction between formal monies (i.e., commodity money, fiat money, and managed money) and domestic money as a category of money that is predicated on *how* the money is actually earned or generated in the first place.

On Money and Money-Making in Indie Video Game Development

By and large, the video game industry is associated with younger people and youthful interests. As one interviewee remarked, "Older people in our industry are like 45. They are the old-timers" (Analyst #1, Male, Swedish Video Game Interest Organization). In addition, video games development is derived from a hobbyist and sub-cultural tradition, wherein primarily adolescent men and boys have developed their interest in digital games (even though younger women and girls always have been part of the gamer community). As the industry has consolidated in the first decades of the new millennium, the industry has fragmented into large-scale developers, the Triple-A game developers that employ perhaps hundreds of employees, medium-sized firms, at times referred to as Double-A companies, and a large number of smaller companies and indie developers. While Triple-A companies develop the flagship games whose forthcoming releases are covered in great detail also in mainstream media, the indie developers are widely regarded to represent the creative fringe of the video game industry that of necessity needs to develop new and creative ideas to be able to be detected in the video game market, and because indie developers do not hold extensive resources that enable them to develop Triple-A genre games.

All of the interviewees argued that the indie scene flourished both in Sweden and Scandinavia and internationally. One of the interviewees spoke about "the indie boom in the video game industry" (Analyst #1, Male, Swedish Video Game Interest Organization) as a fact of the matter. In order to define in more precise terms what the indie scene consists of, several of the interviewees argued, discussed in the previous chapter, that indie does not so much represent the size of the company or the resources committed to video game development, but denotes a broader "attitude" or identity. In this view, indie is a label that is used to actively signal a commitment to certain video game qualities, including an inventive game design, a creative use of computer graphics, or some original game idea. Taken together, indie developers are part of the video game industry, but they actively choose to operate from a more marginal position in the industry so that they can fulfil their dream of developing games that they appreciate and are passionate about. This choice includes a combination of sacrifice and the endorsement of normative ideas that justify such career choices. As part of this credo and justification of career choice, money-making is treated with some scepticism among indie developers.

The Ambiguous Nature of Money-Making

The indie community was widely treated among the interviewees as having a sceptical attitude towards the commercial side of video game development, the upperground segment of the industry. In many cases, the business side of video game development is a necessary evil that needs to be contained within the broader professional commitment to video game development. At the same time, many interviewees argued that one of the principal motivations for video game developers was to achieve recognition from the global gamer community, which implied large amount of downloads and an accompanying reimbursement to the studio. "Most [indie developers] are not primarily in the industry to make money. That is not their primary incentive ... They do not operate within the traditional [business] settings," the director of a video game development incubator said. For instance, the indie developer in Company M argued that his primary motivation was to develop games that he was passionate about, not to "make money":

> I am not doing this to [primarily make money] ... I do this because this is what I want to work with. I am passionate about this, to create an experience. When you go to a game convention, you can see people playing our games. You see how they lighten up, become happy, laugh and have a good time. (Indie developer, Company M)

Being in control of one's own career is a key issue for the indie community.

One of the analysts (#3) at the industry interest organization argued that there were in fact some developers who were intrigued by the business side of the activities: "There are a few [game developers] that are committed to money making. This is because they have that interest and like business and to create ventures." At the same time, he continued, "most game developers are gamers in their hearts" (Analyst #3, Male, Swedish Video Game Interest Organization). His colleague at the industry interest organization even claimed that there were certain indie developers who endorsed "a non-commercial and anti-capitalist agenda." For most part, she continued, "self-declared indie developers ... wants to do their own thing" (Analyst #2, Female, Swedish Video Game Industry Interest Organization). This leaves the indie community as a group with a pro-business and a more "anti-business" fringe, but with the absolute majority being relatively indifferent regarding the business side.

Indie developers themselves expressed a variety of preferences regarding the business side of the development activities, as the developer in Company I underlined: "Some people just want to make enough money so they can buy food. Others feel that they need to provide salaries for team of developers. There's a huge difference [in ambition]" (Indie developer, Company I). Still, the CEO and co-founder of Indie Company D argued that the alleged distancing between the indie community and money-making was overstated:

> Indie as culture denotes the development of experimental games, somewhat odd stuff. In addition, which is almost like a joke now, indies are not

> supposed to be concerned with money. They should lead a bohemia way of life. They do this on basis of artistic convictions. No profit motives expressed ... But that is an unreasonable view. People can do as they wish, but that's not a good life! (CEO and Founder, Indie Company D)

The money-making component of business creation, at best resulting in an inflated market value of the studio and larger personal returns on work efforts, was also regarded with certain scepticism among indie developers. Some experienced indie developers were concerned that incubator directors, business counsellors, and other relatively recently introduced actors in the video game industry actively promoted profit motive, not so much because a return on investment *per se* was an issue, but because the risk of running the indie studio at a loss could easily result in disappointment and disillusion:

> In the past, you was more fully aware that you wouldn't make a nickel on this work. You did it for the fun of it. No longer so. It feels like many gets disappointed when things don't go so well for them. It's a bit more naïve attitude. (Indie developer, Company L)

The third analyst at the industry interest organization clarified that whereas there is a general attitude to "frown at money-making," the actual attitude is more sophisticated as it imposes an *ex ante* and *ex post* view of economic returns. In this view, the analyst argued, it is "disrespectful" to let economic considerations determine the video game development process and the design of the game. For instance, in-game purchases, wherein the gamer can buy items, skills, or other resources supportive of a better performance, violate the gamer ethos that stipulates that gaming should rest on a meritocratic ground, and success in the game should unambiguously be a function of personal or collective skills and acumen. As a consequence, many studios and developers reject in-game purchases as an option even though it would have provided a potential source of income for the studio. This *ex ante* view of the economic potentials of the video game mandates that "the game development process should not be shaped by the ambition to make money" (Analyst #3, Male, Swedish Video Game Interest Organization).

In contrast, once a game is released, making money is more of a matter of the game being well received by the gamer community. In this situation, indie developers suddenly find themselves in the fortunate position to have developed a game that generously, at times conspicuously so, rewards the team for their efforts. The CEO and co-founder of Indie Company D said that monetary return is treated as a form of "confirmation" from the gamer community that the work done was appreciated: "The downloading of games is one confirmation regarding the quality of the outcome, but monetary returns are also welcome. To actually receive money. I would lie if I claimed that didn't matter." As long as this game has not been designed to maximize the revenues, such success cases were widely respected and honoured by indie developers as well as Triple-A and Double-A developers. The analyst referred to one very successful video game developer who in their own minds "continues to be Indie developers despite being millionaires and makes enormous amounts of money" (Analyst #3, Male, Swedish Video Game Industry Interest Organization). According to analyst #3, this studio was unperturbed by their success and was still committed to game development and regarded this work as an "expression of their creativity." The director of the incubator pointed at two similar cases, one being the international case that more or less single-handedly created the upsurge in indie development activities in the 2007–2008 period, and one local case. In the former case, a small group of indie developers have "been working on [a game] for a really long time," and when the game was finally released, "it was a huge success":

> That game suddenly made everyone start to talk about 'indie.' It sold millions of copies for millions [of dollars]. Thereafter, there has been this wave of games wherein you maintain a certain mood based on an aesthetic—sound and graphics. (Director, Video Game Development Incubator)

The latter case was an indie studio that included two owners that released a game that to date has been downloaded by "127 million people." This resulted in the turnover of the studio suddenly being in excess of 30 million Swedish crowns. "They were very successful," the director concluded. There were a sufficient amount of such success stories that circulated in the community to motivate speculations about how to cope with the substantial economic possibilities that a successful game release entails. Analyst #3 addressed this condition:

> Suddenly, you own sixty millions [Swedish crowns, approx. 6 million euros], what do you want to do with that amount of money? To invest them in corporate growth? To increase the portfolio of projects? Become a publisher,

> investing in other developers' games? When you start to think in those terms, you become more an investor than a game developer. If you enjoy doing what you do, that is where you grow your competence. Some do not enjoy such activities, they stay in the development. (Analyst #3, Male, Swedish Video Game Interest Organization)

In many cases, the tensions derived from the *ex ante/ex post* reimbursement of indie developers were handled by jokes about how indie developers shun commercial rules of the game while still being motivated by the possible returns from a massively successful game. For instance, the single indie developer in Company F both referred to himself as being a "corporate whore" when he designed games with a commercial appeal, while at the same time he emphatically recognized himself as being a "product developer" rather than some "artist," and praised games that appealed to a mass market:

> I think that is a matter when it comes to creativity, regardless whether you paint pictures, play in a band, or develop a game, or whatever. What needs to be there is a sense of what is popular in commercial terms. Alternatively, you may think of it as 'my art' ... I don't want to sit like some hermit someplace and develop stuff for my own pleasure's sake. I want the stuff to reach out to be received by someone. (Indie developer, Company F)

By the end of the day, what matters is the capacity to develop games that are recognized by some market participants.

Passionate Game Development

According to the indie developer ethos, making money after the game release is honourable, but to develop a game with the intention to make money on the basis of the gamer's purchases is deemed inappropriate on ethical and cultural grounds. This important line of demarcation between *ex ante* and *ex post* the release was supplemented by further rumination pertaining to the dangers of money-making. The key phrase used when the interviewees defined indie development activities was *passion*. Originally a theological term, denoting an intensive experience of religious faith, passion is today a widespread shorthand term in, for example, entrepreneurship discourses. Passion was seen as a defining quality of the indie developer work, one of the industry interest organization analysts stated:

> Above all, it's a matter of passion, I'd say. Many company owners are not entrepreneurs simply because they are passionate about business, but because they are passionately committed to the idea to materialize their game concept. (Analyst #2, Female, Swedish Video Game Interest Organization)

The director of the video game incubator agreed on this point and referred to the current market rate for the economic compensation of video game developers:

> The interesting thing is that the video game industry is extremely passion-driven. You can see that historically and on the level of the salaries [being comparably low]. Salaries are on the way up, and have been so for some time. A programmer in the video game industry make like one fourth of what they can get elsewhere. (Director, Video Game Development Incubator)

In addition to the passionate interest for video game development and video games as entertainment and cultural expression, several interviewees remarked that the somewhat fuzzy concept of *authenticity* played a key role in the indie developer worldview and self-appreciation. One of the industry interest organization analysts argued that the idea about authenticity and accompanying terms, such as artistic integrity, was imported from the adjacent art world. In the art world, primarily male artists have been able to fashion a serviceable identity for themselves, assisted by a mythology that emphasizes the capacities and integrity of the "lone genius," or the "*auteur*" (a term derived from the film industry and film theory; Bazin 1967): "[T]his willingness to take risks … [is part of the] 'male genius' tradition, wherein you are supposed to 'do your thing.' This male genius thing is part of the indie development work … to be a 'starving artist.' You 'fight against all odds,' and you're 'difficult,' but you do your thing" (Analyst #3, Male, Swedish Video Game Interest Organization). In this passion-driven and authenticity-motivated activity, higher aims than money-making define the activities.

In practical terms, indie developers were prone to dismiss Triple-A companies as sites wherein few new ideas could be tested or implemented as novel thinking risk to disrupt the industrial production of the new version of commercially successful games. The reason for this risk-aversion is primarily a stated concern for bottom-line results and other "managerial" priorities, one of the indie developer argued:

> That is the thing with Indie and Triple-A. Triple-A games will never include any new ideas. They cannot take the risk because of all the money involved. Indies, in turn, has nothing to lose so they can do cool stuff. (Indie Developer #4, Video Game Company A)

His colleague continued:

> [Triple-A companies] only make safe bets. [One Triple-A company] make [the same game] over and over. They did *Under Siege 5* [a pseudonym], and then they did *During Siege*, which is *Under Siege* in a *Star Wars* setting. They develop the same game. (Indie Developer #3, Video Game Company A)

By implication, this tendency to make "safe bets" results in video game development in Triple-A companies being largely characterized by a far-driven division of labour and repetitive work procedures, the indie developer argued: "[In a Triple-A company] you do basically the same thing, very intensively. In smaller company, there are only the ten of us doing everything" (Indie Developer #3, Video Game Company A). In contrast, Indie Developer #4 (company A) said, it is the indie developers that "dare to take some risks and to deliver original stuff." The larger studios, which monitor the industry and the local contributions in particular, may incorporate these new ideas, or more simply try to recruit the creative indie developer.

In Defence of the Business Side of Video Game Development

Some indie developers argued that the disregard for the commercial side of the development work was little more than coquetry or an indication of immaturity of indie developers. To be successful in an industry characterized by fierce and international competition, a first-rate degree of self-discipline was the foremost demand, the indie developer in Company G said: "Working in your own business demands a certain self-discipline that not everyone can maintain. Quite a few have fallen prey to that." The CEO and co-founder of Company E, herself being business-minded and concerned with creating a successful, viable company, was quite impatient regarding the indie scene. When being asked, "What's 'Indie' for you?," she replied bluntly, "A crap company!" Then she softened her opinions: "No, you mustn't say that! I don't know. I really do not care ... Okay, it's a small company ... It feels like a threadbare term, I'd say" (CEO and Founder, Company E). The principal concern expressed by the CEO of Company E was the ignorance of the business activities, always making the game development work *per se* the overarching priority. She made a comparison with start-ups in other industries, propelled by the prospect of a return on investment:

> What is indicative of these video game companies is this naivety that are not so common in start-ups. Start-ups are commonly founded on the idea that 'Let's make some money!' These companies have the greatest potential to make money. In many video game companies, this is profit motive is not considered at all. (CEO and Founder, Company E)

The developer in Company M was another informant that fully recognized the commercial side of the development work:

Q: Would you say that making money is frowned upon in the indie scene?
A: Absolutely not! I don't think so. I believe that if you do a lot of money on a game, you have done something just right. Unless you really maximize the profit, I cannot see any problems. If there are buyers, they are the people who actually appreciate it. (Indie developer, Company M)

The indie developer in Company H said that the "indie attitude" is to be "concerned with *what* is being developed rather than how viable it is as a product." Also the indie developer and culture sector entrepreneur, who himself was quite tolerant of an unpredictable and not very sizeable income ("There's no massive surplus, but I can live with that," he said), emphasized that "You need to develop something that is possible to sell." Using the American musician Frank Zappa as an example of an artist who was able to move back and forth between commercial music and classic composition, and who uses commercial output as a means to finance less market-oriented work, the informant claimed that this could be a sustainable business model for indie developers. On the other hand, he continued, there is always the risk that commercial activities become too time-consuming so that the aspiring indie developers never reach the point where they can realize their plans, and get stuck in a line of work they are less intrigued by. At the same time, the indie developer in Company G advised against overstating the difference between "commercially viable" and "artistic" games as he reported that in his portfolio of games released in the market, which included more conventional indie games and more "artistic" and "experience-oriented" games, it was the more artistic games that were downloaded to a higher extent. "[Games] that would be considered more commercial do actually sell less than my more artistic games," the developer said. He explained this outcome on the basis of lower competition in the artistic games genre: "I believe that my artistic games are located in a relatively unchartered territory, where the competition is lower. It is easier because people just discover something unique, an idea that they simply like" (Indie developer, Company G).

In the end, indie developers are portrayed as the inventors and creators of the video game industry, not yet burdened by past successes, nor employing hundreds of developers who need to have their salaries covered by video game sales revenues, and thereby being the hothouses for novel thinking and ideas. It is noteworthy that Triple-A developers are not treated as non-creatives nor devoid of the capacity to develop new ideas. They just operate within a corporate system and a business model wherein a failed project would result in a considerable loss in income and ensuing layoffs. Such a profit motive, which for most parts serves as the ultimate measure of the success of the development work, to some extent violates the indie ethos that stipulates an uninhibited capacity to develop video games as they are conceived by the indie community. Expressed differently, money is the lifeblood of the industry and the capitalist mode of production, and return on invested efforts in the development work is a legitimate evidence of recognition in the gamer community, but what ultimately matters is to remain true to the credo that video games are the primary commitment of developers, and especially indie developers.

The Fickle and Ambiguous Nature of Money and Money-Making

Economists (e.g., Decker et al. 2017) and entrepreneurship researchers (e.g., Åstebro et al. 2013) are concerned with faltering enterprising motives in the contemporary economy, and emphasize the lower return on entrepreneurial investment as one explanatory factor. This is particularly cumbersome evidence as innovation-led growth demands calculated risk-taking and finance capital committed to uncertain business activities. At the same time, to exclusively emphasize monetary returns and economic compensation misses some of the underlying rationale for enterprising, especially in the community of transactional entrepreneurs who are highly educated and motivated by other objectives than to merely make money (Schoar 2010). Among this category of entrepreneurs, which includes indie video game developers, creative and aesthetic motivations are combined with entrepreneurial incentives to build and run an individual business wherein operational autonomy and innovative ideas are honoured, and also non-monetary rewards and forms of compensation need to be considered. Still, when opening up for a broader view of entrepreneurial incentives, money and money-making become more ambiguous as direct economic compensation needs to be understood within the framework of wider social relations, social norms, and meaning. Just like in the case of Fine's (2003) folk artists, expected to act as culture carriers and as ambassadors for a specific culture or cultural expression, and therefore cannot signal an interest in money-making as their primary motivation as that would compromise their alleged authenticity, indie developers tend to fashion a similar identity for themselves. That is, in the day-to-day-practice to develop new video games, monetary interests cannot influence the video game design or mechanisms as such choices violate stated ideals and ideologies regarding video games as a cultural expression or distinct art form, having a social value in its own right. At the same time, the digitally mediated and global outreach of video game development and distribution provides the possibility to "make it big time" as positive feedback and reputational gains can spread rapidly once a new and innovative video game becomes recognized in the global community. In its consequences, money-making is simultaneously an objective surrounded by norms and restrictions, still being one of the principal, yet distant, motivations for embarking on a career in the indie video game development segment of the industry.

Speaking in more formalist terms, money-making may be restricted as an *ex ante* incentive, prior to the video game being developed and published, whereas economic returns *ex post* are celebrated for most part, especially if the video game that generates the income is treated as a genuine contribution. In the former case, when money-making is surrounded by admonitions, the very term "money" assumes a metonymic function.

"Metonymy builds on contiguity instead of similarity: something nearby is substituted for the original phenomenon," Czarniawska and Sköldberg (2003: 343) write. Money is thus not primarily a symbol or index of commercial interest and its benefits and possible dysfunctions, but is rather its correlate or implication. In this metonymic use of the term "money" (and versions derived therefrom, e.g., money-making), the term denotes a series of activities or qualities, for example, the use of strict project management development models, detailed managerial oversight, the submission to narrowly defined video game genre conventions, a commitment to bottom-line financial results, and so on, all of which indie developers are eager to surround or escape altogether. The ambiguity of money and money-making, in themselves containing various social practices and diverging norms, is thus endemic in the indie community. Making money is an honest activity, whereas a commitment to such goals prior to the development process compromises social norms that indie developers hold in esteem.

Summary and Conclusion

Most developers enter the video game industry on the basis of their love of gaming and video games, and the belief that individual skills and ambitions can make a contribution to the industry. The opportunity to make money, and especially to make enormous amounts of money, is secondary to the original motive. However, as the industry has proven its growth potential and ability to generate economic returns, industry policy has been geared towards actively supporting business venturing in the video game industry. Tertiary education and occupational training equally emphasize the business side of video development work, but this emphasis on business venturing in terms of profit motives and job creation (both being in the policy makers' and their defined agencies' interests) runs counter to the gamer community ethos that regards the video game as an art form and a source of entertainment and community-building. Consequently, there is a tension between the "old school" tradition to consecrate the video game development work *per se*, and to downplay all other objectives and concerns, and the new generation of developers who are trained within an educational and institutional system wherein the business venture side of the activities is not only recognized but also actively encouraged. For the majority of the developers, this shift in focus is indicative of the industry coming of age and is therefore a tolerable condition, but a few hardcore indie developers deplore the tendency to promote business objectives as they believe that, for example, incubator counsellors underrate the difficulties involved in making innovative video games. In the end, these developers contend, those who lack the genuine passion for video game development will end up disappointed as the business objectives promoted by, for example, incubator business counsellors will be complicated to reach unless that criterion is fulfilled. Under all conditions, the whole issue of money-making is introduced as what balances a variety of professional ideologies and social norms vis-à-vis other objectives so that it can be permitted, but only after these ideologies and norms are recognized.

References

Abolafia, M. (2001). *Making markets: Opportunism and restraints on Wall Street.* Cambridge: Harvard University Press.

Agarwal, S., Chomsisengphet, S., & Lim, C. (2017). What shapes consumer choice and financial products? A review. *Annual Review of Financial Economic, 9*, 127–146.

Akerlof, G. A., & Shiller, R. J. (2009). *Animal spirits: How human psychology drives the economy, and why it matters for global capitalism.* Princeton and London: Princeton University Press.

Amir, O., & Lobel, O. (2008). Stumble, predict, nudge: How behavioral economics informs law and policy. *Columbia Law Review, 108*(8), 2098–2139.

Anteby, M. (2010). Markets, morals, and practices of trade: Jurisdictional disputes in the U.S. commerce in cadavers. *Administrative Science Quarterly, 55*(4), 606–638.

Åstebro, T., Braunerhjelm, P., & Broström, A. (2013). Does academic entrepreneurship pay? *Industrial and Corporate Change, 22*(1), 281–311.

Axelrod, R. (1985). An evolutionary approach to norms. *American Political Science Review, 80*(4), 1095–1111.

Baker, W., & Jimerson, J. (1992). The sociology of money. *American Behavioral Scientist, 35*, 678–693.

Bandelj, N., Wherry, F. F., & Zelizer, V. A. (Eds.). (2017). *Money talks: Explaining how money really works.* Princeton: Princeton University Press.

Bazin, A. (1967). *What is cinema?* (H. Gray, Trans.). Berkeley, Los Angeles and London: University of California Press.

Becker, H. S. (1982). *Art worlds.* Berkeley; Los Angeles; London: University of California Press.

Bermiss, Y. S., & McDonald, R. (2018). Ideological misfit? Political affiliation and employee departure in the private-equity industry. *Academy of Management Journal, 61*(6), 2182–2209.

Brown, J., & Matsa, D. A. (2016). Boarding a sinking ship? An investigation of job applications to distressed firms. *Journal of Finance, 71*(2), 507–550.

Czarniawska, B., & Sköldberg, K. (2003). Tales of organizing: Symbolism and narration in management studies. In B. Czarniawska & G. Sevón (Eds.), *The northern lights: Organization theory in Scandinavia*. Malmö; Oslo; Copenhagen: Liber; Abstrakt; Copenhagen Business School Press.

Dalton, M. (1959). *Men who manage: Fusion of feeling and theory in administration*. New York: Wiley.

Decker, R. A., Haltiwanger, J., Jarmin, R. S., & Miranda, J. (2017). Declining dynamism, allocative efficiency, and the productivity slowdown. *American Economic Review, 107*(5), 322–326.

Desan, C. (2005). The market as a matter of money: Denaturalizing economic currency in American constitutional history. *Law & Social Inquiry, 30*(1), 1–60.

Dodd, N. (2014). *The social life of money*. Princeton and London: Princeton University Press.

Dorner, M., Fryges, H., & Schopen, K. (2017). Wages in high-tech start-ups—Do academic spin-offs pay a wage premium? *Research Policy, 46*(1), 1–18.

Eisenberg, M. A. (1999). Corporate law and social norms. *Columbia Law Review, 99*, 1253–1292.

Fine, G.-A. (2003). Crafting authenticity: The validation of identity in self-taught art. *Theory and Society, 32*(2), 153–180.

Goodhart, C. A. E. (2009). The continuing muddles of monetary theory: A steadfast refusal to face facts. *Economica, 76*(s1), 821–830.

Hausman, D. M., & Welch, B. (2010). Debate: To nudge or not to nudge. *Journal of Political Philosophy, 18*(1), 123–136.

Hirsh, C. E. (2009). The strength of weak enforcement: The impact of discrimination charges, legal environments, and organizational conditions on workplace segregation. *American Sociological Review, 74*(2), 245–271.

Katz, A. (1996). Taking private ordering seriously. *University of Pennsylvania Law Review, 144*, 1745–1763.

Kim, J. W., Kogut, B., & Yang, J.-S. (2015). Executive compensation, fat cats, and best athletes. *American Sociological Review, 80*(2), 299–328.

Lane, C. A. (2010). *The company of one: Neoliberal faith and the post-organizational man*. Ithaca: Cornell University Press.

Lipkin, N. (2013). Examining Indie's independence: The meaning of "Indie" games, the politics of production, and mainstream co-optation. *Loading... The Journal of the Canadian Game Studies Association, 7*(11), 8–24.

Matsa, D. A. (2018). Capital structure and a firm's workforce. *Annual Review of Financial Economics, 10*, 387–412.

Matten, D., & Moon, J. (2008). "Implicit" and "explicit" CSR: A conceptual framework for a comparative understanding of corporate social responsibility. *Academy of Management Review, 33*(2), 404–424.

Maurer, B. (2006). On the anthropology of money. *Annual Review of Anthropology, 35*, 15–36.

Meuris, J., & Leana, C. (2018). The price of financial precarity: Organizational costs of employees' financial concerns. *Organization Science, 29*(3), 398–417.

Neff, G. (2013). *Venture labor: Work and the burden of risk in innovative industries*. Cambridge and London: The MIT Press.

Posner, E. A. (1996). Law, economics, and inefficient norms. *University of Pennsylvania Law Review, 144*, 1697–1744.

Resnik, D. B. (2007). *The price of truth: How money affects the norms of science*. Oxford and New York: Oxford University Press.

Schoar, A. (2010). The divide between subsistence and transformational entrepreneurship. *Innovation Policy and the Economy, 10*(1), 57–81.

Simintzi, E., Vig, V., & Volpin, P. (2015). Labor protection and leverage. *Review of Financial Studies, 28*(2), 561–591.

Turco, C. J. (2012). Difficult decoupling: Employee resistance to the commercialization of personal settings. *American Journal of Sociology, 118*(2), 380–419.

Vohs, K. D., Mead, N. L., & Goode, M. R. (2006). The psychological consequences of money. *Science, 314*(5802), 1154–1156.

Zelizer, V. A. (1989). The social meaning of money. *American Journal of Sociology, 95*(2), 342–377.

Zelizer, V. A. (2011). *Economic lives: How culture shapes the economy*. Princeton and Oxford: Princeton University Press.

Zelizer, V. A. (2012). How I became a relational economic sociologist and what does that mean? *Politics and Society, 40*(2), 145–174.

CHAPTER 6

In the Venture Capital Market: Raising Funds and Dealing with Investors and Financiers

Introduction

To raise capital to finance an economic venture has been a long-standing concern for aspiring entrepreneurs. Shakespeare's *The Merchant of Venice* is one illustrative work of art, written by the end of the sixteenth century, which addresses how Venetian traders borrowed money from the local Jewish finance agents who were in charge of the lucrative but sinful money-lending business, and describes how this credit relation could easily result in social conflicts and commotion whenever a venture fails (in this case, a long-distance trade venture goes bankrupt as a ship is lost at sea). Money may be sterile, as Aristotle suggested, but the social relations that financial contracts and agreements engender are for most part spirited and animated. The millennial ban on usury in the Catholic Church, making money-lending a sin as it exploited the factor of time in God's creation when charging interest (Le Goff [1986] 1988), was still an indirect concern for the early modern finance system agents. In the early modern period of the eighteenth and nineteenth centuries, the Catholic Church's ban on usury was marginalized as a modern finance system was developed, but credit relation was still dependent on social norms, including the borrowers' social position and "credibility" more widely. This made money-lending a business that essentially favoured certain groups that already enjoyed many social and economic advantages and were located at the apex of the social organization (Crowston 2013). The early modern finance system thus blended elements from what Fontaine (2014) refers to

A. Styhre, *Indie Video Game Development Work*,
https://doi.org/10.1007/978-3-030-45545-3_6

as the "aristocratic economy" and "the market economy," that is, creditworthiness was in many cases based on an assessment of the borrower's social position and inclusion in social networks rather than his—women were not yet regarded as full legal subjects—business acumen or track records as investors or business promoters. As stipulated by *The Gospel According to St. Matthew*, reading "For unto every one that hath shall be given, and he shall have abundance," the already privileged were granted further advantages in the early modern finance system. "The role of social status, reputation, and networks in the formation of personal credit remained crucial in the eighteenth century, on both sides of the Atlantic world," Giraudeau (2018: 132) writes. Credit was ensconced in an "economy of obligation," wherein the rules of "gentlemanly civility forbade seeking profit for itself," at least openly (Giraudeau 2018: 132). When violating such more or less explicit rules, the borrower could be accused of profiteering, which would result in costly, at times devastating reputational losses. The handling of money still operated in the long shadow of the Christian liturgy and the Catholic Church, which rendered money-lending a deeply problematic social and economic practice, yet vital for the increasingly differentiated economic system.

To leapfrog into the late modern era, wherein the global financial system displays a complexity that is almost impenetrable for any observer, also insiders (Jacobides 2005), the term *venture capital* plays an important role in the contemporary economy as being a share of the stock of finance capital committed to risky and uncertain development work, and commonly associated with the promise of above-normal returns on investment. The very term "venture capital" was first used by DuPont—a pioneering firm in terms of advancing a modern view of finance capital and its circulation (Giraudeau 2018)—and was mentioned in a Wall Street editorial on January 13, 1938 (Kenney 2011: 1686). The British Private Equity & Venture Capital Association (BCVA) defines venture capital accordingly:

> VC [venture capital] is 'the process of external equity finance by professional investors in a new or young (i.e., early stage) company to create new assets for the primary purpose of reaping substantial economic gains through a market flotation [Initial Public Offering (IPO)] or trade sale.' (BCVA-NESTA, cited in Hopkins et al. 2013: 907)

In practical terms, venture capitalists raise money from large pension funds, mutual funds, insurance companies, or any finance industry actors that hold large stocks of finance capital and being willing to commit some of this capital to fund-of-funds investments. Roughly 2 per cent of the fund value in venture capital funds serve to cover managerial costs (Hopkins et al. 2013: 908), that is, the remaining 98 per cent of the capital raised are invested in a portfolio of companies for a period of time, stipulated to be around ten years, before the venture capital investor makes an exit, either by selling the company to another company or through an IPO.

Venture capital investment receives considerable attention from news media and the scholarly community, but venture capital market is oftentimes relatively thin inasmuch as there are few investors that have a robust track record from venture capital investment, and consequently a relatively small proportion of all companies that seek to raise venture capital are successful in their pursuits. In the mid-1990s, investment in early stage business development accounted for less than 0.01 per cent of GDP in the 15 European Union economies, but in the 2001–2005 period, a period of quick finance industry expansion (unfortunately ending with the spectacular finance industry meltdown of 2008), the amount of equity committed to early stage business development grew by around 10 billion euros per annum (Deeg 2009: 566). In the period, European venture capital markets thickened, yet remained relatively small in comparison to other forms of investment. Taken together, as Leyshon and Thrift (2007: 102) put it, venture capital has been "the object of almost obsessive attention."

What is particularly challenging are the difficulties involved in assessing the future market value of a venture that develops a novel technology in a market that is yet in the making. "One in three ventures fail within the first 2 years, and 50% of them terminate operations within 5 years of founding," Vedula and Kim (2019: 827–828) report on the basis of U.S. statistics. A consistently high failure rate is an endemic condition in business venturing. The current risk management models are heavily geared towards "taming chance" (with Hacking's 1990, apt phrase), but as uncertainty is defined as non-parametric risk, only imprecise estimations of future market values and cash-flows can be made. This renders venture capital investment a professional domain of expertise that demands knowhow in a variety of, say, technological, medicinal, or scientific fields, and a tolerance for uncertainty and ambiguities in addition to an intimate understanding of the finance industry and its institutional and operational logics.

Another issue to consider is that the total stock of venture capital investment reported is a somewhat deceiving measure as roughly 75 per cent of that capital stock are not committed to early stage business development, but are invested in buyouts, wherein existing businesses are acquired with the intention to run the business with greater efficiency than under the previous management, or to otherwise realize market potentials. Early stage business development investment should preferably be isolated from buyout investment to better signal to market actors how large the stock of venture capital dedicated to the former objective is for the time being. Statistical material also indicates that the average buyout investment is considerably larger (27 million euros in Deeg's data) than the average investment in early stage business development.

An additional imbalance in venture capital investment is that male entrepreneurs receive the absolute largest proportion of the capital invested. In the U.S. for instance, only about 2 per cent of venture capital investment benefit female entrepreneurs, despite the fact that women today own 38 per cent of all businesses in the U.S. Needless to say, such gender imbalances have been subject to critical scrutiny by management and entrepreneurship scholars (Lewis 2006; Jonsson Ahl 2002). Finally, venture capital markets are, despite the last decades' legal and regulatory reforms to promote a global finance market, essentially local in orientation, Vedula and Kim (2019: 833) argue: "Even with the ubiquity of technologies that enable long-distance connections, venture capitalists and angel investors still prefer to invest in geographically proximate ventures because of the high costs and uncertain outcomes of early stage commitments." This preference may be less pronounced in indie development, a venturing activity that is "born global"—from its inception oriented towards international video game markets and geographically dispersed gamer communities.

This chapter reports the empirical material that pertains to the issue of how to raise capital to finance the development work in indie video game development teams. Already here, it can be remarked that actual venture capital investment by professional venture capital firms in indie studios is an exception, and therefore indie developers raise capital from any source they can identify and successfully extract capital from. In some cases, indie studios are simply run on the basis of the Swedish student loan system, quite generously designed to provide operational freedom for presumptive students, and therefore *de facto* a convenient source of capital for indie developers. Needless to say, this use of student loan funds violates the legislator's intentions as such funds were created to democratize higher education and to incentivize students to make the effort to develop specialized professional skills, a necessary investment in economies propelled by innovation-led growth. At the same time, such enterprising or even audacious use of existing social services systems is arguably indicative of the low degree of institutionalization of the video game industry, still being merely in its second decade of operation as a full-scale industrial activity.

Investing and Raising Venture Capital in Indie Video Game Development

As a vignette to the question of how to raise capital to finance development work, it needs to be remarked that the absolute majority of the indie video game developers enter the profession, the trade, and the industry on the basis of their perhaps life-long love of video games and video gaming. Some of the developers eventually figure out that they have an interest in or a talent for either the business side of the activities or administrating network of actors in, for example, an incubator setting, but such insights and epiphanies are commonly secondary to the original motivations. Business Counsellor #1 in the video game development incubator #3 addressed the fact that money and the prospect of earning a private wealth were rarely key motivators for the neophytes: "It is quite rare than someone comes here and tells us that they intend to make bucket-loads of money. That has never happened" (Business Counsellor #1, Video Game development Incubator #3). At the same time, the news stories and urban legends about indie developers such as Markus Persson, better known under his developer alias Notch, the creator of the indie hit Minecraft and today a billionaire video game celebrity, create a fascination for the idea that what is originally marginal and little attended to may suddenly blow up out of proportions in the era of digital distribution. In the period of 2010–2019, Sweden was in a hazy stage of experiencing an unprecedented digital media boom with digital objects and services such as Minecraft, The Candy Crush Saga, Spotify being introduced, and the YouTuber with the largest number of subscribers in the world for a considerable period of time, Felix Kjellberg, better known among YouTube-users as PewDiePie being on the rise, all being media darlings and portrayed as the pioneers and heroes of the emerging digital economy. This self-confidence in Sweden's and more largely Scandinavia's capacity to exploit the new business possibilities enabled by digital media naturally spilled over to the indie video game development scene. In this new business folklore, any creative and innovative indie developer could turn into an overnight sensation, and, by implication, millionaire by the click of the finger if such activities took place in millions of places in the nodes of the global Internet system. In the new era of digital media and digital businesses, anything was still possible by the end of the 2010s in the eyes of several interlocutors.

Digital Distribution on a Global Market: Coping with Market Risks

In order to better understand the difficulties involved in investing in indie development projects, the central activity of the development process is the release of the video game on the predominant distribution platform Steam. The director of Incubator #2 addressed the issue that a common rookie problem was that aspiring developers did not fully understand the need to create a market demand or a community, supportive of the video game to be launched, prior to its release on Steam:

> It is quite common to release your first game on your own … What happens is that is just vanishes … Even though it is a digital product, it is still a product. You need to market it. If you're a small team and a single publisher, you don't have the muscles to market it: you lack the money, the time, the skills, etc. The marketing is never done because it is not planned in the project. It is like an afterthought and suddenly everyone is surprised it all went down the drain. (Director, Video Game Development Incubator #2)

Needless to say, such experiences are discouraging and easily lead to cynicism among indie developers who fail to see how they can practically reach the gamer community without holding a sizeable marketing budget. Indie developer #1 in Company B addressed how indie developers had no choice but to operate on the Internet as publishers and mainstream media have limited capacities for covering all new games being released:

> [Indie games] are largely invisible because they are not marketed. They do not hold large funds or publishers who back them up and actively promote them. The newspapers do not write about them because they cannot find

them. [Journalists] get all information from marketing companies and publishers. (Indie Developer #1, Company B)

This predicament in turn calls for creative uses of digital marketing and community-building to send a signal through the market noise. The director of Incubator #2 argued that one key lesson to learn is to try to figure out how the algorithm of the Steam distribution platform works, and to take measures to ensure that the game being released remains visible for a longer time than it would be without such pre-release intelligence work:

There are much money to make by learning to understand the conversion attention model, what you need to do to crack Steam's algorithms ... [To learn how to] make the end-user buy the game the day it is released, and then remain in focus for some more hours ... It is a matter of optimizing the activities. That has nothing to do with creativity. (Director, Video Game Development Incubator #2)

The inconvenient truth is that not everything in indie development work pertains to game development and gaming experience *per se*, the director argued. In order to become commercially successful and to generate a cash-flow that finances planned development projects, the business side of the operations needs to be recognized by at least the top management team of the indie studio. The digital distribution of video games thus cannot be understood as an exposure to a random selection of games to succeed, but needs to be approached as a problem to be solved.

The CEO of Company C had the comforting experience of producing a video game that generated a satisficing cash-flow even the first time the studio released a game. Company C was heavily influenced by another company, located at the same incubator, which had successfully managed to decode the Steam algorithm, and could now use it to their advantage. First of all, the CEO remarked that "Steam is the totally dominant publisher on the market." In order to promote a large number of new games being released, and to maximize its own revenues, the Steam distribution site was strictly based on the use of algorithms: "There are no manual marketing or commercials any longer ... For the indie developers, algorithms are what matters," the CEO said. When, say, an indie developer releases a new game on Steam, the site displays the game to presumptive consumers (gamers who shop around for new and intriguing games to purchase) a few times for free. But unless the video game demo (a promotion video that conveys the basic narrative of the game and advertises its mechanisms) acquires "a sufficient amount of clicks, and you don't get a sufficient amount of purchases," the CEO continued, "then the algorithm decides that this game will not make any money for Steam." The Steam algorithm is thus based on a unforgiving "attention economy" business logic (see, e.g., Davenport and Beck 2001), wherein the Steam home page visitors more or less immediately need to direct their attention towards, and preferably also buy the game within a relatively short period of time. Unless the video game demo is successful in attracting this attention (measured in terms of clicks; this performance metric is also used by news journalists who publish articles online; see, e.g., Christin 2018) and ensuing purchases, "then your game is no longer on display," the CEO says: "You end up in the ditch. After that, it is really complicated to get back on track" (CEO, Company C).

This digital media distribution business logic is uncompromising. A comparable "old economy" model would be that a fashion designer was given a chance to sell her most recent collection at a major department store, say, Sachs Fifth Avenue in New York City, or at Harrods in London, but only during, say, 30 minutes during a defined date and not thereafter unless this 30-minute sales period shows the market demand for the collection. In order to optimize the attention and the number of purchases during this relatively short period of time, the designer needs to build a community of presumptive consumers and to ensure that they show up at the department store on the particular date and at the right time. Only then can she ensure that her collection will remain on display for a period extending the assigned period of department store display. The CEO pointed at the primary implications of the digital distribution business logic: the need to build and maintain a community of gamers who are supportive of the development work, and that comply with this business logic and actually participate in the video game release when it is finally taking place:

> You need to bring a critical mass of people to Steam [when you release a game]. Without that support, it is really difficult. It is hard to think of successful releases without this critical mass of gamers that build the case. (CEO, Company C)

The CEO said that his own team was inspired by another local indie studio that actively used the digital distribution platform Discord to build a community. This "fan-base" constitutes the core of the studio's consumers, now including between fifty and hundred thousands of followers on their Discord channel, the CEO claimed.

One of the major implications of the digital distribution model is that video game development companies spend long periods developing, testing, and refining the video game prior to its release, whereas the cash-flow that generates an income is acquired in a comparably short period of time. "There are very short [sales] cycles now. You bring back home the whole year's sales in a week or two," an incubator director (Video Game Development Incubator #2) remarked. That is, for developers with limited funds, the release of a newly developed game is a critical moment that "make or break" the studio. If being successfully released, the coming few days or even hours can secure the survival of the studio in a medium-term perspective (keep in mind that the temporal horizons of video game developers differ from other industries, with "the past" not being so very distant, and "the future" not being very far away). This makes the release of a new game a quite exciting but also stressful experience, being the moment of truth wherein months or even years of work need to be translated into documented clicks and online purchases to locate the studio "in the money."

User Reviews, Clicks, and Media Attention

The two indie developers that jointly run Company B, largely on the basis of joint game preferences and aesthetic principles, did not share their views of what mattered the most for them professionally: to get good reviews on Steam by gamers, or receiving favourable or even enthusiastic reviews from, for example, video game journalists and web-based influencers. Indie developer #2 said that "good reviews on Steam" was what truly mattered to him; "You can read that people like you. That's very important" (Indie Developer #2, Company B). His business partners questioned the honesty of this claim, and compared to the value of good reviews from more expert commentators:

> Wouldn't you say that it is more cred to have a cool reviewer writing positively about your game in comparison to user reviews? That is my impression from the indie community. The large majority knows nothing about game [development], as opposed to the reviewer. (Indie Developer #1, Company B)

Indie Developer #2 responded by imposing a dual reviewer structure, each having its own benefits:

> You can separate the two [types of reviewers]. The popular games [it works with user reviews] ... whereas in the case of more experimental author-games, then it is the reviewer that matters. [The latter categories of games] can be quite rudimentary, but they convey a certain 'mood' that the average gamer simply ignores. (Indie Developer #2, Company B)

That is, the higher the artistic and aesthetic content (and by implication, the degree of risk-taking in the game design), the higher the value of expert reviews. As indie developers may choose to either develop more commercially oriented games, or games with a higher artistic ambition (or combinations thereof), they rely on different classes of reviews. Under all conditions, what unified the two types of games is that they are *sensu stricto* never developed for a "local market," and therefore "local reviewers" were relatively marginal in the trade: "The whole market is very international. There are strictly speaking no 'local' games," the CEO of Company C said.

This international orientation of video game development underlines that indie developers cannot sit idly and await consumers to download and pay for their games. This demand is to some extent inconsistent with what the CEO of Company C referred to as the "introvert" character of many indie developers. To a high extent, such developers prefer to "show stuff when they are done," the CEO argued. Unfortunately, he continued, "the problem is, by then it is already too late [to adjust to market demands]" (CEO, Company C). Business Counsellor #2 at Incubator #3 argued that the key to a successful career in video game development, and especially for newcomer on the indie scene, was to "build a community" that shows an interest in what the studio is currently developing. This community can serve as a test group, as advisors, and, most importantly, as future paying clients that ensure a sufficient cash-flow when the game is released:

> As the business is run these days, you need to build a community, to maintain the community, and make the community the source of the success of the product and the studio. Everybody does not have that capacity. (Business Counsellor #2, Video Game development Incubator #3)

The developer in Company M, with a series of internationally successful games on his CV, also stressed the community-building activities as being of central importance: “One strength in indie is that you build a fan-base. Then you can know with almost 100 percent certainty that the next time you release a game, the community will buy it.”

The CEO of Company C had extensive experience from such community-building efforts, and he admitted that indie developers with limited or no marketing budgets were increasingly dependent on intermediaries such as influences with their own YouTube channels to promote their games and to create attention in the gamer community:

> We wanted to be indie developers and do our own thing. But overall, you are dependent on influencers and Youtube-streamers. There are other influencers you can use, depending on what type of games you develop. People at Instagram [can be engaged] ... We cater for the influencers, i.e., we must determine what they need. They need content—good content—to attract an audience at the lowest possible effort. They just want to make their channel grow, that is what they care for. (CEO, Company C)

The CEO defined an influencer in functional terms, as “someone who produces content to maintain their followers.” In his mind, it is important to target the right influencer that speaks directly to the gamer community that would potentially be interested in buying the video game:

> The important influencers are those with followers that include the customer segment that the game targets ... If you do a horror game, then it is a more mature customer segment. Possibly someone who is a grown-up with a job, potentially having a shortage of time. (CEO, Company C)

Taken together, indie video game development is not strictly a matter of simply developing a game, but the business activities increasingly concern the capacity to create attention for the new game to be released. In this new regime, indie developers cannot simply isolate themselves from the gamer community and rely on their technical and game design skills. They also need to develop or hire social and communicative skills so that the video games being develop can more easily find its end-users. Marketing in emerging field of digital distribution is a critical business activity that is continuously developed as new platforms and media are engaged, and as the gamer community establishes new ways to communicate with the video game development companies.

Raising Funds and Dealing with Investors and Financiers

A pressing concern for all indie developers is how to raise the finance capital needed to finish the development work. One of the pioneers of the Swedish indie development scene, also being experienced from being one of the early co-workers in one of the Swedish flagship Triple-A companies, underlined the importance of not ignoring the issue of how to finance the development, a question that was in fact not that easy to handle, and surrounded by myths and susceptible to wishful thinking:

> I think that is a form of myth, like 'Quit your Day job, you're an indie developer and you will make loads of money.' Minecraft is the exemplary case. But I have felt all the time that, 'Hey! That cannot be true! It is still a market economy out there, and how are you planning to get through the noise?' Now there are talks about the 'Indie apocalypse' and so forth. Things do not run as smoothly no longer. For me, nothing has changed. The competition has always been fierce, and games have always been difficult to develop. We compete over people's time and money, and so forth. (Indie developer, Company F)

Another experienced indie developer with a considerable track record in video game development shared this concern that the difficulties involved were largely understated by, for example, incubator directors, business counsellors, and education programme directors:

> [T]he general vibe is, 'This is quite easy! Come join us and develop a game.' I have been around in this business for some time, and have helped like children to make games. That's a good thing. But there can be too much of it's easy to make computer games. But it is easy to be disappointed. (Indie developer, Company K)

Consequently, most of the indie developers told their own version of a similar story that included a shortage of finance capital during the early stages of the development work, like the one presented by the CEO and co-founder of Company E: "After graduating, we had a tough period of time. We used our own money, and were trying to raise capital. There was no venture capital. No one was willing to invest. So that was really rough." At the same time, some developers took pride in not being financed by investors who claim the authority to have a say about the design of the game. In some cases, money emerged from unexpected sources, as in the case of the developer in Company L, who for some time operated under the patronage of a wealthy individual with an interest in video game development: "[An early indie developer I knew] had some contact with some dude who owned some game tool and who made an obscene amount of money. He donated 1,000 dollars per month to ten persons. I received that grant for two years" (Indie developer, Company L). Based on this experience, the developer consistently refused to accept any funding from investors:

> I never received any financing. We made the choice to not accept that. When you get a publishing deal and gets financing, you get a smaller proportion of the income. As we both have money and could make it through the development period, we decided to not accept [external funding]. (Indie developer, Company L)

Other indie developers testified to their hard-nosed attitude "to run the show until it stops" (as the developer in Company K expressed it): "I need to continue to do exactly what I want until it is no longer an option. That is after all what I like," he said. He continued: "It would be stupid to quit before all options have been exhausted." Needless to say, not all developers share this passionate commitment to the video game development work, and for the incubator directors and business counsellors that took on the responsibility to turn indie development work into regular business-venturing activities, this stock of hardcore indie developers was more of a liability than an asset.

Fortunately, these days, the hardware and software used are easily acquired at comparably low costs, but salaries including various taxes and fees need to be paid, which demand finance capital. The director of a university education programme addressed this predicament:

> The thing with video game development is that it is quite costly. You just cannot make a video game by spending a few hours in the afternoon cobbling together something ... A computer is not that expensive and neither is the software. But people sitting down to work together, and do this as their

day-job, that is quite expensive. There you need a number of competencies. (Director of game development education program)

At the same time, the majority of incorporated businesses being active in video game development were run at a profit, and industry representatives took pride in being a commercially successful industry, not dependent on grants from tax-money-based funds. In contrast, the Swedish film industry, another media-based business, was used as a warning example by several of the interviewees. By tradition, film production in Sweden has been part of the state's culture policy, and most of the films produced rely on finance capital from the state and its defined agent, primarily the Swedish Film Institute. As neither the quality of the films produced, nor the integrity of film production workers, subject to various politicized rules and red tape, impressed video game developers, a state-based funding model was rejected out of hand. Video game development should primarily operate as a commercial activity outside of the influence of the political system. The director of the university education programme flatly stated that the Swedish film industry "is not an industry, it is merely a cost-based activity." "There are no revenues in Swedish film industry, it is totally financed by tax-money," she said.

As large-scale and medium-sized companies were for most part running at profit, which constitute video game development as a *de facto* industry in its own right, there were few incentives for policy makers to financially support the video game industry. In addition, as video games are widely understood in policy-making quarters as a form of entertainment rather than an artistic expression, for example, indie developers with artistic and aesthetic ambitions were still not eligible for the various culture grants that, for example, artists with an art school diploma can apply for. This locates the indie developers in the shadow of the commercially successful video game companies, and outside of the regulator grant-based activities that finance the Swedish culture sector. To cope with this situation, indie developers use a "mixed strategy" approach, wherein they considered all possible ways to raise the funds needed to maintain their development work. The first way to ensure sufficient funds is to conduct so-called outsourcing work, that is, to conduct specific services for other firms, either other studios or companies in other industries that need expertise in, say, programming or gamification more widely. Vedula and Kim's (2019: 840) study of business ventures and the role of regional entrepreneurial ecosystems indicated that "ventures that exclusively offered products were more likely to close operations than those that offered both products and services." Thinly capitalized ventures may finance their product development work on the basis of professional services provided, and therefore demonstrate a higher survival rate. One of the indie studios (Company A) was, for instance, conducting contract work with the Swedish Civil Aviation Administration (Luftfartsverket), with whom they further refined simulation models that were used when training air traffic control officers. Needless to say, outsourcing work was regarded as a necessary evil among video game developers as it took time and energy away from the regular video game development activities. In addition, the CEO of Company C remarked that once a studio starts to conduct outsourcing work, it needs to acquire the skills and the competencies needed to conduct such work, and that tends to result in "hybrid teams" that move back and forth between the two production activities. That *per se* creates its own traction, and also generates tensions in the studios that are not always easy to manage. In the best of worlds, outsourcing work would thus be relatively marginal to the core activities.

Another way to finance the ongoing development work is to live off income already acquired, or the income from sales. As remarked above, today the lion's share of the income from a new game may be collected during a relatively short period of time, and therefore indie studios need to manage its own capital funds wisely to be able to maximize the time they can finance new development work. "We lived off [the first game developed] for a while, like a year ... In total, the revenues where half a million [Swedish crowns per year]," Indie Developer #1 (Company B) said. Being a textbook case of a studio being essentially self-funding and autonomous from external investors, this model creates a peace of mind among the co-workers. The two developers of Company B were lucky to more recently have received venture capital from a Chinese investor, who now owns shares in the game being developed (in practically terms, the investor holds a contract that defines a certain percentage of future game sales revenues). Indie Developer #1 (Company B) described the contract as "a rather peculiar deal," being a new form of contract in venture capital investment inasmuch as the investor does not own shares in the company *per se* but only in one of its assets, a video game in the making whose future revenues remain uncertain.[1] The principal objective for the studio

[1] LoPucki (1996: 6) refers to the ownership of claims against assets as a form of "avoidance of liability." The traditional way to invest and own assets is to hold stock in public companies

was therefore to ensure that the investors made a sufficient return on their investment so that they would be incentivized to supply finance capital to the studio also in the future, beyond the release of the current video game being developed:

> The deal right now is that we have received a sum of money from investors, and they naturally want a return on that investment when the game is released. So that is the first level we want to reach first. (Indie Developer #1, Company B)

"Our ambition is to continue to produce games and lead the life we have today," Indie Developer #1 (Company B) summarized the short-term strategy of the studio.

The CEO of Company C, which generated its own funds and is now able to plan for the forthcoming activities in at least a medium-term perspective, addressed the concern that investor may not only supply finance capital, but also make contributions in terms of business know-how and network contacts that benefit the development of the studio:

> If we would raise venture capital it would be to access new competence in the board. An owner that can help us on basis of qualified input. It would not be for the finance capital per se necessarily ... Someone to guide us into the future and help us develop by addressing the larger somewhat more

(what LoPucki 1996: 29 refers to as "business securitization"), but securitization and global securities markets enable investors to hold claims against assets, not entire businesses ("asset securitization" in LoPucki 1996: 29, vocabulary). The case of the investor who holds claims against a specific game and its projected future sales revenues is therefore not an idiosyncratic ownership contract, but rather reveals new ways of holding claims against assets rather than businesses *per se*. These changes from ownership in corporations to ownership of assets need to be understood within broader changes in corporate governance and corporate financing. For instance, Lund (2019) examines the recent tendency among, for example, Silicon Valley companies to issue both non-voting and voting stocks, which essentially protect top management and majority owners from the market for managerial control. This dual structure of the stock seems to be tolerated by market traders as non-voting shares trade at a relatively small discount to voting shares, "generally observed to be between 3% and 5%" (Lund 2019: 730). Similarly, Cohney et al. (2019) examine financial innovations such as *Initial Coin Offering* (ICO) as the recent shift to new ways for financing corporate development work. Such changes in corporate financing and the emergence of new corporate asset ownership contracts are predicted to generate new possibilities for technology-savvy entrepreneurs and developers (Lin 2014).

> difficult issues. Someone with experience, extensive contact networks, or whatever it may be. (CEO, Company C)

This is a key point made in the venture capital literature that investors not only secure the continuation of development work but also assist the firm in acquiring commercial and leadership skills that help the studio take another step in its development towards being a regular and profitable business. It is noteworthy that some studios may express only a marginal interest for moving in that direction as they may have opted for an indie developer career precisely to avoid becoming a conventional business. Yet, while many indie studios prefer to remain relatively small in size (say, in the range of 20 co-workers or less), they still regard commercial success as a factual evidence of the appreciation of the development efforts. As commercial success is in most cases followed by new challenges (e.g., how to invest the existing funds in various development activities), the input provided by investors is in most cases welcome.

Generally speaking, several interviewees argued that investing in video games is not an easy activity for outsiders as the industry is characterized by a variety of idiosyncrasies and specific market conditions that make it difficult to predict outcomes. This condition may result in the situation wherein those "who access finance capital may not regard this as a financially lucrative investment," the director of the university education programme argued. In addition, the marginal social and cultural status of video game—more entertainment than art or education, more a pastime of adolescents than a concern for mature and high-brow audiences—served as an another hurdle that needs to be passed: "It may also be that [investors] fail to see video games as the cultural expression that they actually are," the director said. In such situations, indie developers are starved of finance capital and need to consider other opportunities to maintain the work.

A Word from the Investors

A more recent phenomenon in the video game industry is the presence of investors specializing in financing video game development. One of these defined investors (here referred to as Company J) employed "four and a half person" (one co-worker was employed on a 50 per cent worktime contract), and was a spin-out from one of the most renowned video game incubators in Sweden. "The goal is to find small but strong indie companies, or small developers and provide them with funding and to help them with technical issues, or game design, or business development," one of the video game development investors said. The investor currently held a portfolio of Swedish studios, located all over Sweden. In addition, the investor co-financed industry infrastructure projects such as video game development incubators in cities and towns in three regions in Sweden. This investment was made to assist the output of investable companies, and to signal to, for example, policy makers that incubators were in need of proper financiers. In comparison to, for example, the film industry and dramatic theatre, the investor in Company J regarded the video game development industry as being "disfavoured" and "underdeveloped" in terms of political attention, subsidies, and direct financial support. At the same time, video games have been developed outside of the pretention of being "high art" and have been oriented towards commercial ends from its very beginning, so the lack of political initiatives and support has apparently not prevented the video game industry from thriving.

In terms of day-to-day work activities and investment process *per se*, the investor argued that everyday work essentially consists of "a fair share of scouting," the work to detect and communicate with companies with a potential to develop a successful video game. A certain share of the work consists of more conventional due diligence activities, as in the case to examine the technical assets and legal contracts of the targeted studio. The investor argued that they were looking for "a healthy balance between a high degree of enthusiasm and a realistic view of what can be practically delivered" (Game development investor, Company J). The development team thus needed to display both technical skills and enterprising capacities. In addition, the core asset of any developer remains the games already being developed, or in the portfolio:

> Even if we wanted to, we cannot ignore the quality of the game ideas. Because the game ideas and game demos are the only expression of the competence. So the game idea needs to be explored. (Game development investor, Company J)

Furthermore, the investor preferred to hold shares in the entire company so that they can influence business decisions that can be made through the company's primary governance function, the board of directors. In practice, this means that Company J does not, unlike, for example, publishers, invest in specific projects in the company's portfolio:

> We are contacted by people who apply for funding of individual projects … They might not be interested in letting go of the full control of their companies, and therefore they build a portfolio of projects. But what they are looking for is actually a publisher or a distributor. (Game development investor, Company J)

As indicated by Company J's investment in incubators in three locations, the investor regarded his and his colleagues' role as being somewhat broader than being a more conventional venture capital investor. To ensure the growth of the industry and the output of new and innovative companies, the investor in Company J at times also advised companies wherein they do not invest:

> We get to see an incredible amount of video game developers. If we get the chance, we pass on some business advice … That provides me with an opportunity to develop the industry from a fairly low level. (Game development investor, Company J)

In this view, Company J, in its role of one of the very few specialized venture capital investors, served a community-building function:

> In a way, were sitting on two chairs when we're in the field. The one role is as the investor, and then we might by a bit critical and say, 'Well, no, this is not our thing, really.' But the other role is to help the companies, to serve as a form of mentor, or advisor. (Game development investor, Company J)

The business mentoring or advisor role thus contributed to the sharing of know-how and expertise across segments of the industry and between regions. In the end, such activities contribute to an increased business orientation among also junior video game development companies, still being in the process of establishing adequate business functions and routines.

Alternative Sources of Funding: Crowdfunding

Structural changes and innovation in the finance industry, not the least the introduction of so-called cryptocurrencies (Omri 2013) or "virtual currencies" (Magnuson 2018: 1184), and the development of fintech (Brummer and Yadav 2019; Arner et al. 2015) have enabled new ways of financing innovation work. Magnuson (2018: 1174) defines fintech ("financial technologies") as "[t]he new breed of companies that specialize in providing financial services primarily through technologically enabled mobile and online platforms." In August 2013, Germany officially recognized Bitcoin, the perhaps most widely known cryptocurrency, as "private money." Two week prior to this event, a federal judge in the U.S. ruled that Bitcoins and other cryptocurrency should be subject to securities regulation, that is, Bitcoin was *de jure* established as money (Omri 2013: 39). Video game companies and indie developers more specifically are not particularly affected by such technological changes and legal reforms for the time being, but as they are both born "global" and "digitally," it may be that fintech can provide new pathways for financing the development work. For instance, structural changes in the finance industry generate legal reforms and regulatory policies that either directly or indirectly affect how, for example, crowdfunding can be organized. Currently, in the U.S., crowdfunding platforms are regulated on the basis of securities law (Magnuson 2018: 1199, footnote 156), but as crowdfunding is predicted to grow in scope (in terms of the variety of industries financed on the basis of crowdfunding platforms) and in magnitude (in terms of sheer turnover)—crowdfunding companies raised $16.2 billion in 2014, and the World Bank predicts that "the industry could grow to $96 billion by 2025," Magnuson (2018: 1175) reports—legal and regulatory reform can be expected.

Planells (2017: 625) examines the use of crowdfunding in indie video game development and suggests that "[c]rowd investment pretends to help small entrepreneurs or start-ups that have difficulties attending traditional financing." Crowdfunding is also supportive of the gamer community-based digital distribution model that is dominant today. Consequently, crowdfunding is "one of the most popular" social models among indie developers (Planells 2017: 625). Crowdfunding is also consistent with the gamer community as a form of "prosumer," wherein the producer/consumer identities merge, and being a relation wherein the gamers conduct "playbour" (i.e., the work to play the game) for the benefit of themselves and the developer, Crogan (2018: 681–682) argues: "The player as critical interlocutor and cocreative supporter and collaborator, as coinvestor, as community member, these are all formulations of the desired dream of the rise of the indies."

Crowdfunding is a practice that is based on what Fisher (2019: 280) refers to as *online community advantage* (OCA), which Fisher describes as an "underrecognized yet increasingly important source of firm advantage":

> OCA comes about when firms engage with one or more online communities as a key stakeholder group to form a source of competitive advantage that comes from the firm's ability to generate information, influence, and solidarity benefits from engagement in the online community. (Fisher 2019: 281)

Fisher here contrasts employees, who work within the boundaries of the firm and being compensated for their efforts, and "online community members" (e.g., the gamer community) who "mostly operate beyond the boundaries of a firm and are not remunerated for doing so" (Fisher 2019: 279). In many industries, Fisher 2019: 279) argues, "[*o*]*nline communities* are becoming a distinct and increasingly important stakeholder group for many firms." Not the least in the video game industry, thoroughly grounded in "technology-based forums" that "facilitate communication and exchange among individuals and entities with shared interests" (Fisher 2019: 279), online community advantages can be exploited to benefit the firm. More specifically, Fisher (2019: 291) identifies three classes of online community advantages: "Information, influence, and solidarity benefits." Crowdfunding is arguably best understood as a combination of the three advantages, being a "solidarity benefit" that is based on the gamer community's access to information about previous video games developed by the studio and ongoing development work, disclosed by the studio through its Internet channels (i.e., the site Discord), and the influence crowdfunding investors believe they can have on the end-product. Indie developers are thus oftentimes skilled in exploring online community advantage, either because that is at the very heart of the industry and the gamer community ethos, or out of sheer necessity, as in the case of crowdfunding.

Radoynovska and King (2019: 782) examine how crowdfunding contributors review various investment or donation alternatives (depending on perspective and legal frameworks), and argue that what they refer to as "likability" is a "critical mechanism" that determines the relationship between the perceived authenticity of the fundraising organization and audiences' support of an organization. Likeability is a rather loosely defined category that nonetheless "taps into the intuitive appeal of an individual or group," Radoynovska and King (2019: 783) write. Furthermore, Radoynovska and King (2019: 783) introduce a distinction between two types of authenticity that crowdfunding contributors assess. The first is referred to as *craft authenticity*, which denotes "how something is produced and demonstrates its fit within a particular category." Craft authenticity thus relates to the quality of the work conducted within a specific domain of jurisdiction or genre. The other category is *idiosyncratic authenticity* that denotes "an actor's moral commitment to a particular—unique/quirky—set of beliefs common to moral authenticity" (Radoynovska and King 2019: 783). In this view, crowdfunding contributors not only assess the competence and skills of the fundraising organization, but also value how committed its co-workers are to complete the stipulated project, that is, crowdfunding contributors introduce moral categories to assess investment/donation alternatives. Likability increases the chances of contributors committing money to the stipulated project, and likability is *per se* a matter of the perceived authenticity of the fundraising organization. "Authenticity thus creates a form of personal connection to an organization with which an individual has little or no previous experience," Radoynovska and King (2019: 784) contend.

As the video gamer community is quite dense and closely connected by digital media and Internet technologies, the step to ask the gamers themselves to make contributions to ongoing development work or planned video games is not dramatic. At the same time, crowdfunding is a relatively new mechanism for supplying finance capital, and there are not yet any strict and unambiguous rules regarding how to use this model and how to return capital to the small-scale investors that make contributions. As a consequence, indie developers tended to regard crowdfunding as a curiosity, or even a marketing activity *per se* that essentially failed to provide a competitive alternative to more conventional venture capital investment. Indie developer #1 in Company B said that they had "raised capital via crowdfunding at Kickstarter [a crowdfunding site] twice." In his view, this activity, regardless of the success of the initiative, "[i]s just as much a public relations activity as a fund-raising activity supportive of the development work" (Indie Developer #1, Company B). Furthermore, a crowdfunding initiative is at times quite unpredictable inasmuch as certain campaigns can raise funds vastly in excess of the sum that was originally targeted, developers argued:

> Just like a publishing on Steam can generate an indie hit, so can a Kickstarter campaign virtually explode. There are cases of people who asked for 5,000 dollars that ended up with 5 million dollars. (Indie Developer #1, Company B)

The use of crowdfunding was also complicated by fiscal policies, not being up to date with Internet-based operations. For instance, if a globally distributed community is eligible for a return on investment after the video game is released, is each recipient expected to declare this as a taxable income, and if so, in what country?: in Sweden, being the domicile of the indie studio in this case, or in the country of residency of the crowdfunder? According to the indie developers in Company B, such issues remain obscure in the current fiscal policy framework. In the end, crowdfunding remains a complementary funding model for most indie developers as the model is unpredictable and thus costly to manage, at least within a weakly institutionalized regulatory framework. The video game industry may be based on the ideal of community, but to rely on the community of gamers to supply capital for the development work is arguably not yet a sustainable business model.

Culture Grants and Other Forms of State Funding

In the absence of qualified venture capital investors, or at least a shortage of such capital in comparison to the demand for finance capital, indie developers and other industry actors also considered the possibility of the state subsidizing and partially funding an innovation-led segment of the economy. For instance, in the field of life science innovation, the Swedish state provides generous funds to support basic research in medicine, biotechnology, medical technology development, and so forth, and thereafter finance incubator and science parks services to assist the commercialization of research findings. Public health and the quality of health care services are naturally politically prioritized areas, and therefore there is only limited disagreement regarding the political support in this field of research and development. Video games, in contrast, are safely couched within the entertainment industry, and therefore receive only scant political attention. Recent changes in the video game development business suggest that video games are increasingly associated with cultural production, and therefore it would be possible to include video games within the responsibilities of the, for example, Swedish Arts Council, the primary state-controlled agency dealing with culture project support. Still, the enthusiasm over a convergence between culture production and the video game industry was moderate, arguably on both sides, the director of the university education programme noticed:

> There is a very weak interest among other culture sector workers to share a budget with an industry that otherwise performs well financially. Coming from the gaming community, I guess we need to tread carefully in these domains. Now, we're supposed to claim a share of the culture sector budget as well? (Director of game development education program)

Indie developer and culture sector entrepreneur accounted for his experiences from communicating with regional policy makers, being only modestly successful: "We tried to initiate lobbying activities supportive of video games as an art form." The only accomplishment was that video game development was recognized in the formal culture policy document being published and circulated in the region, but video game development was nevertheless portrayed as a curiosity:

> [In the region's culture policy document] you could read, 'And then there are some folks developing games and that's a good thing.' Of course, that was expressed in more fancy terms, but that is basically what is said. (Indie developer and culture sector entrepreneur)

The two business partners in Company B accounted in somewhat amusing terms of how they had participated in a seminar where a culture grant application process was explained to an audience of presumptive applicants. "There was nothing about video games in that area," Indie Developer #1 (Company B) concluded. On another occasion, the developers examined the possibilities for applying for a grant from the European Union's *Creative Europe* programme, an initiative that at least formally recognized video games as a species of cultural expression and thus being eligible for funding. According to the developers, the instructions for the grant application were "very odd" (Indie Developer #1, Company B) inasmuch as the financiers prohibited video game developers from producing a prototype of the game. The reason for this red tape was that the European Union considered prototype development as a form of "production activity" (Indie Developer #2, Company B), which falls outside of the *Creative Europe* programme. "It is almost impossible to develop a game without making a prototype because you need to test the idea to see if it works," Indie Developer #1 (Company B) remarked. Discouraged by these experiences, wherein video game development, regardless of the form or content of the game, was either excluded altogether from culture fund applications or surrounded by regulatory rules that *de facto* exclude presumptive applicants from the video game industry. The two business partners of Company B reached the conclusion that they were not working in a grant-based industry, and that they therefore needed to finance their development projects otherwise.

When being asked if the state and industry policy could make a material difference for, for example, indie developers who do not yet generate a cash-flow and sufficient revenues to finance ongoing development work, the idea was recognized but commonly associated with a limited sense of urgency among policy makers. "Some kind of indie development grants from the state would have made a massive difference, really!" Indie Developer #1 (Company B) said. He continued:

> This year, prior to the investment, has been difficult. We have lived off change money. But things go up and things go down. But some kind of grant from the state, something quite simple, not demanding too much paper work, which would have made a huge difference. We are not the only ones who think that would be the case. (Indie Developer #1, Company B)

Based on the unpredictable nature of the video game development industry, and the numerous documented cases wherein seemingly small contributions eventually generate massive income, Indie Developer #1 claimed that also small sums of money could make a significant difference: "It is a comparable small amount of money exposed to high risks, but also small sums can lead to considerable outcomes." To date, the Swedish industry policy does not provide such small grants, but several interviewees pointed at Finland that offered such funding through a state-controlled innovation agency, Tekes (also known as Business Finland), assigned the role to support innovation-led growth. In Sweden, the only operational state-funded grant was the student loan services, by default serving as a financier of indie development activities, the director of the university education programme argued.

> We have students who have started their own companies on basis of student loans. They sign up for courses to be able to develop games. That sounds like a small sum of money, but for them raising their burden of debt, it is not minor issue. That is the concern. (Director of game development education program)

As the proportion of indie developers who make sufficient returns on their video games to cover such loans is relatively small, the current system serves to build up a stock of student loans that are to be repaid by individuals. As the state can tax income and new businesses create new jobs, industry policies that include grants for indie development activities can be justified, especially as industry data reveals that the Swedish video game industry is an exemplary high-growth industry that runs on profit. Such a policy reform would also reduce the student loan stock that burdens a generation of students being in the age where they form families and buy homes, in themselves costly and mortgage-driven activities.

In summary, indie developers use a variety of activities to raise the finance capital needed to continue their development work: they accept contracted outsourcing work assignment, they communicate with venture capital investors that specialize in video game development, they browse culture agency's homepages to see if they are included in posted campaigns and initiatives, and they make use of existing financial services, including the state-funded student loan system, to supply capital to the development work.

Indirect Support of Indie Developers: The Role of Incubators in Making Indie Studios Business-Like

Some interviewees argued that venture capital investors have only limited understanding of the video game industry, and that this was to the detriment of, for example, the indie video game community as they were starved of capital despite the fact that the industry at large being a high-growth and profitable business. Indie developers are at times not attracted by the business side of the operations, several interviewees claimed, more prone to care about the video game and the gaming experience as such. In this situation, many of the representatives of various incubators that were set up in various part of the Sweden argued that one of their foremost responsibilities was to train the indie developers to better communicate their visions and business models in a vocabulary that resonates with investors.

The director of Incubator #2, located in a metropolitan area, argued that his primary assignment was to transform leniently managed indie companies into proper business ventures that could compete over finance capital investment, generate a cash-flow of its own on the basis of the portfolio of assets, and provide stable and qualified job opportunities. This process included the establishment of new attitudes among the developers, no longer located in boys' or girls' rooms, or cellars hosting some gaming team, but actively working to develop new games: "As part of our assignment, we need to eliminate all misconceptions and faulty identities and to rebuild them. This is a boot-camp," the director argued in a militaristic vocabulary to underline a sense of urgency (Video Game Development Incubator #2). The director even admitted that this straightforward focus on business creation and growth would deter certain indie developers who reject such processes as a violation of their artistic freedom, integrity, and ideologies endorsed *tout court*: "If you're a hardcore indie developer, You wouldn't be here," the director said. One of the business counsellor in Incubator #3, located in a smaller university college town, one hour away from a larger city, shared this commitment to business creation: "This is our assignment: To generate economic growth and to create jobs," the business Counsellor #1 (Video Game development Incubator #3) said. The director in Incubator #2 expressed the same idea: "In the end, we would like to build sustainable companies. That is the primary objective."[2]

In the eyes of the director and the two business counsellor in Incubator #3, indie developers have the right technical skills and an intimate understanding of the gamer community's expectations and passionate interests, but are still far too introvert when it comes to how they exploit such resources. Rather than to nourish a self-indulgent outsider identity, and to recognize no broader economic, social, and cultural connections to the broader community, the incubator staff actively instructed developers to regard their expertise as critical resources within a business venture that added to innovation-led growth on the aggregated level. The director of Incubator #2 argued that there was currently a tendency to promote indie video game development as a cottage industry as a variety of incubators or platform initiatives opened at numerous locations in Sweden, also in

[2] Needless to say, some of the indie developers were not equally impressed by the business counselling that was provided by the incubators. The CEO of the Company E, for instance, which develops casual games intended for mobile phones and tablets, was concerned about the lack of understanding of the emergent global casual game market: "The business coaches [in the incubator] didn't know nothing about mobile games, and they always said like 'I've got no idea!' We couldn't get proper help to address things we thought were problems." Despite such criticism, it is reasonable to assume that indie developers who were not fortunate to acquire accurate business advice benefitted indirectly from the incubator activities.

smaller towns and communities, to exploit local competencies and skills. Internationally, the same tendency was observed, with countries previously being invisible on the map now suddenly developing video games. To preserve the competitive advantage of Swedish video game industry, the incubator's role was not so much to further strengthen the video game development skills *per se*, but to actively integrate and align such capacities and skills within a corporate structure, but without harming the creative ethos and skills of the indie developers. Whenever this process started to generate its own momentum, the director felt a sense of self-fulfilment as he could see the benign consequences of such accomplishments: "I enjoy observing the development teams develop. It is more a matter of organization and human development [than video game development]" (Director, Video Game Development Incubator #2).

In an economy characterized by innovation-led growth, it is complicated for policy makers and regulatory agencies to actively instruct market actors how to deal with business challenges. Yet, the funding and support of intermediary agencies, including incubators, business labs, science parks, and so on, have been a widely used mechanism to align macroeconomic policies and interests and firm-level venturing. In the case of video game development, the industry has grown from the margin to the centre, being essentially a hobbyist activity in the fringe of the economy that has proved its economic significance, in many cases to the surprise of less informed agents. Incubators are thus legitimate agents in innovation-led growth that serve to align interests in a network of actors, and that assist market-based actors in better communicating with, for example, venture capital investors.

Summary and Conclusion

Any new business needs to raise some funds to finance the development work that eventually can generate the cash needed to finance further development work. Alternatively, the development work is conducted during the spare time of the developer, being some kind of leisure activity comparable to playing football with friends or being in a book club. The term *entrepreneur* presupposes that the business promoter is indebted, that is, acquire finance capital from investors who are willing to commit their residual cash to a business venture that is run on the basis of the promise that sufficient cash will be generated so that debt can be repaid and a surplus is generated to finance ongoing and future projects. However, finance capital owners consider a wide variety of opportunities for how to reinvest their cash, which includes reinvestment in the finance industry itself. By and large, business ventures that can provide credible calculations of risk and minimize the presence of uncertainty (i.e., non-parametric risk) are more likely to be successful in terms of raising venture capital. By implication, video game developers need to not only promote their own passionate commitment to video games and to display their skills, experience, and documented track records, but also engage in calculative practices as expected from investors. For some developers, this ability to promote their business venture in financial terms is challenging as they may lack this expertise, or even reject the idea that video game development is like any other business venture activity. Anecdotal evidence also indicates that the market for video game industry venture capital investment is thin as major investors such as banks and insurance companies largely refrain from investing. In Sweden, there is currently only one venture capital investor specializing in video game industry investment. In contrast, industry insiders such as publishers and distribution platform companies have signalled that they are willing to develop investment activities for the benefit of the industry. These tendencies indicate that the video game industry may increasingly generate its own financial surplus that can be reinvested in new studios and development activities. Similar to the Silicon Valley computer industry cluster, relying on successful entrepreneurs to reinvest their surplus, the video game industry may prove to have the finance capital and investment skills to self-finance its development work.

References

Arner, D. W., Barberis, J., & Buckley, R. P. (2015). The evolution of fintech: A new post-crisis paradigm. *Georgetown Journal of International Law, 47*, 1271–1319.

Brummer, C., & Yadav, Y. (2019). Fintech and the innovation trilemma. *Georgetown Law Journal, 107*, 235–307.

Christin, A. (2018). Counting clicks: Quantification and variation in web journalism in the United States and France. *American Journal of Sociology, 123*(5), 1382–1415.

Cohney, S., Hofman, D., Sklarof, J., & Wishnick, D. (2019). Coin-operated capitalism. *Columbia Law Review, 119*(3), 591–676.

Crogan, P. (2018). Indie dreams: Video games, creative economy, and the hyper-industrial epoch. *Games and Culture, 13*(7), 671–689.
Crowston, C. H. (2013). *Credit, fashion, sex: Economies of regard in old regime France*. Durham: Duke University Press.
Davenport, T. H., & Beck, J. C. (2001). *The attention economy: understanding the new currency of business*. Boston: Harvard University Press.
Deeg, R. (2009). The rise of internal capitalist diversity? Changing patterns of finance and corporate governance in Europe. *Economy and Society, 38*(4), 552–579.
Fisher, G. (2019). Online communities and firm advantages. *Academy of Management Review, 44*(2), 279–298.
Fontaine, L. (2014). *The moral economy: Poverty, credit, and trust in early modern Europe*. New York and Cambridge: Cambridge University Press.
Giraudeau, M. (2018). Proving future profit: Business plans as demonstration devices. *Osiris, 33*, 130–148.
Hacking, I. (1990). *The taming of chance*. Cambridge: Cambridge University Press.
Hopkins, M. M., Crane, P. A., Nightingale, P., & Baden-Fuller, C. (2013). Buying big into biotech: Scale, financing, and the industrial dynamics of UK biotech, 1980–2009. *Industrial and Corporate Change, 22*(4), 903–952.
Jacobides, M. G. (2005). Industry change through vertical disintegration: How and why markets emerged in mortgage banking. *Academy of Management Journal, 48*(3), 465–498.
Jonsson Ahl, H. (2002). The construction of the female entrepreneur as the other. In B. Czarniawska & H. Höpfl (Eds.), *Casting the other: The production and maintenance of inequalities in work organizations*. London and New York: Routledge.
Kenney, M. (2011). How venture capital became a component of the US National System of Innovation. *Industrial and Corporate Change, 20*(6), 1677–1723.
Le Goff, J. ([1986] 1988). *Your money or your life: Economy and religion in the Middle Ages*. New York: Zone Books.
Lewis, P. (2006). The quest form invisibility: Female entrepreneurs and the masculine norm of entrepreneurship. *Gender, Work and Organization, 13*(5), 453–469.
Leyshon, A., & Thrift, N. (2007). The capitalization of almost everything: The future of finance and capitalism. *Theory, Culture, and Society, 24*(7/8), 97–115.
Lin, T. C. W. (2014). The new financial industry. *Alabama Law Review, 65*, 567–623.
LoPucki, L. M. (1996). The death of liability. *Yale Law Journal, 106*(1), 1–92.
Lund, D. S. (2019). Nonvoting shares and efficient corporate governance. *Stanford Law Review, 71*(3), 687–746.
Magnuson, W. (2018). Regulating fintech. *Vanderbilt Law Review, 71*, 1167–1126.

Omri, M. (2013). Are cryptocurrencies super tax havens? *Michigan Law Review First Impressions, 112*, 38–48.
Planells, J. A. (2017). Video games and the crowdfunding ideology: From the gamer-buyer to the prosumer-investor. *Journal of Consumer Culture, 17*(3), 620–638.
Radoynovska, N., & King, B. G. (2019). To whom are you true? Audience perceptions of authenticity in nascent crowdfunding ventures. *Organization Science, 30*(4), 781–802.
Vedula, S., & Kim, P. H. (2019). Gimme shelter or fade away: The impact of regional entrepreneurial ecosystem quality on venture survival. *Industrial and Corporate Change, 28*(4), 827–854.

CHAPTER 7

Expanding the Video Game Concept: The Perceptual and Epistemological Bases of the Digital Objects

Introduction

The previous chapters of this volume have addressed how indie developers have coped with a variety of practical concerns in the day-to-day work to be able to actually fulfil their dream of producing their own video games on the basis of novel game concepts and individual preferences. This empirical chapter shifts the focus from practical concerns and business decisions, and re-located the video game within a broader historical domain wherein the human faculty of visual perception is examined. In the long history of media, beginning in ancient Sumeria and the invention of writing as a means to keep track of cattle in the agrarian economy, video game is a relatively recent media invention, stretching back to the early 1960s and 1970s when original games such as *Spacewar!* (1962) and *Pong* (1972) were developed as technological curiosities in the fringes of the new computer science discipline. In comparison, the visual medium of cinema is close to a century older, and film theory and media theory more widely can shed some light on how video games can be understood in the *longue durée* of media history. The film theorist Jonathan Beller (2006: 275) cites the renowned Russian film director Sergey Eisenstein, speaking about film as "a tractor ploughing over the audience's psyche." Movies were a core component in the Soviet era propaganda apparatus, and Eisenstein does not mince his words when it comes to the possibilities he saw in film production. The agricultural metaphor is also telling as it is indicative of the period's doctrines regarding public relations, here

A. Styhre, *Indie Video Game Development Work*,
https://doi.org/10.1007/978-3-030-45545-3_7

portrayed in terms of the physical manipulations of natural resources, such as the soil. Eisenstein's enthusiasm over the by then relatively new film medium nevertheless lives on, today projected onto other media such as video games and digital objects, and not the least, more recently, when being combined with artificial intelligence and algorithm governance. The continuity over centuries of media history and the theories of perception that have dominated during different periods demands a more comprehensive theoretical framework for understanding the significance of new media, including video games.

The media philosopher Vilém Flusser (2011a: 63) suggests that "[if] we want to instigate a human society, we must understand their new technologies, not higher values." Flusser proposes that the invention of linear writing has dominated human societies (and Western societies in particular, as these societies use linear rather than pictographic writing) for centuries, but that this epistemological dominance is now challenged by the invention of image-based media such as cinema and digital media. "Print-based thought is about to be overhauled," Flusser (2011b: 52) announces. In Flusser's view, the invention of image-based media is a human invention at the same scale as writing. Writing is a form of abstraction of lived first-hand experience, and images are in turn a further abstraction based on writing. Flusser thus proposes that the history of media (e.g., writing, images, motion pictures, digital media) is a paradoxical process wherein the media *per se* becomes "structurally more complex," while for the user, the medium of choice becomes "functionally simpler" (Flusser 2011b: 17). For instance, the invention of television, the broadcasting of visual images, is based on a variety of technological innovations, but in the eyes of the end-users, the viewers, the operational difficulties are minimal: press the button and get seated, and you are all set! In fact, this functional simplicity has been the grist-for-the-mill for critics of new media, who have suggested that media instil a passivity that is harmful to the viewer's health, result in an apathy that may even undermine the democratic society, and a variety of additional malaises that the protagonists of new media need to take into account.

Regardless of such concerns, Flusser (2011b: 17) suggests that increased structural progress in combination with functional simplicity is above all the "mark of progress." Flusser here introduces the concept of *apparatus* as the medium (e.g., a camera) that fulfils the desires of the user, but only those desires that can be functionally handled by the apparatus: "The apparatus does as the photographer desires, but the photographer can only desire what the apparatus can do" (Flusser 2011a: 20). Expressed differently, "a man gives an apparatus instructions that the apparatus has instructed him to give," Flusser (2011a: 74) writes. In this view, the camera is not so much a tool in the conventional sense of the term as what demands skills and experience to use efficiently (say, a pair of scissors or a golf club), but becomes a "plaything": "The camera is not a tool but a plaything, and a photographer is not a worker but a player: not *Homo faber* but *Homo ludens*" (Flusser 2000: 26). The possibilities of the camera qua apparatus reduce the operational freedom of the user, and he or she is no longer the *homo faber*, the creating human, but becomes *homo ludens*, the playing human, functionally limited to what the apparatus can accomplish. Flusser does not suggest that this reduces the value of the camera, but he insists that the self-enclosed nature of the camera imposes limitations for the user: he or she cannot transcend the "possibilities contained within the program of the camera" (Flusser 2000: 26). The new medium *is what it is*, and *does what it can*, but beyond that point, the medium becomes inept, incapable of functionally responding to the user's desires.

Flusser's concept of the apparatus is of relevance when it comes to theorizing the role of the digital object of the video game, being a most complex apparatus whose programmes contain almost innumerable (but never unlimited) possibilities. First of all, video games are epistemologically speaking grounded in computer code, the machine language that is used to instruct computers to execute operations. As Galloway (2012: 16. Original emphasis omitted) notices, code is "the only language that is executable," that is, whereas other forms of writing, say, poetry, are a means to represent certain ideas, emotions, and social relations, and thus subject to interpretation and discussion, code does not serve this role but instead generate other effects:

> Code is machinic first and linguistic second: an intersubjective infrastructure is not the same as a material one ... To see code as subjectively performative or enunciative is to anthropomorphize it, to project it onto the rubric of psychology, rather than to understand it through its own logic of 'calculation' or 'command.' (Galloway 2012: 71)

Expressed differently, code is a medium that is "more than a medium" inasmuch as it accomplished certain things and materialized certain ideas or intentions. The code is not to be read as text *per se*, but needs to be considered only in terms of its material implications, for example, as what emerges on the surface of the computer screen, the user's interface. Speaking in Flusser's (2000) vocabulary, computer code is mid-way between the linear writing paradigm and the image-based paradigm that Flusser believes will displace linear writing for most parts; the code is the passage point between the linear computer instructions and the visual images generated on the basis of these instructions. Furthermore, code is *infrastructural* inasmuch as it is, first, widely taken for granted by lay audiences as long as it performs its operations as expected on reasonable grounds, and, second, the capacity to understand and to manipulate the code is a professional domain of expertise in its own right, beyond the reach of lay audiences. If Flusser's (2000) proposition that digital media is based on visual and primarily cinematic images is the mark of technological progress that future societies will rely on when the era of linear writing is coming to an end, then computer code is the key social resource to manage, to interfere with, to manipulate, and to gain control over. Hayles (2006: 152) proposes that the French philosopher Jacques Derrida's aphorism, stressing the grammatological embedding of the human mind in texts—"*Il n'y a pas de hors-texte*," there is "no outside of the text," Derrida famously stated—is now being replaced by the dictum "*Il n'y a pas de hors-code.*" Code is everywhere as part of the human predicament, operating "behind the scene" and yet only enabling the users to accomplish what is always already written into the programme of the digital medium. When Ada Lovelace, the first documented computer programmer, started to calculate Bernoulli numbers by using Charles Babbage's Analytical Engine in 1843 (Galloway and Thacker 2007: 113), she possibly did not anticipate that such code would define the human condition some fifteen decades later.

This final empirical chapter will examine how video games as digital objects and programmed apparatuses can be defined in novel terms and to incorporate new processes, activities, and experiences. To date, the name given, *video games* is telling, being based on the principle to include some kind of competitive moment, and preferably an element of chance to avoid a sense of deterministic predictability in the game. But digital objects can be virtually anything, and video game technologies that combine digital media, interactivity, and specific forms of visual perception can be used in a variety of settings, from the training of airline pilots and surgeons to more low-brow, yet enriching cultural experiences, such as re-constructing famous buildings in, for example, *Minecraft*. In order to better recognize the capacities of video game technologies, a theory of visual perception is presented, better couching the more recent debate and discussion regarding the future of video games. This chapter therefore to a lower extent examines how video game developers cope with actual issues and concerns, and instead stresses how the expertise and skills developed in the industry over the last two decades (most interviewees speak about the mid-1990s as the point of origination of Swedish video game industry) can be deployed when taking video game technologies farther, into new applications and to provide new experiences, yet to materialize.

The Modernist Theory of Perception: Seeing as Trained Capacity

To better explore the possibilities of video games as a technology and cultural expression, the concept of visual perception as a socially enacted concept is examined. The scientific and philosophical idea of an "epistemology of seeing" is closely entangled with modernity and the basic tendencies: Urbanization, which results in a shift in how visual perception is understood, and the technological development of visual media, both scientific (e.g., the medical visualization technologies such as the X-ray) and communicative (e.g., rudimentary visual media, cinema, and television). Crary (1995: 46) speaks about the first half of the nineteenth century as the period wherein a "relatively sudden emergence of models of subjective vision in a wide range of disciplines" is observed. The "classical of visuality" was abandoned, and vision was enacted as a trained capacity of the individual human, who could learn to see differently by actively paying attention to details in his or her life world and domain of work. In the classic model of visual perception, the visual apparatus, the eyes and the mind, passively records what occurs within the visual field of the observer. Pliny, the Roman intellectual, argued that the eyes "[a]cts as a sort of vessel receiving and transmitting the visible portions of the consciousness" (cited in Leppert 1996: 6). In this way, visual perception is for most part given as what it is, a form of biological capacity, and little else. In the modern enactment, visual perception is instead what is subject to individual skills and capacities; as vision not only is contingent on external conditions but also includes cognitive processes, visual perception is subject to "external techniques of manipulation and simulation" (Crary 1999: 12). The visual field is never fully given, but the capacity to, for example, detect significant details is a question of the "psychophysics" of the individual subject. As an implication from this shift in focus, from seeing as an evolutionary condition to a trained skill, visual perception is lending itself to a variety of formal measures and recording activities, which ultimately embed human perception in the domain of quantifiable performances (Crary 1999: 12). Not only does visual perception differ from person to person, but these diverging visual performances can be expressed in measures and quanta, and serve to commensurate individual performances.

In the increasingly urbanized European and North American societies of the mid-nineteenth century, one specific feature of visual perception was emphasized by scientists and social reformers, and thereafter also business promoters and their assigned managers: the individual's capacity to *pay attention* to specific entities or events. The urbanized and capitalist society, emerging in the mid-nineteenth century, produced a new life world, a "social, urban, psychic, industrial field" increasingly saturated with "sensory input" (Crary 1995: 47). This "thick" social environment differed considerably from the rural life world, wherein people lived in less densely populated communities, and where change was determined by the seasons of the year, not by new technologies or economic conditions. In this new environment, the individual's attentiveness was put into new contexts, Crary (1995) argues:

> It is possible to see one crucial aspect of modernity as a continual crisis of attentiveness, to see the changing configurations of capitalism pushing attention and distraction to new limits and thresholds, with unending introduction of new products, new sources of stimulation, and streams of information, and then responding with new methods of managing and regulating perception. (Crary 1995: 47)

In the rural society and the agrarian economy, the individual's attention needed to recognize slower changes in, for example, weather. In contrast, the cultural logic of capitalism and its imprint on the urban landscape demands a capacity to rapidly switch the attention from one thing to another in the blink of an eye. The circulation of capital that is the underlying mechanism of the cultural logic of capitalism emphasizes exchange and circulation, which in turn generate a "human perceptual adaptability" (Crary 1995: 48). This perceptual adaptability, the capacity to shift the focus of the attention comes at a price: Distraction and the failure to detect perceptual signals that are significant, that is, to effectively separate noise from genuine perceptual information. The cultural logic of capitalism disciplines the individual to swiftly shift the attention from one issue to another, but it fails to provide the tools for how to determine what perceptual signals that are worthy of the attention, and which that needs to be ignored or overlooked.

William James, the pragmatist philosopher, stated that "my experience is what I agree to attend to" in his *Principles of Psychology* (James [1890] 1950: 402). This proposition downplays the idea of visual perception as a passive recording of the visual field, but instead renders visual perception an active faculty, subject to effort and the individual's willingness to participate. In Crary's (1999: 361) view, James here introduces the individual as an "autonomous self-choosing, world-creating subject, liberated from the *receptive* status of a subject for whom experience was 'the mere presence to the senses of an outward order.'" By implication, if visual perception is an act of will, then this capacity is also what is possible to influence and manipulate: "Within modernity," Crary (1995: 51) argues, "vision was merely one layer of a body that could be captured, shaped, directed by a range of external techniques, a body that was also an evolving sensory-motor system capable of creating and dissolving forms." Attention thus became a key concern for scientists and social reformers amidst the crisis of perception of the nineteenth century, the gateway through which the perceptual apparatus and the cognitive processes of the mind, which jointly generate the faculty of visual perception, could be accessed and rendered a legitimate study object:

> Within the general epistemological crisis of the late nineteenth century, attention became a makeshift and inadequate simulation of an Archimedean point of stability from which consciousness could know the world. Rather than perceptual fixity and the certainty of presence, it opened onto flux and absence within which subject and object had a scattered, provisional existence. (Crary 1999: 64–65)

It would be inadequate to claim that the urbanization singlehandedly justified the renewed interest for visual perception as the nineteenth century was characterized by the swift growth of scientific know-how and expertise, in, for example, the field of clinical medicine. In France, medical schools had been established outside of the regular university system by the first decades of the century, and in Germany, states such as Prussia created new connections between university-based researchers and industry, which resulted in more problem-solving-oriented research agenda.

Modern Visual Media

The nineteenth century was the period wherein visual media was developed and commercialized on broad scale. The development of visual media can be separated into scientific and medical visual media and entertainment media, but the two categories of media shared the same underlying scientific principles and know-how. The Belgian scientist Joseph Plateau developed the phenakistoscope that generated moving images in the early 1830s, and by 1833, the device was sold in London (Crary 1990: 107–109). William G. Horner invented the zoetrope in 1834, and the German mathematician Simon Stampfer developed the stereoscope the same year. By the mid-1850s, the stereoscope was commercialized (Schiavo 2003: 113). Crary (1990: 116) portrays the stereoscope as "most significant form of visual imagery in the nineteenth century, with the exception of photographs," an invention that equally paved the way for a new concept of visual perception. In the field of entertainment media, the pace of the development was not lower. Already in the mid-1740s and the mid-1750s, a device referred to as a zograscope, a device that could produce what today would be referred to as 3-D animations, was manufactured and marketed in, for example, English magazines and newspapers (Blake 2003: 1). To use the zograscope, wealthy consumers had to purchase engraved, hand-coloured images that were offered in the emerging market for visual gadgets. The development of cinema, the invention that is oftentimes credited to the Lumière brothers, Auguste and Louis, who organized the first film premiere in 1895, was preceded by various inventions, including Emile Reynad's *Praxinoscope* (1876). This device was introduced in a variety of versions under different brands, including *Praxinoscope-Théâtre* (1879), *Praxinoscope à projection* (1892), and *Théâtre Optique* (1892) (Crary 1999: 260–267). Taken together, all these technological inventions in combination with the intellectual work to re-formulate a new model of visual perception, better aligned with the life conditions of the urban, resulted in what film theorist Jonathan Beller (2006: 2) speaks about as the "the cinematization of the visual." The cinematization of the visual denotes how visual perception is entangled with a set of "socio-technical institutions and apparatuses" under the influence of the capitalist mode of production, and the interests of capital owners (e.g., the concern for the issue of the individual's capacity to pay attention). The development of new visual media in the nineteenth century further accentuated the connections between visual perception and economic interests.

Visual Perception and Imaginative Capacity

Throughout the twentieth century and into the new millennium, doctrines regarding visual perception, originating in the nineteenth century, were further accentuated and refined. The visual field was increasingly subject to scholarly research, and new visual media were continuously developed and introduced, not the least merging the computer technology, yet another nineteenth-century invention. To better understand how video game development rests on changes in the doctrine of visual perception and exploits the new possibilities provided by computer technologies, yet another "wetware" (i.e., human) issue needs to be addressed: the human capacity to integrate visual perception, media (and digital media in particular), and human imagination. Studies of visual perception may reveal how humans navigate in a visual field, and how they pay attention to details or fail to do so. Visual technologies introduced may either assist the perceiving subject to enhance their "visual performance" or serve to re-direct the individual's attention to new details. Nevertheless, the visual apparatus, constituted by hardware, software, and wetware, does not say very much, regardless of its degree of technological sophistication and complexity, about what humans are intrigued by and attracted by intellectually and emotionally. To fully understand the potential of video games as a cultural expression, and as a form of entertainment, the human capacity of imagination needs to be introduced.

George Simmel (1980: 174–175) states that humans only "exist in the present," being the only temporal horizon that "qualifies as reality." The past is in the domain of the memory, whereas the future "lies within the domain of fantasy or imagination." This existential predicament wherein humans are temporally determined to live exactly where they are and no place else has been subject to philosophical reflection, not the least in the writings of Søren Kierkegaard who regarded life as essentially incomprehensible as the individual cannot fruitfully make sense of the temporal horizon wherein the humans live their lives. Fortunately, Simmel (1980) not only introduces an existential predicament but also points at a solution or a remedy, the escape route that fantasy and imagination provide. Plato introduced the concept of *Eikasia* ("imagination") in his dialogue *Republic*.

Hegel proposes the concept of *Einbildungskraft* ("imagination") in his philosophical vocabulary. Also less formalist philosophers than Plato and Hegel have been concerned with the human capacity to imagine. Gaston Bachelard, indubitably a heterodox philosopher in the pantheon of thinkers, suggests that imagination is factually not a matter of "forming images of reality." Rather, Bachelard (1987: 15–16) argues, imagination is to use the cognitive faculty to form images that "go beyond reality, which *sing* reality." Bachelard characterizes the imaginative capacity as a "superhuman faculty" inasmuch as the capacity to "go beyond the *human condition*" transcends the temporal determinism of the human condition:

> Imagination is always considered to be the faculty of *forming* images. But it is rather the faculty of *deforming* images offered by perception, of freeing ourselves from the immediate images; it is especially the faculty of *changing* images. (Bachelard 1987: 19)

The renowned Russian psychologist Lev Vygotsky introduced the research programme of *art psychology* and placed imagination at the centre of the inquiry. Vygotsky's (1971: 199) research programme includes three branches of theoretical psychology, the "study of perception, the study of emotions, and the study of imagination and fantasy," all being combined in the theoretical framework. In Vygotsky's (1978: 93) view, grounded in laboratory research on the cognitive development of infants, imagination is distinctively human capacity, emerging when the child is in the age of three. Imagination is consequently "not present in the consciousness of the very young child," and it is "totally absent in animals," Vygotsky (1978: 93) remarks. When a child below the age of three is instructed to tell what happens in a picture (say, in a picture book), the younger child can point out the entities in the picture (a car, a ball, a child), whereas the older child can also tell stories about what is about to happen in the image, or what has happened previously. This cognitive capacity to move from the constitutive elements of the picture to tell an engaging story about the relations between the entities is an act of imagination, a dynamic capacity to "go beyond" that which is immediately given by visual perception. This human capacity is the centrepiece of Vygotsky's research programme (which was never completed as Vygotsky died untimely of tuberculosis at the age of 37 in 1934) and remains the core capacity in any abstract human activity.

Needless to say, culture workers of all kinds have embraced the imaginative capacity as a mark of the creative and inventive mind. The English literature critic Cyril Connolly (1945: vi) portrays art as "man's noblest attempt to preserve Imagination from Time." Saul Bellow (2015a: 127), American Nobel Prize laureate in literature, refers to Arthur Schopenhauer, who argued that imagination rather than opinion is the qualifying mark of art to substantiate his claim that writing is essentially an act of imagination. In Bellow's 2015b: 80) view, a novelist begins with "disorder and disharmony" and creates a meaningful structure in the literary text on the basis of what he characterizes as "an unknown process of the imagination." No one can thus say what this imaginative capacity is, but it generates material effects and manifests itself as a form of "action," as stipulated by Vygotsky (1978). Imagination is therefore not some passive faculty, awaiting to be mobilized in the process of work, but is better described as what is co-produced with a specific action, for example, the writing of a novel. The imaginative capacity is thus part of what Piaget ([1950] 2001: 7) described as *intelligence*, a form of coordinated mobilization of a variety of cognitive, perceptual, and emotional capacities to handle an actual assignment:

> [I]ntelligence itself does not consists of an isolated and sharply differentiated class of cognitive processes. It is not, properly speaking, one form of structuring among others; it is the form of equilibrium towards which all the structures arising out of perception, habit, and elementary sensori-motor mechanisms tend. It must be understood that if intelligence is not a faculty this denial involves a radical functional continuity between the higher forms of thought and the whole mass of lower types of cognitive and motor and adaptation; so intelligence can only be the form of equilibrium towards which these things tend. (Piaget [1950] 2001: 7)

Simmel's (1980) claim that only the present is qualified as "reality" is a sociologically accurate observation, but humans employ their imaginative capacities to transcend temporal determinism. Especially in science, invention, and art, the imaginative capacity is central to the activities. This balancing of sociological necessity and psychological possibilities is nicely captured by Oscar Wilde (cited in O'Doherty 2007: 184), who stated that, "Imagination is a quality given to man to compensate for what he is not, and a sense of humour is provided to console him from what he is." The unbearable temporal determinism of the human condition is overcome on the basis of the capacity to imagine and invent social worlds that do not exist and that will never be, what transfers the human experience beyond what is immediately given. This ambition to create experiences that "go beyond" what is a matter of fact propels the video game development industry and serves as its credo.

Video Games and the Technology of the Fantastic

Lucie Armitt (1996) introduced the concept of "the fantastic" in literature theory, a term that denotes literary works that seek to apprehend what is in excess to what humans experience in everyday life. This literature includes a variety of genres including fantasy, sci-fi, stories about mythical and folklore-based creatures such as werewolves, vampires, and zombies, and experiences that move beyond what is physically possible, for example, shifting the physical embodied form (e.g., Virginia Woolf's *Orlando*) or travelling in time. The culturally and artistically fantastic has always been appealing to large audiences, but it is also criticized for being a form of escapism that ignores day-to-day problems and concerns and is therefore culturally and politically ambiguous. Needless to say, video games are for most part embedded in the technology of the fantastic inasmuch as one of the principal ideas with the video game is to provide experiences that go beyond what everyday life can offer. Such fantasy-oriented games are frequently accompanied by state-of-the-art computer graphics that render such experience visually and aesthetically pleasant, which reinforces the sense of transgressing what Jean Baudrillard referred to as the "desert of the real," the all-too-familiar and grey everyday life that is the human condition and predicament, but also the platform for creation.

Under all conditions, there is a difference between *homo faber*, the creating human who conducts some kind of substantial work, and *homo ludens*, the playing human, who uses the apparatus of video game and its programmed choice alternatives to exploit his or her imaginative capacities. This does not mean that *homo ludens* passively submits to the apparatus of the video game, but that the gamer actively uses the video game to accomplish certain goals that have a benefit for the gamer and the gamer's community. Seen in this view, the video game is not already made and done, now awaiting its users to engage with it to reach a varying degree of excellence, but rather the video game displays performative capacities inasmuch as it becomes what it is through its use. Galloway (2012: 30) examines this performativity concept and says that it is "[q]uite common to understand interfaces less as a surface but as a doorway or window." That is, a vocabulary of "thresholds and transitions" enacts the interface not as "something that appears before you," but rather serves as a "gateway that opens up and allows passage to some place beyond" (Galloway 2012: 30). The interface is thus characterized by its former morpheme, *inter*, rather than the second, *face*; the gamer is located *in medias res*, "in the middle of things," in-between his or her imaginative capacities and the technical apparatus that is the video game. The world of imagination and fantasy of the gamer's mind and the computer code being laid down in the digital artefact is mediated by the individual gamer.

Given these propositions, that the individual's imaginative capacity is always already part of the interaction with any media (e.g., books, movies, visual art, video games) and that the apparatus of, for example, the video game is the canvas onto which the gamer can project such cognitive capacities, the empirical question is then how far the video game can be taken? What are the artistic, aesthetic, and game-concept limits of the media of video game technology and the underlying video game technology. The empirical section of remainder of the chapter will address this issue in more detail.

Developing the Video Game Technology: Novel Applications and New Thinking

One of the issues addressed by the interviewees was how video game is a form of cultural expression that is complicated to define strictly on the basis of the digital media *per se*. Rather than being strictly the digital object that is downloaded through servers and the Internet infrastructure, the video game is part of a wider socio-cultural framework. The director of one of the oldest university-based video game development education programme discussed video games in such terms, as a modality of a broader cultural tradition:

> I consider video games as being part of a broader subculture wherein for instance Anime and Manga is included.[1] Fan fiction is another thing. There

[1] Similarly, Johns (2006: 173) remarks that the Japanese software industry draws largely on *manga* and animation films (*anime*) for inspiration and creative inputs. Furthermore, Johns (2006: 177) proposes that "when placed within the broader context of global flows of culture," the high degree of "interconnection between the video games industry and other cultural industries is especially apparent."

> are quite a bit of sub-cultural expression that are related to video games. (Director of game development education program)

Furthermore, the director argued that video games, as opposed to other cultural media, are closely tied to the competitive component, the game design that structures the experience around the quest for some pre-defined goal or objective. The staging of the video game experience as univocally being a matter of winning in a competitive sphere is limiting the scope wherein the video game technology can be applied, the director argued:

> There are a considerable proportion of culture for children that is not directed towards acquiring facts or expertise in areas, but that essentially is about listening to a story and become engaged in something. With games, that is not really tolerated. Games never acquire that cultural status as such. I think that is deeply problematic. There are for instance quite a bit of low-quality literature for children, but that's okay, simply because it is a book. (Director of game development education program)

As video games are coming of age and maturing, it is a good environment for reconsidering how a video game can be designed and now the gaming experience unfolds. The director called for critical reflection regarding the possibilities of video games:

> It more a matter of how we regard games. How can we use games in new contexts? How can we work with games and young adults, and how can we create an interest for games as a form of creative expression. (Director of game development education program)

In the director's view, thanks to increased expertise in the industry and lower costs for hardware and software, to produce modified versions of past successes or clones thereof is no longer a challenge: "Anyone can produce a 'Call of Duty game,'" the director argued. The real challenge is instead to create new video game genres so that new consumer segments can be attracted: "I think it is a question of providing the video game culture to everyone," the director argued. This ambition to explore new territories for video games, and video game technology more widely, is not so much a matter of supporting market-based operations as it demands actors who are capable of moving beyond familiar concepts (e.g., first-person shooter games), the director said:

> I am not overoptimistic regarding the market ... It may solve [issues] for the larger community but not for the more narrow group ... Sure, we can make games that appeals to 80 percent of the consumers, but the remaining 20 percent, who will serve that segment? I don't see the market being able to solve that. Not as long as a commercial success is the measure of all things. (Director of game development education program)

This line of reasoning, which stipulates that video games have considerable potential to provide entirely new experiences that no other medium can offer, but that this development is complicated to accomplish in a market context wherein only bottom-line results are what matters, was mirrored in the widespread scepticism regarding Triple-A company development activities, almost univocally portrayed as risk-averse and uninventive by indie developers. The director of Incubator #2 argued that Triple-A companies were today basically run like any other business, functionally organized into a hierarchical and essentially bureaucratic structure. As corollary, the daily work took place during office hours, an indication of the "wild years" being over for some of the most commercially and artistically successful studios: "To work for large corporations is a nine-to-five occupation these days," the director of Incubator #2 said. Despite such changes, one of the business counsellors at Incubator #2 said that "many indie developers frown at Triple-A companies" (Business Counsellor #2, Video Game development Incubator #3). The two business counsellors argued that this dismissive view was partially explained on the basis of immaturity and a lack of business experience in the indie developer community, but also recognized that the strategy in Triple-A companies, to reproduce past successes with additional features and modified graphics, was regarded as a form of calculated risk-aversion among ambitious indie developers. The CEO of the indie development company C expressed such concerns, especially since he did not regard their principal output, their games, as particularly engaging:

> There is not so much innovation in Triple-A development work. I have tried to play those game. Overall, I am not so intrigued because I think they are quite boring. That is because they always look the same. (CEO, Company C)

"Every single game feels like the last one, but in new colours," he continued. The inability to create new video games is ultimately a matter of an unwillingness to take risks, the CEO argued: "Triple-A studios have become more risk averse recently ... They do not expose themselves to risks. They only make safe bets" (CEO, Company C). While the CEO understood that larger studios, at times hiring hundreds of developers and employees and actively engaging with and serving a sizeable gamer community, could no longer ignore previous successes to pursue entirely new development activities, the predicament of Triple-A companies is precisely this inability to maintain the indie developer's explorative ambition and innovative capacities when being bestowed with commercial successes. To some extent, the success of a video game developer also marks the end of its innovative period, this narrative suggested. In contrast, the CEO argued, "the innovations always emerge on the indie scene. That is where the artistic ambitions are."

The indie developers in Company B argued that the primary reason for applying for a job position in a Triple-A company is the relative economic safety that such a career choice entails: "It's a matter of security [to choose to work in a Triple-A company]. I can fully understand this choice of career" (Indie Developer #2, Company B). Unfortunately, this preference for economic security, undoubtedly an "appealing feature" of the work in Indie Developer #1's (Company B) view, still has "little to do with game development." In the indie developers' view, the individual developer has to make a trade-off choice between economic security and the freedom to create: Triple-A developers "suffer from this feeling that 'I cannot be creative and accomplish what I want,'" Indie Developer #2 (Company B) stated. Business Counsellor #1 (Video Game Development Incubator #2) expressed these concerns in terms of being a consequence of the larger size of the functionally organized Triple-A company, which develops new video games as a form of modularized process, wherein each development team only oversees a smaller component of the entire digital object:

> Everyone emphasizes the disadvantages of large corporations. They are too demanding and boring, and all too bureaucratic. If you ask company representatives, no one wants to employ like ninety [employees] but would prefer like 20. (Business Counsellor #1, Video Game Development Incubator #2)

One of the consequences from this growth of the Triple-A companies is that they may maintain contacts with the indie scene and indie developers to get a sense of what is happening in the creative fringe of the industry. On the other hand, indie developers appeared to be less intrigued by such collaborative activities beyond the prospect of being funded by the cash-rich Triple-A developers: "Triple-A companies may feel they want more contact with indies, whereas indies does not necessarily share such interests," Indie Developer #1 (Company B) said.

The Skills Needed to Conceive of New Game Applications and genres

One lingering question is to what extent video game development is a function of creativity. For many interviewees, creativity is the *sine qua non* for all video game development activities, but more experienced interviewees, with a somewhat broader overview of the industry, rendered the question of creativity more complex. First of all, as one of the incubator directors argued (Video Game Development Incubator #2), "it is difficult to claim what creativity is in this industry." In his view, indie developers are all too narrowly focused on honouring their own video game experiences to be able to take a broader and more comprehensive view of video game development as a business creation activity and business practice:

> In many cases, your own gaming experience matters for you. In most cases, they are hardcore gamers to start with. You only wants to accomplish what you already like. It is hard to claim that is an innovative mindset. There are preciously few individual who has this genuine talent for creativity and can use new technology to create something entirely new ... Is there a value in being innovative and creative? Not necessarily so! (Director, Video Game Development Incubator #2)

Furthermore, the CEO of the commercially successful indie development company C argued that creativity cannot be examined in isolation from the broader business activities and industry structure. In his experience, there are for most part a "'business-clever' solution" and a "the creative solution" to a specific problem. Unfortunately, these two solutions "rarely coincide—they never converge," the CEO said. Furthermore, it is a leadership and group-based (in smaller companies, with fewer employees enabling more direct communication) challenge to strike a balance between business interests and creative ambitions, being two oscillating sinus curves that rarely converge: "I'd say that it is a matter of day-to-day mood. At times, you get energized by creative inspiration and tend to forget about the business issues. Then it is just so inspiring to create and create" (CEO, Company C). The CEO told a long story of how the company's first hit, developed for PC, was intended to be transformed into mobile phone version, a business decision that first appeared to be a "no brainer," but that eventually proved to be a tormenting experience for the developers as the transition from the one medium to the other demanded considerably more work than anticipated. This allegedly "uncreative work" drained the team of energy and ambition, and ultimately delayed the development of the studio's second video game. In the end, the CEO regretted making the business decision that appeared to be a safe bet. If nothing else, this story is supportive of the claim of the indie developer in Company H, who remarked that "there's a huge difference between what is fun to play, and what is fun to develop. These are two different actions."

In contrast to this view, wherein creativity is defined as the capacity to realize market potentials, and to materialize commercially successful video games, several of the indie developers argued that creativity could in fact be defined in more self-referential terms, outside of business metrics and downloading statistics. Several interviewees committed time to define generic qualities of what they regarded as qualified games. The CEO and co-founder of Indie Company D argued that what characterized all innovative games is what he referred to as a "hook"—a music production term, which denotes a feature of the song that captures the listener's attention, as in the case of catchy chorus, guitar lick, or baseline, or some good bridge between sections in a song: "There got to be some hook in the game, something that is appealing" (CEO and Founder, Indie Company D). The CEO also argued that in order to generate a commercially successful game, the gamers need to include some central components in the game design from previous games: "To make something popular, there need to be 50 percent old and 50 percent new things, to make it stick with the users," the CEO said (Indie Company D). The indie developer in Company I argued that what characterizes all good video games is the capacity of the developers to integrate diverse gaming mechanisms and functions into a coherent, functional, and seamless unity, wherein all components assist each other to enhance the gaming experience:

> The one single thing I like best about games is this totality composed of individual components. Games that have successfully managed to combine a unified aesthetic, wherein you can notice how sound and image and text and programming have been subject to much effort. Everything comes together, weaved into a singular thing. (Indie developer, Company I)

Other indie developers shared this image of "the perfect game" as a *multiplicity*, a functional whole composed of discrete parts: The developer in Company K listed a handful of qualifying criteria: "[The game needs] a certain artistic leverage, stringency, lacks bugs, to be beautiful ... You want to get the feeling that 'This is as good as it gets.' You have reached your peak performance" (Indie developer, Company K). The developer in Company M added that games also need language translations that were credible in the eyes of local gamers, a relatively substantial cost for the developers: "There are many components [in good games]. You need music, sound effects, a good story, and good translations in German, French, Spanish, and Italian" (Indie developer, Company M). The developer in Company L defined a good game in ostensive terms, that is, as something that could be pointed out whenever it appears, but being more complicated to define in propositional terms:

Q: So what is a 'good game,' for you?
A: Something that gives you a new experience, I would say ... Nothing I can put the finger on. But I know when I have a good time gaming and when I do not. (Indie developer, Company L)

Based on this proposition—games are assemblages—the indie developers argued that there are in fact universal qualities that can be examined in rather objective terms when, for example, reviewing a video game:

> There are certain universal qualities when it comes to all types of games. For instance, to have good feedback mechanisms. If I push a button, I need to understand that something happened. The menus need to be easy to understand so that I don't feel lost when opening a gamer. Nice sound. (Indie developer, Company H)

Stipulated performance criteria and an intimate understanding of what ultimately makes a game appealing do still not explain *how* new gaming ideas and concepts are established. Neither can developers for most part pin down what makes certain games so mesmerizing that gamers commit a considerable proportion of their lives to them. Several developers mused about the nature of these skills. In many cases, this "it factor" in the video games was explained on the basis of residual factors such as the developer's "personality" and similar constructs. The indie developer in Company F preferred to introduce the term "emotions" (and "emotionality") to explain why he considered his games to be relatively commercially successful:

> My biggest advantage is that I am driven by emotions and can build or construct emotional tableaus [in the games]—to put it like that. If you look at [the video game] and disassemble it, and examine the graphics and all the components, there's nothing special to be found. But I have noticed that the cake I have made, that is something special, right? (Indie developer, Company F)

The developer in Company M shared this view that personality or similar constructs matter, and predicted that the branding of individual studios would become more accentuated in the future: "I think people increasingly appreciate individual studios. They can even consider buying a game more than once when it is released on different platforms, simply because they appreciate the studio." Based on this evidence and his genuine developer experience, the developer advised neophytes to find their own idiom rather than to imitate current industry activities: "You need to try to find your own way. To not be too distracted by what others do. You cannot just imitate" (Indie developer, Company M).

The ability to express emotional experiences via the complex digital medium of the video game was here portrayed as a personal competence. More largely, the indie developer was sceptical regarding the possibilities to formalize and theorize the game development process in propositional terms, at least in terms of reaching into the interiority of human imagination. The indie developer in Company F used the concepts of design and design work to convey this sense of an indeterminable quality in the development work: "I have read many design books, and most of it is just mumbo jumbo ... It is hard to find something that works. Even in the case where something works, it is hard to fully understand why that is the case" (Indie developer, Company F). In some cases, the informants spoke about new ideas for games as something that merely spring to mind during everyday activities. Such developers tended to think of the creative work to generate new ideas as partially a sub-conscious process, moments wherein new thinking appeared in the mind, like an angel passing through a room, as the saying has it:

> I get an incredible amount of gaming ideas ... Every time I take a shower there's something popping up. If I sit in my bed, I write down all my gaming

> ideas. I have this notebook where I keep all my scribblings regarding gaming ideas. (Indie developer, Company M)

Another residual factor to consider in relation to what makes games appealing is "personality," a form of signature quality that carries through all the technological systems and devices being involved in the video game development process. "Generally speaking, regarding marketing and Youtube and all such things, it seems like personality actually makes a difference. That is something I have always felt since I was a kid. Wouldn't personality matter in creative work?" the indie developer (Company F) asked. In this view, it is complicated and costly to define in more formal terms what qualities the video game developer needs to demonstrate, but the difference between an emotionally engaging and intellectually intriguing game and games that do not induce this sense of commitment nevertheless remains. How to exploit this distinction between the spectacular and the more average game remains to be determined, and consequently is a managerial concern and business potential to be further explored.

New Thinking and New Ideas as the Driver of Innovation

The science and technology literature indicates that innovation is likely to emerge in the fringes of a specific field. In, for example, the domain of music production and performance, new music instruments—Bijsterveld and Schulp (2004) use the term *organology*, "the study and knowledge of musical instruments"—are invented by creative individuals whom themselves believe they have little status to defend or risk to lose. Such individuals are part of the "creative marginality" of a field, that is, they are skilled, yet marginal figures (in organology, this group includes music-teachers, performers-composers, etc.) who need to demonstrate a "mixture of audacity and traditionalism" (Bijsterveld and Schulp 2004: 667). Famous instruments that combine new technology and traditional music instrument components include the theremin, the world's first electronic instrument, displayed at New York Metropolitan Opera in January 1927, where its Russian inventor Leon Theremin played a series of popular songs including Franz Schubert's "Ave Maria" on his eponymous instrument (Sconce 2000: 119). Another more recent case is the Moog synthesizer developer by Robert Moog from the mid-1960s, and being demonstrated at the pop festival in Monterey in 1967 (Pinch and Trocco 2002). Pinch and Trocco (2002: 308) portray the synthesizer as a "liminal entity," developed in-between traditional music production and electric engineering.

In a similar manner, innovation in video game development was expected to emerge from its margins. The director of the game development programme argued that one of the challenges for the industry was the conservatism of the hardcore gamer community, who claims the authority to police and discipline the gamer community and to define what a true game and a gamer are:

> The problem is that there is always someone who claim the right to point out who's a gamer. What types of games you play. In many cases, it is a matter of being a man … At the same time, there are many people sitting someplace and playing games and think, 'I am not that much of a gamer.' 'But I can see how you play Candy Crush!' 'Yes, but is that a game?' 'Yes!' (Director of game development education program)

This may sound like a marginal concern, but the hardcore gamers in many cases quite aggressively advocated their worldview and interests, which at times resulted in long-standing disputes and evidence of intolerable behaviour in, for example, web forums. Furthermore, also inside the community of video game developers, there were attitudes that served to exclude certain groups, or that acted against their interests, some informants argued. The CEO of Company E was concerned that casual games, video games developed for the mobile phone platform, were lowly rated in terms of status among many mainstream developers[2]: "There's no respect for

[2] Even though indie developers take pride in venturing beyond the point that Triple-A developers regard as financially sound projects, causal games being played on mobile media such as smartphones or tablets have relatively lower prestige among indie developers than other game genres. One explanation may be that the current generation of indie developers was raised prior to the introduction of hand-held devices, during what Johns (2006) calls the "console era," and therefore does not fully recognize the sophistication of casual games. Another condition pertaining to the status of causal games is that "[c]asual games are often played by 'bodies-in-waiting,'" Keogh (2015: 157) writes. A significant proportion of video game developers are themselves committed gamers, but the casual game genres invite also non-conventional gamers, who regard video games as a form of light entertainment, which also provides the benefit of coming in handy during shorter periods of waiting, say, when communing. This "gaming practice" may deviate from the full commitment of the hardcore gamer community. Ultimately, Keogh (2015: 157–158) proposes, causal games serve to re-

mobile games," she said. The director of the university education programme argued that in order to embrace a broader and more inclusive view of video games, and to find new application for video game technology, there is a need for a fruitful debate within the industry and with other sectors of the culture sector. The director compared video game development with the music industry, hosting a considerable degree of diversity and a variety of genres:

> [Video games] is a platform. Just as in the case of music, there is much possibilities for variety. Music is based on certain parameters that taken together make music what it is. But music can be many different things. There are narrow genres, and there's popular genres. This goes for all forms of cultural expression, actually. (Director of game development education program)

The director identified a challenge in developing the video game industry in analogy with music production inasmuch as there are barriers that need to be passed to make other culture industry workers see the potential of the video game: "Not everything in the gaming culture is super-interesting if you arrive from other culture disciplines" (Director of game development education program). Several of the more experienced indie developers, now in their early to mid-forties, were concerned with how indie games have failed to fully exploit its artistic potential as the industry has increasingly endorsed a business ethos. "In the past, you could see this wave of attempts to do small and beautiful games. It feels like everyone has left that path. It is a bit boring [now]," the developer in Company K said. The developer in Company L recalled that in the "early days of Indie" more "characters" were attracted, people advertising their own idiosyncratic views of video games as cultural expression: "In the beginning," the developer said, "there were more eccentric people around, no doubt. These were quite funny characters" (Indie developer, Company L): "[The indie concept] has changed over the years. In the past, there was less emphasize on money in a way. The creative part was what mattered." The developer in Company K argued that the emphasis on commercial interests tends to promote the development of "silly devices" that could become Internet memes and hits on the global scale:

define gaming and thus pose a threat to the "outsider" identity of certain gamer communities: "Traditionally an outsider identity held by geeks and hackers as a badge of honour, videogames are now mainstream and ubiquitous, played on trains by businessmen and on computers by parents and on airplanes by small children" (Keogh 2015: 157–158).

> It is this trend that what you do is just silly devices. I am more interested in artistic and serious activities. If you sit down to express something more personal than to do 'The Donald Trump Simulator' [it takes more effort] … I am not so keen on helping such companies. But people who do interesting stuff, I am willing to support. (Indie developer, Company K)

At the same time as the limited interest for video games in other culture sectors was deplored, the director of the video game development education programme anticipated a variety of areas wherein video game technology could be exploited in meaningful ways. The director referred to one of her colleagues who ran a "project about cultural heritage" wherein video game technology was included to provide a new form of cultural experience. "There are certain qualities in video games that are very efficient to combine with other types of products," the director claimed.

Gamification and Its Uses

The concept of gamification has been discussed frequently in both the industry and in the scholarly literature.[3] The Indie developer in Company

[3] The scholarly literature on gamification will not be subject to any comprehensive review in this volume. It is still worth noting that the debate regarding the value of and possibilities for gamification—the use of video game technology for other purposes than mere entertainment, say, education and training purposes—is disputed. Scholars such as Robson et al. (2016) provide both "positive" and "negative" cases of gamification, but the basic assumption is that gamification is a potential that can be realized with net economic welfare following. Other commentators are more sceptical. Dale (2014: 83. Original emphasis omitted) defines gamification quite broadly as "the use of game thinking and game mechanics to engage users and solve problems." The gamification market has grown considerably and has been estimated (in 2014) to be worth £3.4 billion ($5.5 billion) by 2018 (Dale 2014: 82). Sceptical commentators such as Woodcock and Johnson (2018: 543) discriminate between what they refer to as "gamification-from-above" and "gamification-from-below," wherein the former represents the use of game technology to achieve already stipulated goals. Woodcock and Johnson (2018: 543) explain this distinction in greater detail:

> Gamification-from-above is the imposition of systems of regulation, surveillance and standardization upon aspects of everyday life, through forms of interaction and feedback drawn from *games* (*ludus*) but severed from their original *playful* (*paidia*) contexts. By contrast, gamification-from-below represents a true gamification of everyday life through the subversion, corruption and mockery-making of activities considered 'serious.' (Woodcock and Johnson 2018: 543)

In this view, an uncritical application of gamification-from-above means that "game elements" are imposed on people, "purporting to improve their experiences without genuine engagement or dialogue" (Woodcock and Johnson 2018: 547). Under such conditions, gamification

I had a firm belief in the relevance of gaming technology in the future society, and argued that gamification is one among many ways that gaming technology can serve other ends than to merely entertain. This line of reasoning was tangential to existential conditions of contemporary

is treated, not entirely unlike other media such as digital technologies, as "an inherently and unproblematically *progressive* force," Woodcock and Johnson (2018: 543) argue. Other commentators have argued that gamification applications that are introduced to serve pre-defined managerial interests easily result in conformism and generate other unintended consequences, or consequences inconsistent with formally acclaimed qualities of gamification and games more generally. For instance, DeWinter et al. (2014: 116) examine the case of what its proponents refer to as "lean training," wherein a trivial case of how to instruct a group of trainees how to draw a pig illustrates the concern with the gamification-from-above model:

> In this exercise, all participants are asked to draw a pig in a prescribed amount of time, and the skill levels range from excellent to very bad. Then the group is given a set of instructions to draw a pig, such as 'draw a circle,' and 'draw a sideways 3 for the ears'. At the end of this process, everyone's pigs look similar, and this norms the group. What is sacrificed is the outliers, which means that the people who were excellent are also normed to the group. (DeWinter et al. 2014: 116)

In the end, such uses of gamification to impose standards and to eliminate outliers on the basis of group decisions regarding tolerable performance are indicative of the unintended consequences of Woodcock and Johnson's (2018) gamification-from-above concept. In the end, regardless of the praise and acclaims of the use of games and other forms of play in working life settings, DeWinter et al. (2014: 123) contend that play and games tend to converge towards economic and financially defined ends, which make play far less "free" and "creative" as early proponents of play and games claim: "[P]lay belongs to games, games belong to algorithms and algorithms represent the intellectual and manual labour processes of high-stakes economics" (DeWinter et al. 2014: 123).

Rosenblat and Stark's (2016) study of the algorithm-based monitoring of Uber drivers is an illustrative case of DeWinter et al. (2014) point. Rosenblat and Stark (2016) explicitly speak about this line of work as a form of "algorithmic labour." "Through tools such as dynamic, algorithmic pricing and a number of other elements of the Uber application's design, Uber is empowered via information and power asymmetries to effect conditions of soft control, affective labor, and gamified patterns of worker engagement on its drivers," Rosenblat and Stark (2016: 3759) write. Rather than using direct disciplinary measures on drivers, the Uber business model uses weekly performance metrics that reveal how well Uber drivers conform towards the behaviour and/or performance of other drivers. As such statistics are also revealed to presumptive Uber customers, the algorithm-based control has homogenizing effects that, if nothing else, undermine the claim that Uber drivers represent a class of entrepreneurs, simply because there is little room for entrepreneurial decisions as the algorithm-based model incentivizes Uber drivers to provide "a standardized service" (Rosenblat and Stark 2016: 3772). In the end, the gamification element in the Uber business model is distinctively and unambiguously a case of gamification-from-above inasmuch as Uber drivers are actively encouraged to participate in game-like competition that is supposed to be engaging and fun, but the divers themselves are not invited to participate in the creation of the rules of the game they eventually submit to.

everyday life, wherein basic elementary needs were for most parts already satisficed, the developer argued:

> I believe games will be extremely relevant in the future ... Already today, we are less and less dependent on [satisfying] our basic needs. Like we need to get food, or else we die, we need to get access to water, or else we die, we need a house, or else we die, and we need to procreate, or else we die. These demands are there, but they are almost gone today. I think this trend will continue. So what can we do it our lives then? We can already today largely design our own worlds. (Indie developer, Company I)

In the developer's view, the concept of gamification is "a fairly threadbare term," but he still believed that "there are projects wherein games are needed." For instance, the developer explained some of the details of a project, finance by the EU, where the project co-workers use gaming technology to help younger children cope with the experience of undergoing MRI scanning, an advanced medical visualization technology. The developer argued that gamification is commonly considered in terms of creating new possibilities for on-the-job training and similar activities, that is, gaming technologies are used to create a situation that demands cognitive engagement and induces emotional responses from the gamer. In such cases, gamification generates a certain level of (allegedly) positive stress as gamers know they are competing over something, and are subject to monitoring and assessment, in most cases in metric terms. But the same gaming technologies can also be used to accomplish other, relatively limitedly documented experiences, such as gaming experiences that are relaxing and otherwise rewarding through other means than to participate in competitive games. Under all conditions and regardless of what ends gamification eventually serves, video games are "an integral part of society, what we currently breathe," the Indie developer argued. This does not mean that all types and classes of games are equally efficient or widely recognized. The developers referred to experiences from developing and using Virtual Reality (VR) technology,[4] being hyped for more than two decades as the

[4] In scholarly circles, Virtual Reality (VR) technology was introduced in the early 1990s as the latest thrust in visual media technology. Steuer (1992: 74) defines virtual reality as the "[e]lectronic simulations of environments via head-mounted eye googles and wired clothing enabling the end user to interact in realistic three-dimensional situations." A few years later, Zettl (1996: 86) defined VR as "a computer-generated three-dimensional image and stereo sound that displays events (objects and environments) and that is interactive with the user."

future of digital media, as being essentially disappointing, not the least in terms of how long gamers are able to participate in this type of games or gaming experiences in comparison to more regular PC or console games:

> The VR hype a few years back [is now over] It wasn't exactly what people thought it was. It's a bit overrated. Sooner or later, that will be the big thing, but the technology is not yet fully developed. It is still quite expensive. The technology demands too much space and you need a quite powerful computer to run it. (Indie developer, Company G)

Even though the developer is sceptical regarding the current VR technology, he is characteristically optimistic regarding future technologies being able to solve what today are treated as shortcomings of video games. The firm belief in technology as the solution to a variety of social and economic malaises tends to stand strong even among sceptical commentators.

By the end of the day, a more progressive view of what gaming technology can accomplish and as what gradually merge with other cultural practices and cultural and artistic expression is far from uncontroversial among,

In this case, Zettl (1996: 86) adds, "interactivity means that we change from mere observers or viewers to event participants." As such, the gamer exercises some control over "the event display" (Zettl 1996: 86). By and large, VR was introduced and marketed as an "immersive" visual medium, which means that the visual medium "submerges the perceptual system of the user in virtual stimuli" (Biocca 1992: 25). More simply put, "The more the system captivates the senses and blocks out stimuli from the physical world, the more the system is considered immersive," Biocca (1992: 25) writes. Steuer (1992: 75) uses the term *presence* to underline that VR is not primarily the technological apparatus that needs to be assembled and integrated into a functional unity, but being a matter of a "human experience." Presence here means the "the sense of being in an environment," with which the subject interacts (Steuer 1992: 75. Original emphasis omitted).

The term "presence" underlines that VR technology is part of a long tradition of visual media, best characterized as "technologies of illusion," whose purpose is "to convince the viewer that he or she is occupying the same visual spaces as the object in view" (Bolter 1996: 113). The perspectival *trompe l'oeil* paintings of the Renaissance period thus differ in degree rather than in kind from contemporary VR technology. Despite Steuer's (1992) ambition to release the VR technology from the physical devices that constitute the medium, VR has been consistently associated with the failure to provide a sufficiently immersive, functional, and not the least affordable technology so that the VR promise can materialize. The technology has been successfully implemented in various forms of training, say, invasive surgery (e.g., Gallagher and Cates 2004), but the technology has, on balance, failed to live up to the hype of the early 1990s. Consequently, few of the indie developers and other video game industry functionaries addressed VR as a serious contestant to, for example, PC or console-based video games.

for example, hardcore gamer. This group tends to fiercely resist perceived threats against status quo. Also more moderate developers tend to regard video games as a cultural expression in its own kind, albeit to date primarily associated with mere entertainment, adolescent amusements, and not sufficiently recognized in high-brow segments of the culture industry. For instance, indie developer and culture sector entrepreneur expressed the concern that video games should not be too closely associated with gambling, as that was "not a positive thing." For this informant, the "line of demarcation" between economic interests and gaming was important to maintain to ensure the integrity of video game development. Also the developer in Company M shared this concern regarding what he referred to as "casino games":

Q: Is there something you wouldn't like to do?
A: Well, casino games, work on one of all these gambling sites on the Internet.
Q: Why is that?
A: I really don't know. There's a certain shame about all these damn commercials everywhere. And there is little innovation. Only this cool, flashing design. The games are the same being used since the 19th century. (Indie developer, Company M)

Certain indie developers did not want to participate in activities they did not approve for ethical or creative reasons, and the quickly expanding web-based casino game business was clearly outside of the indie developer's immediate interest.

Business Concerns and Creative Inspiration in Video Game Development

Several of the interviewees argued that video game development is like any other form of cultural production, a field wherein original ideas and concept are included in new development work activities. As a consequence, indie developers constantly browse web pages and attend game jams, workshops, and conventions in their relentless search for new and inspiring ideas. "We poach concepts all the time: 'We have this design problem, how can we handle that? Where are those who did this previously? Let's do it like this and use this specific solution' To be inspired by others is a prerequisite for being creative," the CEO (Company C) declared. By and large, creativity was regarded as being important, albeit in many cases indirectly and not in ways that external observers may intuitively believe, but even more important is the passionate commitment to the development work. Indie Developer #1 in Company B, for instance, argued that what he and his colleague cared for is "the curious stuff that that is not exactly mainstream." He continued: "We are always intrigued by all that. But we need to consider to what extent we can afford to develop it" (Indie Developer #1, Company B). This latter passage is indicative of what several of the interviewees argued was the lost potential of the otherwise inventive and adventurous indie community, the difficulty to learn how costs and benefits are part of any business venture and how such conditions inevitably influence the development work. The director of incubator #2 expressed some of his grievances regarding the immaturity of some of the indie developers he had encountered over the years, and especially their inability and unwillingness to transcend their adolescent fascination for the video games *per se*:

> To let your daydream and imaginative capacity guide you, there's no value in that. It is only expensive. You cannot afford that attitude in a start-up. What really distinguishes the winners are their capacity to act strategically. To abandon relations, close doors, choose a direction. (Director, Video Game Development Incubator #2)

To learn to act strategically was thus the primary recommendation that the director gave to aspiring indie developers.

The two business partners in indie development company B had learned the lesson to not let their personal preferences and ideals overshadow development decisions, but to make pragmatic decisions that targeted what is possible to accomplish within stipulated budgets and planning horizons: "We had these ambitious ideas to include various emotions, not previously explored, in a [forthcoming] game ... But we dropped that idea. We did this action games with much blood and monsters" (Indie Developer #1, Company B). This ability to drop early ideas is an important part of the development process, and it helps the developers to learn from the process. The historical record reveals that developing games is a matter of failing, yet being able to continue the work despite setbacks until the development team strike gold:

> By experience, we know this is a craft. Your third, fourth, fifth game [may be profitable]. By then you have learned to know the market, what people appreciate, and how to develop the game. The games become better over time. You can just as well develop your first games, dump them, and then move on. The craft work is a very important component. (Director, Video Game Development Incubator #2)

Such scenarios may appear discouraging for aspiring developers, but in many cases, the passionate commitment to video game development helps to overcome such rational reactions to stated facts. Not the least the flourishing indie development activities, now a cottage industry of its own, are indicative of this ambition and wiliness to endure uncertainty and to work against better odds.

Summary and Conclusion

Video game developers repeat time and again that video game development is in fact not as easy as laypersons may believe. Being a committed gamer is one thing, and to actually develop a complex video game is another, it was remarked. Furthermore, the video game as such is an assemblage of heterogeneous components that need to be brought together into functional unity: The game narrative, graphics, game mechanics, and music need to blend seamlessly to create a gaming experience wherein few glitches are detected by the hyper-attentive end-users. At the same time, being able to develop existing ideas is one skill, admirable in itself, but the professional ideology emphasizes the capacity to participate in second-order thinking, to formulate new ideas regarding what video games are, and how gaming technology can be applied in new ways and settings. Video games were originally constructed as a form of technology of the fantastic, wherein escapism remains an important component, which renders video games as a technology of the self (as discussed by Michel Foucault) wherein an all too familiar everyday life can be transformed into an adventure. While developers take pride in such accomplishments, some interviewees address their concern that the game design options are after all too limited, too much geared towards certain aesthetic expressions and competitive situations in particular. As video games can be basically anything the developer wants them to be, there is consequently room for more aesthetically appealing games and gaming experiences, but the challenge is to identify the community that appreciates this category of work. When this is done, not the least supported by a new generation of gamers (e.g., female or middle-age gamers), not of necessity been raised playing video games, there may be a larger variety of possibilities for video game developers. The genre of first-person shooter games is the typical case of an adolescent, competition-oriented, and markedly violent category of video games, the type of game being a concern for generations of regulators, worried parents, crusaders, and others who have been vocal regarding alleged risks of video gaming. The visionaries in developer community anticipate an industry wherein such "genre games" (in analogy with the film industry vocabulary) may be complemented by games and gaming experiences that are more aesthetic in orientation, or being even curated by more conventional artists and creatives of all sorts, collaborating with developers. Much of this work already exists, but constitute the fringe of the indie scene, but arguably being in a stage wherein new audiences are targeted.

References

Armitt, L. (1996). *Theorizing the fantastic*. London: Arnold.

Bachelard, G. (1987). *On poetic imagination and reverie*. Dallas: Springer.

Beller, J. (2006). *The cinematic mode of production: Attention economy and the society of the spectacle*. Duke Hanover: Dartmouth College Press.

Bellow, S. (2015a). Where do we go from here? The future of fiction. In S. Bellow (Ed.), *Simply too much to think about: Collected nonfiction* (pp. 121–130). New York: Penguin.

Bellow, S. (2015b). Distraction of the fiction writer. In S. Bellow (Ed.), *Simply too much to think about: Collected nonfiction* (pp. 76–91). New York: Penguin.

Bijsterveld, K., & Schulp, M. (2004). Breaking into a world of perfection: Innovation in today's classical musical instruments. *Social Studies of Science, 34*(5), 649–674.

Biocca, F. (1992). Virtual reality technology: A tutorial. *Journal of Communication, 42*(4), 23–74.

Blake, E. C. (2003). Zograscopes, virtual reality, and the mapping of polite society in eighteenth-century England. In L. Gitelman & G. B. Pingree (Eds.), *New media, 1940–1915* (pp. 1–30). Cambridge and London: The MIT Press.

Bolter, D. J. (1996). Virtual reality and the redefinition of self. In L. Strate, R. Jacobson, & S. B. Gibson (Eds.), *Communication and cyberspace: Social interaction in an electronic environment* (pp. 105–119). Cresskill: Hampton Press.

Connolly, C. (1945). *The condemned playground: Essays 1927–1944*. London: Routledge.
Crary, J. (1990). *Techniques of the observer: On vision and modernity in the nineteenth century*. Cambridge and London: The MIT Press.
Crary, J. (1995). Unbinding vision: Manet and the attentive observer in the late nineteenth century. In L. Carney & V. R. Schwartz (Eds.), *Cinema and the invention of modern life* (pp. 46–71). Berkeley: University of California Press.
Crary, J. (1999). *Suspensions of perception: Attention, spectacle, and modern culture*. Cambridge and London: The MIT Press.
Dale, S. (2014). Gamification: Making work fun, or making fun of work? *Business Information Review, 31*(2), 82–90.
DeWinter, J., Kocurek, C. A., & Nichols, R. (2014). Taylorism 2.0: Gamification, scientific management and the capitalist appropriation of play. *Journal of Gaming and Virtual Worlds, 6*(2), 109–127.
Galloway, A. R. (2012). *The interface effect*. Cambridge and Malden: Polity.
Gallagher, A., & Cates, C. (2004). Virtual reality training for the operating room and cardiac catheterisation laboratory. *The Lancet, 364*, 1538–1540.
Galloway, A. R., & Thacker, E. (2007). *The exploit: A theory of networks*. Minneapolis and London: The University of Minnesota Press.
Flusser, V. ([1983] 2000). *Towards a philosophy of photography*. London: Reaktion Books.
Flusser, V. ([1987] 2011a). *Into the universe of technical images?* (N. A. Roth, Trans.). Minneapolis and London: The University of Minnesota Press.
Flusser, V. ([1987] 2011b). *Does writing have a future?* (N. A. Roth, Trans.). Minneapolis and London: The University of Minnesota Press.
Hayles, N. K. (2006). Traumas of code. *Critical Inquiry, 33*(Autumn), 136–157.
James, W. ([1890] 1950). *Principles of psychology* (Vol. 1). New York: Dover.
Johns, J. (2006). Video games production networks: Value capture, power relations and embeddedness. *Journal of Economic Geography, 6*(2), 151–180.
Keogh, B. (2015). Between Triple-A, indie, casual, and DIY. In K. Oakley & J. O'Connor (Eds.), *The Routledge companion to the cultural industries* (pp. 152–162). Routledge.
Leppert, R. (1996). *Art and the committed eye: The cultural foundations of imaginary*. Boulder: Westview Press.
O'Doherty, D. P. (2007). Heidegger's unfunny and the academic text: Organization analysis on the blink. In R. Westwood & C. Rhodes (Eds.), *Humour, work and organization* (pp. 180–203). London and New York: Routledge.
Piaget, J. ([1950] 2001). *The psychology of intelligence*. London and New York: Routledge.
Pinch, T., & Trocco, F. (2002). *Analog days: The invention and impact of the Moog synthesizer*. Cambridge and London: Harvard University Press.

Robson, K., Plangger, K., Kietzmann, J. H., McCarthy, I., & Pitt, L. (2016). Game on: Engaging customers and employees through gamification. *Business Horizons, 59*(1), 29–36.

Rosenblat, A., & Stark, L. (2016). Algorithmic labour and information asymmetries: A case study of Uber's drivers. *International Journal of Communication, 10*, 3758–3784.

Schiavo, L. B. (2003). From phantom image to perfect vision: Physiological optics, commercial photography, and the popularization of the stereoscope. In L. Gitelman & G. B. Pingree (Eds.), *New media, 1940–1915* (pp. 113–138). Cambridge and London: The MIT Press.

Sconce, J. (2000). *Haunted media: Electronic presence from telegraphy to television.* Durham and London: Duke University Press.

Simmel, G. (1980). *Essays on interpretation in social sciences.* Manchester: Manchester University Press.

Steuer, J. (1992). Defining virtual reality: Dimensions determining telepresence. *Journal of Communication, 42*(4), 73–93.

Vygotsky, L. S. (1971). *The psychology of art.* Cambridge: The MIT Press.

Vygotsky, L. S. (1978). *Mind in society: The development of higher psychological processes* (M. Cole, V. John-Steiner, S. Scribner, E. Souberman, Eds.). Cambridge and London: Harvard University Press.

Woodcock, J., & Johnson, M. R. (2018). Gamification: What it is, and how to fight it. *The Sociological Review, 66*(3), 542–558.

Zettl, H. (1996). Back in Plato's cave: Virtual reality. In L. Strate, R. Jacobson, & S. B. Gibson (Eds.), *Communication and cyberspace: Social interaction in an electronic environment* (pp. 83–94). Cresskill, NJ: Hampton Press.

CHAPTER 8

Passionate Production in the Shadow of the Market: The Prospects of Innovation-Led Growth

Introduction

The popular literature on video game development is at times conspicuously hyperbolic regarding the role of video games and its projected role in a future society. McGonigal (2011: 4. Emphasis in the original) justifies the role of video games on strictly instrumental arguments: "The truth is this: in today's society, computer and video games are fulfilling *genuine human needs* that the real world is currently unable to satisfy." This is an unconvincing argument as any social practice or purchase decision can recursively be justified on the basis of some purportedly endogenously given "genuine human needs" that the proponent of the current practice believes need to be honoured. Anyway, advocacy of certain practices as they are confirmed on the basis of empirical evidence may be one line of argument, and prediction about the future is another thing. Here, McGonigal's (2011: 10) enthusiasm is equally pronounced: "[I] look forward and I see a future in which games ... are explicitly designed to improve quality of life, to prevent suffering, and to create real, widespread happiness." Being optimistic is in many ways an admirable quality, but overoptimistic predictions oftentimes reveal an incapacity of the spokesperson *ex post facto* to recognize and effectively process, for example, discordant data, data that appears to be inconsistent with stipulated analytical models and/or desirable outcomes. Furthermore, when predictions fail and the spokesperson becomes anxious to defend an inaccurate analytical model, only open-ended and fuzzy prophecies about what may happen in

A. Styhre, *Indie Video Game Development Work*,
https://doi.org/10.1007/978-3-030-45545-3_8

some future, near or distant, and given certain conditions, remain. As such prophecies are considerably less useful for, for example, policy makers and legislative entities, and not so impressive for audiences that may not share a commitment to the underlying analytical model, the slippery slope from accurate predictions to more lofty but imprecise prophecies reveals the inadequacy of the analytical model being endorsed.

The key point here is not to discount McGonigal's (2011) faith in video games as such (after all, video games may correspond to defined human needs, and it is not unreasonable to assume that gaming makes people happy, at last some people and when they dedicate a sound proportion of the time to it), but to stress that virtually all new social practices may be subject to expectations that are complicated to live up to. Video game is a distinctively contemporary artefact (whereas games, and more generally play, are as old as humanity itself), and the professional business of developing, marketing, and investing in video game development is even younger, in the range of two to three decades as a specific business activity. Video game development is also associated with a number of features related to innovation-led growth, including enterprising, business creation, advanced engineering and design skills, novel ways to build communities and user-groups around video games, and a variety of related practices.

This volume has reported empirical material from this field of video game development, and has emphasized that being an indie video game developer is to navigate in a domain beset by considerable difficulties regarding, for example, the ability to raise sufficient funds to complete planned development work, to create video game concept that is appealing to a mass audience, and to create business models that ensure the long-term survival of the studio. Despite being first-hand entrepreneurs in an innovation-led growth economy, indie developers are also a form of "norm entrepreneurs" (in Skeel's 2001, sense of the term) as they actively advocate video games as a distinct form of cultural and artistic expression, which also offers an entertainment an interactivity potential that few other genres of creative arts cannot match. This commitment to the video game as such, and to business creation, makes video game developers a distinctive species in the regime of innovation-led growth. Many other creative arts actors rely on either direct subsidies from the sovereign state or patronage, but the video game industry has been commercially oriented from the beginning. Consequently, policy makers have only been weakly incentivized to formulate policies or programmes that have been oriented towards supporting video game development. From its inception, the video game industry has been self-sufficient, relied on the financing derived from sales, or, indirectly, from the public sector student loan services that in many ways have financed early stage video game development activities, at times being formalized into proper incorporated businesses at a later stage.

This final chapter will address a specific quality of the indie video game community (arguably indicative of the attitude of the entire video game industry), its downgrading of heroic images of creative work, and the emphasis on team production efforts (with Blair and Stout's 1999, term) in the domain of development work and its functional specialization that still demands the capacity to integrate all the components of the video game. This attitude, belief, or *modus vivendi*, wherein creative artefacts are collectively developed but without the need of the idea to inscribe extraordinary creative skills into specific participants (say, chief game designers, programmers, etc.), is arguably indicative of the passionate commitment to the video game artefact *per se*, and the long-standing business orientation of the industry. In comparison to, for example, the film industry, closely entangled with a celebrity culture to better promote its products in a world wherein a variety of competing product offerings impose market noise and marketing costs, and the tax-sponsored culture sector in several European welfare states, which need to introduce the idea of extraordinary talent and creative vision to justify the transfer of public resources to self-declared elite institutions, the video game industry has only limited use of such narratives. On the contrary, the video game industry thrives in a milieu sheltered from the public gaze and wherein anonymity is preserved.

In addition to empirical observations, the chapter examines the principal learnings from the field work and sketches theoretical and managerial implications. In the end, the study of indie video game developers adds to a more detailed understanding of new innovation-led growth that is modified, oftentimes accomplished, on the basis of a combination of economic and financial incentives, regulatory control, and social norms that actively encourage, for example, risk-taking and participation in entrepreneurial ventures. Such insight may be of great interest for policy makers who are intrigued by the idea that by the end of the day, it is the human capacity to develop new business concepts and to produce innovations, largely unassisted by centrally enacted policies and campaigns, which make a difference in terms of economic and social welfare.

A Post-Heroic Theory of Creativity

Osbourne (2003: 519) calls for "a *post-heroic* conception of creativity," which means that the concept of creativity should be separated from the conventional view, wherein creative work is based on either extraordinary talent or strong will power, and instead should be associated with organized activities that are more mundane, down-to-earth, and non-spectacular. In science and technology studies, Bijker (1995: 270) argues that an artefact (in this case the bicycle) "does not suddenly appear as the result of a singular act of heroic invention." Instead, an artefact is "gradually constructed in the social interactions between and within relevant social groups" (Bijker 1995: 270). Also managerial practices have been theorized outside of the influence of the heroism narrative. For instance, Weick and Roberts (1993: 378) argue that an organization culture that "encourages individualism, survival of the fittest, macho heroics, and can-do reactions" tends to concentrate decision-making authority to the apex of the organization structure. No matter how visionary, smart, or forward-looking such decision makers may be, this model fails to recognize the contribution of all participants and therefore is at risk to overlook much valuable know-how and insights.

Based on these premises, that creative and innovation-oriented work remains bound up with a heroism narrative, and that there is a need for a more elaborate image of creative work, this chapter shows how the video game developers enact the complex and transdisciplinary development process as a form of team production activity. On the contrary, the anonymity of video game developers and the collective work they participate in are central elements of the video game development industry. The reason for this downplaying of the heroism narrative is that video game developers have little practical use of such a narrative, and that the video game industry at large, and the indie developer community more specifically, have persistently defined themselves as an underground activity or a marginalized community. Furthermore, in comparison to other culture industries (e.g., the film industry), which maintain a symbiotic relationship with a celebrity culture and/or an ideology that stipulates that autonomous high-status contributors accomplish their artistic visions in isolation from the wider community, the video game development culture genuinely values community and team production efforts.

The Post-Heroic View of Creativity in Video Game Development

Heroism is an ideology that promotes individual contributors at the expense of team production efforts. In industries and activities prone to actively support ideologies that emphasize talent, individual vision, and ambitions as the primus motor of business activities, notably creative industries (e.g., fashion, design, architecture, film production) and the art world, heroic conceptions of creativity are widespread, at times even being the defining mark of the activities. In contrast, the video game industry has emerged from within the industrial-military complex, characterized by secrecy, and, on the opposing end of the continuum, an American counter-culture that defies all kinds of authority claims, and that nourishes identities being critical of consecrated individuals—great leaders and individuals purportedly bestowed with the capacity to foresee social changes yet to come. Furthermore, the hobbyist and primarily male adolescent culture that generated the video game industry is oftentimes associated with socially inept and marginal figures, taking refuge in the world of video games to protect themselves against an uncompromising society, demanding social skills and servility in all corners of life. Taken together, the genealogy of the video game industry has effectively vaccinated itself against a heroic image of creativity. In its place, the gamer community and solidarity and joint concerns regarding their love of video games remain the social capital that propels the industry. These cultural traits are arguably constitutive of the industry growth over the last two decades, and are therefore worthy of extended scholarly inquiries.

In order to further explore the relationship between a post-heroic image of creativity and industry-specific features, three themes are addressed. First, the claim that in the video game industry, gaming ideas "does not matter" unless you are able to materialize these ideas in a video game will be examined. Second, and related to the claim that proper ideas are not what propels the industry but the actual team production work, the central role of the video game production team is examined. Third and finally, the post-heroic image of creativity precludes a "cult of personality" in the video game industry, that is, in comparison to other industries that produce creative output (defined in its broadest sense of the term), the video game industry has only marginally promoted individuals and singular contributions. This absence of "big names" in the industry, household names that serve the metonymic function as being poster-boys and poster-girls for day-to-day production activities, is exemplary of underlying business practices. Taken together, these three themes apprehend an industry ethos that renders the video game *per se* "the star of the show," and that leaves the developers in the shadows, not as an act of ingratitude, but as a specific social norm that imposes penalties on individuals that seek to promote themselves at the expense of the community.

The Limited Value of Gaming Ideas

One of the interviewees, a director of a video game development incubator, argued that one of the specific features of the video game industry is that video game ideas are complicated to exploit unless they are accompanied by adequate resources and capacities: "There is this saying in the industry that ideas are worth nothing in video game development" (Director, Video Game Development Incubator):

> Everyone with some experience from the industry … would say to someone who says, 'Hi there, I've got this game idea. Can you please help me find people who can help me develop it?' 'Yes, but your idea as such is not worth anything. Unless you yourself can turn it into a game, then it is worth nothing.' To develop a game is all about the team and their ability to create something very advanced and complex together. (Director, Video Game Development Incubator #1)

The director argued that in video game development work, there is an excessive supply of ideas and images of novel games as practically any business participant or aspiring neophyte entering the industry believe they are in the position to envision new and engaging games and creative game concepts. After all, the love of the video game propels the industry and motivates new business entrants to pursue a career in video game development. A core competence in the industry is instead to be able to discern genuine and "doable" video game design ideas in the vast flow of such proposals, a skill that demands considerable know-how, experience, and development experience. Furthermore, as a matter of practical concern, to imitate ideas, or to opportunistically exploit existing gaming idea, is in the absolute majority of cases inoperable, video game developers argue. One interviewee, an indie developer in a medium-sized company, addressed these difficulties: "It takes so much time to develop a game so that if you notice a certain trend, it is already too late to jump the bandwagon and develop a game according to these rules" (Indie Developer #3, Video Game Company A). Also the video game incubator director shared this view, a condition that Dierickx and Cool (1989) have referred to as "time compression diseconomics":

> If someone has a prototype and it looks real cool: to be able to exploit that idea and to produce a game before the original team is done with their development work, that is extremely rare. It is close to impossible to accomplish. (Director, Video Game Development Incubator #1)

Furthermore, another indie developer in company A added, to recreate historical successes is not a viable strategy either, which leaves the video game developer with the sole option to develop games that they themselves believe in and are happy to develop and play themselves:

> If we would like to develop a [certain] game, we can look at historical successes. But these are idiosyncratic cases so it is hard to make any learnings. We can only hope to develop what we like, and hope that others like it too. (Indie Developer #4, Video Game Company A)

"By the end of the day, you need to develop the game you are passionate about," indie developer #3 (Video Game Company A) summarized.

In this perspective, the video game industry is not so much propelled by genuine ideas as it is focused on the capacity to translate viable video game design ideas into material digital object, released on the global video game market. The transition from idea to the full materialization of the video game involves a considerable degree of resources and expertise, and the capacity to enrol and mobilize such resources and competencies is precisely the expertise of video game companies. In the end, video game companies do not sit idly and wait for new and inspiring ideas to pass by, but are fully occupied with working on the game ideas they target. Consequently, the video game incubator director's claim that "ideas have no economic value" is substantiated on the basis of practical conditions.

The Primacy of the Team Production Activities

If video game ideas are omnipresent in the industry, yet costly to translate into a robust video game concept and thereafter even more costly to develop, the essence of video game development is located outside of the domain of idea generation. Most of the interviewees portrayed team production efforts as the primary mechanism of the video game development industry, being the joint but interdisciplinary work activities that gradually stabilize the video game idea and that make it materialize as a product, eventually encountering the end-user, the gamer community. One of the long-term industry actors emphasized the "collaborative" work in all video game development, that is, she stressed the team work efforts:

> Video game development is about collaboration and transdisciplinarity ... The methodology is very important ... This is not information technology development, it is a form of entertainment, and it is a contribution that benefits an end-user. (Video Game Industry Entrepreneur, Female)

As part of this image of the video game as the outcome from transdisciplinary work, the entrepreneur stressed the key role of team work leadership and leadership in the video game development more widely. According to the entrepreneur, the leadership in this environment, in many cases using a variety of "agile" development methods, adapted from the software industry, was at the forefront of leadership work and would therefore serve as role models for executives in various sectors of the economy. Based on this acclaim, the entrepreneur called for more scholarly research on leadership practices in the video game industry.

Also one of the analysts of the industry interest organization emphasized the key role of teamwork in the industry, but added that in comparison to other purportedly "creative sectors" of the economy, the video game industry was not marked by the presence of "high-brow" visionaries advocating his or her creative visions: "Video game development is a matter of teamwork. You mustn't compare it with film production or similar activities wherein there are a director embodying 'the great artistic vision'" (Analyst #2, Female, Swedish Video Game Interest Organization). Again, the myth of creative capacities and talent played a marginal role in video game development as the industry had little use for such idea in its development work, nor in the marketing work or public image of the industry, primarily branding and marketing video games rather than its developers. Furthermore, the relative lack of interest for flamboyant and attention-seeking individuals is consistent with the both the industry-military tradition that promotes secrecy as a virtue, and the underground and sub-cultural heritage of the video gamer community. In this cultural tradition, which combines two extreme positions, it is the video game that is the primary output, not its developers or sponsors. The video game incubator emphasized this cultural trait of the industry as one of its competitive advantages vis-à-vis other industries, for example, the music industry or the film industry (neither of which is of necessity directly competitors to video game developers), being in constant demand of new stars and iconic figures to promote as part of the marketing activities:

> Games are the outcomes from team production activities. That will always be the case, and there is no one who benefits from individual persons being lifted up above the community. That would only diminish the role of the team … There is also a lack of prestige in the community. (Director, Video Game Development Incubator #1)

The video game industry entrepreneur argued that the autochthonous Swedish culture was conducive to a collaborate mindset, now honoured in video game development activities. Historically, the Nordic climate of Scandinavia and its long and cold winters offer poor conditions for, for example, agricultural production, and in rural communities, farmers collaborated to ensure that the food production would sustain the population. Based on such climatological and socio-economic conditions, collaborate work, low "power-distance," and informal relations are practices and virtues that have informed, for example, the Swedish education system, wherein, for example, team-based work assignments are commonplace:

> The explanation for our skills in developing video games is that we are trained to collaborate in school, but we can be even better at that. That is our best advantage vis-à-vis all other larger countries. We maintain this consensus logic, a collaborative mindset wherein no one is more important than the other. (Video Game Industry Entrepreneur)

Team production is an industry standard and not some Swedish specialism, but the non-hierarchical and egalitarian Scandinavian culture is well tuned to such activities, the entrepreneur argued. Above all, in an egalitarian culture, the role of the allegedly outstanding individual with extraordinary creative impulses and aesthetic sensibilities plays only a marginal role in shaping the work of the community. A post-heroic image of creativity is more aligned with the current development activities.

The Absence of Big Name Character

Third and finally, many of the interviewees emphasized that the global video game industry operates in relative absence of major figures and household names that serve to personalize the industry. Whereas the automotive industry once had Henry Ford and the digital media industry has celebrated innovative leaders and entrepreneurs such as Steve Jobs or Mark Zuckerberg (more recently also subject to criticism), the video game industry is closer to, for example, a finance industry model wherein there is limited interests in, and need for, such public persona. The video game incubator director argued that this has not always been the case, and points at early stage video game developers, including Will Right who developed *SimCity*, Peter Molyneux who did *Populous*, and Hideo Kojima who introduced *Metal Gear Solid*, as being "big name developers." According to the director, these names have not been complemented by a new generation of "star developers":

> There are a few big names in the video game industry's early stages. They still live on, but there are no new names being added ... [T]here are no new profiles in the video game industry. The teams have grown, the production is a team effort, and there is more focus on the brand of the studio, its culture and the mood in the games. (Director, Video Game Development Incubator #1)

Again, the strong emphasis on team production activities, bolstered by the ideals of secrecy and a debunking of the cult of "strong individuals," the video game industry has little need for these "big names" as they may distract developers or even downplay the primacy of team production efforts. "I don't think there are so many celebrities and stars and stuff [in the industry]," the developer in Company H remarked. Instead, the video games *per se* are the stars of the industry, at times being household names as in the case of, for example, *Grand Theft Auto* series, the FIFA football game series, and *Assassin's Creed*, all being commercially successful video games and deemed to be landmark contributions to the field.

In summary, the video game industry, being a bona fide innovation-led and knowledge-intensive industry, which combines a variety of state-of-the-art expertise, represents and actively promotes through its operations a post-heroic image of creativity, an attitude that locates a creative capacity and aesthetic sensibilities not so much to individual actors as what is embedded in team-based relations, and manifested in and through team-production activities. In this view, creativity is a relational construct, emerging within collaborative work efforts rather than being what is inscribed into individuals, the self-declared visionary artist catering ideas for others to follow and materialize. This overtly romantic image of the creative individual, standing out from the crowd simply on the basis of a superior capacity to formulate a vision, and for being sufficiently charismatic to enrol devoted followers in his or her pursuit, appears as an obsolete model within the video game industry. In the situation wherein team production activities are what determine outcomes and future recognition and revenues, antiquated images of creative artists cease to make sense or to inform day-to-day practices. In addition, if there are individuals with extraordinary capacities or the gift of charisma, these individuals are unlikely to portray themselves in such terms as they are better served by other industry-specific norms and ideologies. Consequently, a post-heroic image of creativity is advanced in the video game development community and the gamer community more widely, satisfied with portraying the video game as the contribution to the community and leaving its developers outside of the limelight.

Managing Post-Heroic Creative Work: Practical Implications

Video game development work lacks "poster names" that represent the industry and its business activities or creative output, and instead it is the video games *per se* that are marketed vis-à-vis the gamer community. Furthermore, the production-centred business logic wherein, for example, team work and the use of agile project management methods further undermined a heroic view of the development work. Consequently, as opposed to other "creative industry" activities such as film production and architecture, video game developers are better insulated against a celebrity-infused culture wherein individuals are put above the community. This is remarkable as video game development is an overtly commercial activity with limited subsidies and other exemptions granted by the sovereign state, and an industry that operates in a global market shaped by the digital distribution platforms provided by the publishers. Video game development is thus representative of a new idiom of cultural production, eager to sustain itself on the basis of its creative output and to make team production efforts the principal work method to accomplish such goals.

In this view, artefact (say, a video game) is a matter of team production efforts dependent on "social interactions" (Bijker 1995: 270). The video game industry and its two intellectual but essentially diverging roots, the industrial-military complex and the underground and hobbyist counterculture, have limited use for a heroic conception of creativity. Instead, secrecy and collaborative work are virtues held in esteem. Seen in this view, the anti-heroic ethos of the video game developers is indicative of "capitalist civilization" wherein innovation has been subject to routine work (as Joseph Schumpeter once put it), yet recognizes the sparkle of creativity that eventually makes all the difference.

Passionate Work and Innovation-Led Growth

Innovation-led growth is essentially based on the corporations' capacity to motivate co-workers to bring out their best ideas to the table and to make them materialize within a team production context, that is, in a situation wherein various skills and competencies can be combined in meaningful and ultimately productive ways. As a consequence, incentive to participate in such development work is central in the innovation-led growth model. The video game industry and indie development, in particular, are exemplary cases of innovation-led growth, spurred by a passionate commitment to the video game as digital artefact and a species of cultural expression. Many of the interviewees in the study admitted that they had been intrigued by the world of video games from an early age, and that they are fascinated by the technological and narrative complexity of video games, even to the point where they have committed their lives to develop new games.

To be passionate about something means to be animated by a sense of commitment to a cause, and to fully engage one's cognitive and emotional faculties to optimize the output, produced within the horizon of stipulated goals, and the resources committed to the project at hand. As the theological term *passion* indicates, this is not always an entirely pleasant experience as passion is also associated with suffering—with hard and long-term work, a looming sense of failing to live up to high standards, the risk of disappointment derived from a perceived lack of recognition of the end-product, and so forth. But this passionate suffering derived from the commitment to what is perceived as the greater good is bearable as long as the work done is considered meaningful and there are some rewards—pecuniary, reputational, community-based, and so on—that fuel the passionate commitment. In many cases, for outsiders, this passion for a specific activity, or form of production, can appear slightly odd or difficult to understand.[1] Nevertheless, these are lesser matters as individuals must themselves choose how to live their lives and decide to what end they commit their talents and time. In the end, the innovation-led growth regime, beneath all the policies and regulatory frameworks, its subsidies and insurances provided to market actors, and so forth, rests on quite fragile behavioural conditions, wherein expectations, aspirations, beliefs, and hopes for the future are what serve as the means of justification for neophytes and industry entrants who pursue careers beset by uncertainty of all sorts.

One of the key objectives of policy makers is therefore to provide an institutional framework and a cultural climate wherein risk-taking and venturing appear to be a reasonable, perhaps even an admirable, career choice. There will always be individuals in the margin that are impatient enough to shun a way of life that provides all the safety nets that the contemporary welfare state offers, that seek their own path in life, and that

[1] "What we lack today is not reflection but passion," Søren Kierkegaard (1985: 71) writes in *Philosophical Fragments*. In Kierkegaard's view, reflection refers to the human intellect, which he construed as the cognitive processes wherein everything is packaged into "sterile abstractions which could not be experienced 'completely and personally'" (Golomb 1992: 66). In contrast, Kierkegaard was convinced that passion, authentic pathos, is devoid of "rational content" and therefore cannot be spoken about propositionally (Golomb 1992: 69). In this view, of great importance for, for example, the American pragmatism and the work of, for example, William James, passionate commitment escapes a proper denotative vocabulary, which naturally complicates the intersubjective understanding of the "authentic pathos." As, for example, Richard Rorty (2007: 65), a notably secular writer, remarks, for Kierkegaard and his followers, "the quest for certainty is a cop-out, and that absolute commitment has nothing to do with the ability to win arguments or convince opponents." Being passionate is not a matter of providing evidence to substantiate this conviction, but rather to follow one's inner drives to do so. For Kierkegaard, Golomb (1992: 76) emphasizes, "absolute non-commitment to anything, not even to one's self, results in the self's complete dissolution." While this Kierkegaardian defence of passionate commitment and pathos has been acclaimed in, for example, entrepreneurship theory (see, e.g., Cardon et al. 2017; Chen et al. 2009)—itself a secular theology of sorts, critics contend—what has been more challenging to handle for management scholars is Kierkegaard's emphasis on the limits of rational language and its inability to convey passionate sentiments. Strangely, the staunch defence of passionate commitment resonates with contemporary management theory, whereas what has been treated as tolerance in Kierkegaard for non-rationalist thinking is rejected. One explanation for this piecemeal acceptance of Kierkegaard's thinking is, as Rorty (2007: 58) puts it, that "irrationality," that which fails to be accounted for in a denotative vocabulary or apprehended by metrics and quanta, has "become the secular equivalent of sin."

digress from what risk-averse advisors may suggest—be they bohemians, artists, or sheer adventurers—but for the larger crowd, a life in fringes of the economic welfare society may appear less appealing. In such cases, the sovereign state, which acts through its various agencies and institutions, may ensure that the threshold for venturing is lowered, and the risks associated with, for example, business creation are reasonable. As indicated by the empirical material reported in Part II of this volume, the community of indie developers are on the one hand committed to video game production, but they are also aware that the possibilities for developing qualified and commercially successful video games demand a business framework that serves as the vehicle for such activities. Some of the interviewees argued that the business side of indie development was underdeveloped and secondary to other interests, and this critique is arguably justifiable, but the contrary situation would have been considerably more alarming, wherein an interest in business creation would not be assisted and propelled by a passionate commitment to the video games *per se*. In many cases, the commitment to video games comes first, and the business creation process is consequential, a form of adjustment to the economic, financial, and institutional conditions (e.g., fiscal policy) conducive innovation-led growth. From the policy maker's view, the formal demands and rules can be defined in detail to a varying degree, but it is considerably more difficult to create or assist the behavioural conditions that propel, for example, creative industries. Economic policy is therefore essentially a response to social conditions that derive from the outside of policy-making quarters.[2] Only when favourable conditions are in place, say, as in the case of the community of gamers having a shared interest in a specific class of

[2] Sunstein (1996) argues that norms are shaped by law: "[A]n appropriately framed law may influence social norms and push them in the right direction" (Sunstein 1996: 2026). At the same time, unless there are substantial social norms in place, honoured and reinforced by citizens, it is of no use to enact law to influence a situation. "[W]ithout desirable effects on social norms, there is not much point in endorsing expressively motivated law," Sunstein (1996: 2047) writes. In this view, legislation is a governance device that may be inadequately employed in cases where policy makers use legislations in ways that are inconsistent with social norms. Therefore, legislation should preferably be used only in cases wherein current norms need to be further accentuated and reinforced, not to promote some policy maker's beliefs or to otherwise signal the policy makers' preferences. In such cases, the symbolic use of law risks to undermine the authority of legislative entities and to blur the distinction between personal and community-based preferences, social norms, regulations, and legislation. An indiscriminate use of legislation as governance device may gradually undermine the respect for the rule of law, being a core principle of the modern state and its judiciary.

digital artefacts, policy makers can take action to create possibilities for venturing on the basis of such conditions. In this view, innovation-led growth is not so much a top-down economic growth regime as some of its activities emerge from the fringes and the underground segments of popular culture, in many cases out of the gaze of conventional policy-making communities.

As a practical matter, the single most important condition for innovation-led growth is to ensure an adequate supply of finance capital. As finance capital is the ultimate measure of economic worth, actual or as a projected income flow, the willingness to supply credit to new ventures is indicative of the interest and tolerable level of risk-taking in a specific society and its economic system. A perceived shortage of venture capital and a limited number of active qualified investors are recurrent themes in scholarly studies of venturing and entrepreneurial activities. However, on the basis of elementary Marshallian economics theory, supply and demand need intersect in an economic equilibrium, and whenever the demand is in excess of the supply, it would be logically consistent to also speak about, for example, an excess of entrepreneurs just as well as a shortage of venture capital: these two views are the two sides of the same coin. From a policy-making perspective, for more than three decades tuned to the idea that entrepreneurship is the primus motor of economic growth (a hypothesis that can lend itself to empirical testing, as discussed in Chap. 2), it is more politically complicated to advocate that too many entrepreneurs chase an adequate supply of venture capital. Instead, venture capital supply is deemed to be in short supply, an issue of much lamenting among commentators and industry participants. However, economic theory and finance theory more specifically tend to assume that market actors are informed about market conditions and can effectively process public information, and consequently the supply of venture capital is always already at an optimal level given the preference for risk-taking among finance capital owners. That is, in theoretical terms, it is inconsistent to claim that venture capital is in short supply as that supply is adjusted to current market conditions by rational investors. It is noteworthy that this is a theoretical proposition that is self-referential; the stipulated rationality of investors (and market actors more generally) always justifies current market conditions, but without no further evidence than the reference to the rational choices being made. Nevertheless, in the end, the claim that venture capital is in "short supply" is a statement shaped by an ideology that regards entrepreneurial initiatives as always being honourable, regardless of finance capital investors' assessment of the quality of the venture and the management team that monitors the activities.

Taken these theoretical and policy-oriented issues aside, the community of indie developers, the key actors in this study, tries all conceivable ways to raise funds and provide an income to be able to continue their development work. The commercial orientation of the video game industry has created a risk-tolerant attitude among industry participants. Many interviewees are fully aware that they are dependent on raising new funds in the near future, or that they need to be able to secure sales revenues during the first days, or even hours, when a new game is being released. Video game developers are what has been called "born global" as they always already access a global community of gamers through the Internet-based distribution and communication channels. This "long-tail" phenomenon, wherein a small studio may generate considerable revenues from online game sales, and become a well-known brand in a geographically dispersed community of gamers, is arguably puzzling for policy makers and regulators. Rather than communicating with a handful of large-scale and divisionalized corporations, the General Motors of the oligarchic capitalism system, they now need to monitor fragmented industries constituted by, for example, a thousand tiny specialized indie developers, who all cater to their own communities of gamers, in some cases on the basis of only one single but highly successful video game.

Another feature of the indie video game business is the quick change in how the games are financed, developed, marketed, and distributed. The empirical material reported in this volume indicates that the current developer/publisher/distributor system, for the time being centred on the leading distribution platform Steam, is challenged by various new initiatives. Furthermore, the marketing of games has shifted from being based on conventions and fairs, annual events, and physical sites, to increasingly rely on intermediary actors such as YouTubers, bloggers, pod-casters, and other forms of "expert observers" (Elsbach 2009: 1048) who themselves need "content" to fill their airtime, but who also communicate directly with thousands of the so-called followers. In the end, these idiosyncratic features of the indie development business make it complicated for policy makers to regulate business activities in detail. Instead, policy making is directed towards the creation of stable and predictable rules of the game that secure the rights of developers and that stipulate their responsibilities. Essentially, innovation-led growth policy making is a matter of acting through second-order mechanisms rather than more straightforward subsidies and insurances. Consequently, such policy demands political integrity, prescience, and the capacity to endure period of relatively limited economic growth on the basis of the existing policy.

Innovation-led growth represents an economic system that operates on a high level of abstraction. The motives for venturing do no derive from the need to satisfy immediate elementary needs, but are grounded in a passionate commitment to a social practice (e.g., gaming) that *per se* is abstract in its contours. The output, a digital object, may appear both fluid and infinitely modular (in the end, in material terms, video games are sequences of computer language code) in comparison to physical objects, and the distribution and ownership of the video game are embedded in, and entangled, with advanced technological systems and novel legal contracts. In comparison to, for example, agricultural production, the indie developer appears to operate at safe distance from the common sense understanding of the world. At the same time, these are the factual conditions under which a capitalist mode of production operates in the end of the second decade of the new millennium. An unimpressed common sense view of video game development may in fact say very little about the nature of these production activities. In its essence, indie video game development is a professional line of work that needs to be understood in more sophisticated theoretical terms, and when being subject to such an analysis, its contribution to the contemporary economy and its social and cultural conditions may be better appreciated.

Contributions to Management Studies and Organization Theory

On the one hand, managing passionate co-workers should be an uncomplicated activity as it benefits from the commitment of the co-workers and their willingness to make a contribution to a field of expertise they love and have previously committed considerable time to. Empirical studies of passionate workers and deeply meaningful work, reviewed in Chap. 3, provide a somewhat more moderate view and emphasize that passionate commitment can also be a liability in the case where co-workers nourish too high expectations regarding what they and their colleagues can accomplish, or when they underestimate, for example, the managerial and financial conditions structuring the activities. In such situations, frustration, disappointment, cynicism, and an exit altogether from the industry may be observed. One managerial objective is therefore to explain the systemic features of any creative and innovation-led business activity to neophytes, so that they can oversee how a variety of conditions and relations affect the way the operations are organized and managed. Without such leadership work, individuals are left on their own to figure out how business activities are organized, and for individuals with a more limited interest in the managerial and financial features of, for example, video game development, an inadequate understanding of the industry may result in expectations that are complicated to fulfil. To manage creative and innovation-oriented work is therefore not so much a matter of compiling resources and committed co-workers and to leave them to accomplish the best possible output under determinate conditions, but is a sense-making (Weick 1995) and sense-giving (Gioia and Chittipeddi 1991) activity, wherein co-workers jointly create an image of the industry and a roadmap that serves to coordinate collective action, of necessity functionally discrete and yet making individual contributions to a singular entity or service output. Creative individuals who participate in innovation-oriented development work are oftentimes experts in functionally narrow domains, but oftentimes need to get support to fully understand their role in a wider business model and industry context.

Second, leadership work in creative and innovation-oriented activities is essentially a matter of securing funds that can finance projected development work, also beyond the next delivery and release. As indicated in Chap. 2, the venture capital market for video game developers is thin, and there are previously few venture capital investors that are specialized in video game development studios. Also the idiosyncratic production and distribution model of the industry, wherein the attention of existing and potential gamers remains a core production factor, makes many video game development projects non-investable within the current risk management practices. The degree of uncertainty is simply too high to justify an investment decision. Unlike other sectors of the cultural field, the state and municipalities offer few if any funding possibilities, but the state and local government can still assist video game development work indirectly through a variety of investments in infrastructural activities such as tertiary education programmes, incubator support, and various regulatory practices. By and large, the supply of finance capital remains a core concern in the governance and regulation of innovation-led growth, and such issues cannot be handled by managers in the development studios alone, but should be addressed as a matter of industrial policy.

Third, much of the business-oriented issues are addressed within the incubators that host a broad variety of video game development studios, and a significant proportion of leadership work is conducted by the incubator directors and their assigned business counsellors who work closely with the studios. Some of the hardcore indie developers questioned the industry policy that enacts such incubators as a support for start-up firms as they believe that the business side of operations is dependent on the capacity to develop functional and appealing video games in the first place. To start the process to impose a ready-made business venturing model misses the point that what truly matters in the world of indie development is the capacity to provide intriguing digital artefacts, and consequently represents a form of regulatory mindset that risks to disappoint all participants, both developers and incubator directors and business counsellors. Whether such critique can be substantiated is an empirical question, but the sheer lack of finance capital is indicative of a potential oversupply of entrepreneurs who seek to raise capital. In that respect, video game development is no different from, for example, life science venturing, another innovation-led industry that suffers from an alleged insufficient venture capital supply. A more positive interpretation of the current industry policy is that incubators host and train a new generation of developers and entrepreneurs, whose motivations and skills will serve to further reinforce and institutionalize an innovation-oriented industry that is exemplary inasmuch as it combines computer science know-how, entertainment media, and artistic expressions at the same time as it reaches an entirely global audience and market. Such an accomplishment is indicative of the strength of an innovation-led economy that thrives on ideas and creativity.

Implications for Industry Policy

First of all, outside of the specific empirical data reported in this volume, policy makers need to be able to better discriminate between what Schoar (2010) calls subsistence entrepreneurs and transformational entrepreneurs as entrepreneurs tend to veil the considerable differences between these two classes of entrepreneurs. "[M]any current approaches to development policy implicitly or even explicitly assume that subsistence entrepreneurship is the first step toward transformational entrepreneurship," Schoar (2010: 59) writes. This is a mistake, Schoar (2010) continues, as transformational entrepreneurs (such as indie developers) create a business to exploit either perceived market possibilities or specific skills and interests, whereas subsistence entrepreneurs regard self-employment as a means to provide for themselves and their families. Consequently, economic growth in turnover and in employment primarily derives from transformational entrepreneurship. As indicated by scholarly research, for example, the work of Decker et al. (2014, 2016, 2017), entrepreneurs do not make a contribution to economic growth and job creation in parity with the attention the concept is even given in policy-making quarters and scholarly communities. This does still not disqualify policies intended to support enterprising or render them illegitimate, but a more moderate view of the role of entrepreneurial activities in the economy needs to be taken. Not the least the declared shortage of venture capital is indicative of either unreasonably high expectations regarding the return on investment in new ventures (which *per se* is an issue that needs to be framed within the capital formation process, wherein a markedly more liberal finance market legislation and market regulation pose a formidable challenge for finance capital-raising ventures that now compete with the option to reinvest residual cash in a variety of second-level financial asset), or a too sizeable supply of finance capital-raising entrepreneurs. Policy makers need to determine how they can incentivize finance capital owners to commit their residual cash to forward-oriented innovation activities rather than to invest the residual capital in financial assets.

If policy makers deem the current system, wherein the finance industry has expanded considerably faster than the economy at large, as being indicative of a capital formation process that is efficient and indirectly assists venturing as the supply of credit becomes munificent, then they need to decide whether aspiring entrepreneurs should rely on the finance market to attract finance capital investment, or if the sovereign state, acting through its agencies, should provide additional capital infusions in the form of, for example, research grants and similar subsidies. If this latter scenario is chosen—which scholars such as Gilson (2003) advise against as it induces additional costs and represents a politically costly subsidy to private businesses—then policy makers need to establish routines and assessment and commensuration standards for how to transfer tax-money to new ventures. In either situation, innovation-led growth demands sturdy policy making that optimizes the use of public resources. Funding low-performing entrepreneurs at the tax-payers' expense may, for instance, reduce net economic welfare as these resources potentially generate a better return on investment elsewhere. In the end, the funding of innovation-led growth activities such as indie developers is a matter of making informed choices so that regulation (always needed as the capital-formation process is a legal construct within the realm of the sovereign state) does not spill over into over-regulation (as in the case wherein policy makers reduce net economic welfare on the basis of the implementation of ineffective subsidies and insurances to market participants).

In more hands-on, practical terms pertaining to indie video game development, both indie developers and industry representatives point at the need to finance and sponsor infrastructural activities, for example, video game education programmes both within the tertiary education sector (at the university level) and in the vocational training segment of the education system. The supply of internationally qualified education programmes at the university level seems to work quite well, according to industry representatives. Graduates from the education programme were largely absorbed by the current industry growth (as reported on an annual basis by the Industry Interest Organization), and many of the interviewees argued that graduates would be attractive to employ also in more conventional industries in great need of expertise in digital media production. In addition, regional incubators that host and counsel video game companies were widely regarded as an important feature of the Swedish video game industry. State agencies, local municipality governments, and also private investors (as in the case of Company J) jointly contributed to the funding of these platforms for local developers. At the same time as there are a number of incubators in place and in operation all over Sweden, incubator representatives such as directors argued that political representatives in local government were largely sceptical regarding the economic benefits derived from investments in the activities, which resulted in lengthy discussions and negotiations before any political commitments could be made. This condition can possibly be explained by the "liability of newness" predicament that Stinchcombe (1965) first called attention to. By and large, success in the commercially oriented segments of the culture industry (e.g., music production and video game development) seems to be only indirectly related to policy making inasmuch as these industries are niche segments wherein a limited number of individual may generate considerable returns (as in the case of the music production community, built around the producer and song-writer Max Martin, and Markus Persson *Minecraft* success), but only being attended to by policy makers after the fact, and in many cases without any defined policies that leverage historical accomplishments. Based on such observations, innovation-led growth policy should possibly target infrastructural conditions rather than to provide direct capital infusions and other narrowly defined subsidies and exceptions. In many cases, policy in these domains may appear as a mere afterthought in the face of historical successes.

It is advisable to be sceptical towards the idea that the current innovation-led growth policy is the best one available under defined conditions, which would demand no additional initiatives. But it would be equally mistaken to assume that the current policy actively prevents a thousand flowers from blooming. Potentially, given certain bottom-line demands being satisfied so that market conditions can be defined for all actors, there is perhaps a sort of "good-enough policy making" (comparable to D.W. Winnicott's concept of "good-enough mothering") that incentivizes and motivates aspiring entrepreneurs (e.g., younger gamers) to pursue a career in industries characterized by a high degree of specialized know-how and skills and uncertainty, but without overregulating the activities so that the very purpose of the business is distorted. The crux is to identify the point in policy making and regulatory practices that the majority of market participants can agree that a good-enough policy is formulated. How that is to be accomplished falls outside of the stated ambition of this volume.

Summary and Conclusion

Whenever the material welfare has been raised to a certain level—which, with some exceptions, has occurred with the range of three, possibly two, generations in advanced economies that finance a welfare state—non-elementary human needs may be subject to economic exploration and venturing. The access to video games may appear to be high on, say, a Maslowian hierarchy of needs scale, but the human need for meaning, community, and excitement—qualities that video games embody in the eyes of its protagonists—is generic. In a capitalist society wherein the ownership of production capital is primarily assigned to private business ventures, any product or service that can be sold at a defined or negotiated price can generate a return and are consequently investable assets (as being bundles of skills, resources, production capital, etc.). Video games are today a billion dollar business, and the turnover is higher than in, for example, the music industry. Recent market figures indicate a remarkable growth in turnover and the number of businesses in operation, which makes the video game industry an illustrative case of what has been referred to as innovation-led growth. Nevertheless, the internal activities in the industry have only been subject to sparse scholarly attention, especially in a business school setting, otherwise intrigued by economic growth and notable levels of economic performance. Some conservative actors may regard video game production as being a lightweight business activity in the fringes of popular culture, but such stated belief does little to change the fact that this production of digital artefacts incorporates a series of skills and know-how that are acclaimed as being at the forefront of the innovation-led growth regime. Consequently, a scholarly study of, for example, indie video game development may provide a glimpse of business practices in the making, eventually being appropriated also by more conventional and mainstream industries.

As indie studies are maturing and coming of age, some of the participants learn to appreciate the formal requirement of the business activities, whereas some "hard-core indies" may spend considerable periods of their career outside of the reach of such complications. In some cases, hardcore gamers may not be even fully aware of the finance capital their games in fact have generated (as in the case of the developer in Company F, informed by his accountant that "there was some money on the account"), which is a charming indication of a certain naivety for some observers, but being more puzzling for others. Interpreted in generous terms, the indie market segment of the video game industry provides opportunities for different life style choices: being a specialist in a Triple-A company is one thing, but to lead a more unstructured and enterprising life in the fringes on the industry is not an illegitimate career choice either. Seen in this view, the hard-nosed liberalism of the video game industry is both vocal and actively practiced by its participants. For other observers and policy makers, this fluid and inherently changeable industry structure and day-to-day work, centred in a digital sphere largely inaccessible for lay audiences, impose barriers inasmuch as it is complicated to anticipate needs and to prescribe policies without the active participation and advocacy of industry actors. To some extent, this reduces the risk of overregulating the industry, but it also imposes difficulties such as in the case where it is complicated for mainstream finance industry actors (say, mutual fund managers) to acquire the expertise needed to make informed investments in the industry. Being largely an industry in the making is thus equally a blessing and a concern. At the end, taken aside the persistent critique regarding the social costs derived from gaming as such (not covered in this context, but largely dismissed out of hand by industry representatives as a form of persistent moral panic), the video game industry development over the last two decades is a success story of significant proportions. It may be that the Hollywood film industry starts to explore the video game industry business histories (as they have done with some Silicon Valley computer or social media companies, with feature movies about, e.g., Steve Jobs and Mark Zuckerberg already being delivered), but still today, this is largely an industry that has stayed true to its tradition of underground activities and secrecy, inherited from both its industrial-military complex associations and the counter-culture traditions. The video game industry still sails under a flag that acquires only limited attention, at times to the chagrin of its participants but for most parts to their liking.

References

Bijker, W. E. (1995). *Of bicycles, bakelites, and bulbs: Toward a theory of sociotechnical change*. Cambridge and London: The MIT Press.

Blair, M. M., & Stout, L. A. (1999). A team production theory of corporate law. *Virginia Law Review, 85*(2), 247–328.

Cardon, M. S., Post, C., & Forster, W. R. (2017). Team entrepreneurial passion: Its emergence and influence in new venture teams. *Academy of Management Review, 42*(1), 283–305.

Chen, X.-P., Yao, X., & Kotha, S. (2009). Entrepreneur passion and the preparedness in business plan presentations: A persuasion analysis of venture capitalists' finding decisions. *Academy of Management Journal, 52*(1), 199–214.

Decker, R., Haltiwanger, J., Jarmin, R., & Miranda, J. (2014). The role of entrepreneurship in US job creation and economic dynamism. *The Journal of Economic Perspectives, 28*(3), 3–24.

Decker, R., Haltiwanger, J., Jarmin, R. S., & Miranda, J. (2016). Where has all the skewness gone? The decline in high-growth (young) firms in the US. *European Economic Review, 86*, 4–23.

Decker, R., Haltiwanger, J., Jarmin, R. S., & Miranda, J. (2017). Declining dynamism, allocative efficiency, and the productivity slowdown. *American Economic Review, 107*(5), 322–326.

Dierickx, I., & Karel, C. (1989). Asset stock accumulation and sustainability of competitive advantage. *Management Science, 35*(12), 1504–1511.

Elsbach, K. D. (2009). Identity affirmation through signature style: A study of toy car designers. *Human Relations, 62*(7), 1041–1072.

Gilson, Ronald J. (2003). Engineering the venture capital market. *Stanford Law Review, 55*(4), 1067–1103.

Gioia, D. A., & Chittipeddi, K. (1991). Sensemaking and Sensegiving in strategic change initiation. *Strategic Management Journal, 12*, 433–448.

Golomb, J. (1992). Kierkegaard's ironic ladder to authentic faith. *International Journal for Philosophy of Religion, 32*(2), 65–81.
Kierkegaard, S. (1985). *Philosophical fragments/Johannes Climacus*. Princeton, NJ: Princeton University Press.
McGonigal, J. (2011). *Reality is broken: Why games make us better and how they can change the world*. London: Jonathan Cape.
Osbourne, T. (2003). Against 'creativity': A philistine rant. *Economy and Society, 32*(4), 507–525.
Rorty, R. (2007). *Philosophical papers* (Vol. 4). Cambridge University Press.
Schoar, A. (2010). The divide between subsistence and transformational entrepreneurship. *Innovation Policy and the Economy, 10*(1), 57–81.
Skeel, D. A. (2001). Shaming in corporate law. *University of Pennsylvania Law Review, 149*(6), 1811–1868.
Stinchcombe, A. L. (1965). Social structure and organization. In J. G. March (Ed.), *Handbook of organizations* (pp. 142–155). Chicago: Rand McNally.
Sunstein, C. R. (1996). On the expressive function of law. *University of Pennsylvania Law Review, 144*(5), 2021–2053.
Weick, K. E. (1995). *Sensemaking in organizations*. London: Sage.
Weick, K. E., & Roberts, K. H. (1993). Collective mind in organizations: Heedful interrelating on flight decks. *Administrative Science Quarterly, 38*, 357–381.

Index[1]

[1] Note: Page numbers followed by 'n' refer to notes.

A. Styhre, *Indie Video Game Development Work*,
https://doi.org/10.1007/978-3-030-45545-3

The manufacturer's authorised representative in the EU is Springer Nature Customer Service Centre GmbH, Europaplatz 3, 69115 Heidelberg, Germany. If you have any concerns regarding our products, please contact ProductSafety@springernature.com

Printed and bound by CPI Group (UK) Ltd, Croydon, CR0 4YY
30/09/2026
02225461-0005